WORKBOOK AND STUDY GUIDE WITH COMPUTER LAB SOFTWARE PROJECTS

to accompany

Complete Computer Concepts

GARY B. SHELLY
THOMAS J. CASHMAN
WILLIAM C. WAGGONER

SHELLY
CASHMAN
SERIES

boyd & fraser publishing company

PHOTO CREDITS

 © 1992 by boyd & fraser publishing company
A Division of South-Western Publishing Company
One Corporate Place • Ferncroft Village
Danvers, Massachusetts 01923

Developed by Susan Solomon Communications

Manufactured in the United States of America

ISBN 0-87835-785-8

2 3 4 5 6 7 8 9 0 DH 6 5 4 3

BRIEF CONTENTS

CONTENTS

◆ PART I Chapter Projects 1.1

◆ PART II   Computer Lab Software Projects LAB1

Home Banking

On-Line Information Services

Airline Reservations

Electronic Mail

◆ PART III   Answers to Selected Projects Projects A1

P R E F A C E

This *Workbook and Study Guide with Computer Lab Software Projects* is a supplement designed to be used with *Complete Computer Concepts* by Shelly, Cashman, and Waggoner. It provides learning activities that help students master introductory computer concepts and simulate computer applications not usually available to beginning students.

As authors of this supplement, our goal was to overcome the comments often made about student supplements—that they are worthless and poorly prepared. To meet our goal we present unique and meaningful learning activities in an attractive format. We have used color and have included material to enhance and expand upon the textbook.

ORGANIZATION AND CONTENT

This supplement is divided into three parts—the Chapter Projects, the Computer Lab Software Projects, and the Answers to Selected Projects.

Chapter Projects

Each Chapter Project includes the following study aids:

◆ Chapter Objectives that help students measure their mastery of the chapter content
◆ A Chapter Outline that guides students through the organization of the chapter
◆ A Chapter Review that provides a convenient, rapid summary of the chapter and helps students recall and comprehend key concepts
◆ Key Terms with definitions that reinforce the concepts introduced in the chapter

In addition five unique projects are included. These begin with Project 1—ClassNotes. This project requires students to demonstrate their mastery of the vast majority of chapter content by requiring them to fill-in or otherwise choose correct answers. Project 2—Self-Test provides students an opportunity to simulate a chapter test of key material. This project can be completed in two ways—either by marking or filling in answers in the workbook or by using the PC version, an on-line testing and scoring vehicle. The PC version is available to instructors on a disk in the Instructor's Manual described below. Projects 1 and 2 can also be used with the HyperGraphics version of *Complete Computer Concepts*. Projects 3 and 4 require students to demonstrate their mastery of the material by using their visual skills—identifying photographs, labelling illustrations, and so on. Finally, Project 5 fosters development of oral and written communication skills and encourages original research about computers.

Computer Lab Software Projects

The Computer Lab Software Projects provide students opportunities to see first-hand how computers are used in a variety of applications, not just word processing, spreadsheet, and database applications. The subjects of these six projects and a brief description of each follow.

Home Banking   In this project students enter a telephone number to connect to the bank's computer system and then enter an account number and password to access the home banking system. They can then make inquiries regarding account balances and transactions, transfer funds among accounts, and arrange for an automatic payment.

Information Services   After entering a telephone number to connect to the information services computer, students enter an account number and a password. They can then access information about national news, weather, the stock market, and sports.

Airline Reservations   Students act as travel agents and use an online reservation system, checking available flights and fares, making reservations, giving seat assignments, and accessing previously entered information.

Electronic Mail   In this project students enter an account name and password to access an electronic (email) system. They then review email messages that have been sent to them, send email messages, and perform administrative tasks associated with an email account, such as adding user names and maintaining mail distribution lists.

Desktop Publishing   In this project students develop a customer newsletter that has already been started. They use the import command to merge previously created text, a graphic, and a table into the newsletter. Using a command menu, they edit and revise the newsletter.

Presentation Graphics   In this project students manipulate an eight-slide presentation that already exists. They make changes to the slides and rearrange the order of several slides.

Answers to Selected Projects

The third and final part of the *Workbook and Study Guide with Computer Lab Software Projects* contains all of the answers to Projects 1 and 2 for all of the chapters. These provide students indispensable feedback on their understanding and mastery of the chapter concepts.

SUPPLEMENTS

Instructor's Manual

The *Instructor's Materials* contains answers to all of the Chapter Projects and Computer Lab Software Projects.

Instructor's Disk

The Instructor's Disk is packaged within the *Instructor's Materials*. It contains the simulations for the Computer Lab Software Projects and the PC version software for all of the Chapter Project 2 Self-Tests. This disk is available to instructor's free of charge in 3 1/2" and 5 1/4" formats.

ACKNOWLEDGEMENTS

We express our thanks to the professionals at boyd & fraser publishing company who worked with us so diligently. We also express our gratitude to the many instructors who encouraged us to revise and update this supplement.

Gary B. Shelly
Thomas J. Cashman
William C. Waggoner

PART I
Chapter Projects

CHAPTER ONE

An Overview of Computer Concepts

- ◆ Explain what a computer is and how it processes data to produce information
- ◆ Identify the four operations of the information processing cycle: input, process, output, and storage
- ◆ Explain how the operations of the information processing cycle are performed by computer hardware and software
- ◆ Identify the major categories of computers
- ◆ Describe the six elements of an information system: equipment, software, data, personnel, users, and procedures
- ◆ Explain the responsibilities of information system personnel
- ◆ Explain the use of computers in our world
- ◆ Describe the evolution of the computer industry

◆ CHAPTER OUTLINE

CHAPTER ONE

Chapter Review

 Chapter 1 provides an overview of what a computer is, how it processes data into information, and the elements that are necessary for a successful information system. Many of the terms and concepts introduced in this chapter are discussed in more detail in later chapters.

A computer is an electronic device that can operate under the control of instructions stored in its own memory unit to accept data (input), process data arithmetically and logically, produce output from the processing, and store the results for future use. While the term computer can be defined many ways, generally it is used to describe a collection of devices that function together to process data.

All computers perform four operations, which are called the information processing cycle. These operations are: input, process, output, and storage. During the input operation, the computer receives data; raw facts such as words and numbers. During the processing operation, data is converted into a meaningful and useful form called information. The production of information by processing data on a computer is called information processing, or data processing (DP). People who use either the computer directly or the information it provides are called computer users, end users, or simply users.

Computers are powerful devices because they can quickly, accurately, and reliably perform the four operations of input, process, output, and storage. Data flowing along a computer's electronic circuits travels at close to the speed of light which allows processing to be accomplished in billionths of a second. The capability of computers to store and process large amounts of data is another reason why computers are so powerful.

Computers perform the operations of the information processing cycle by following a detailed set of instructions called a computer program, program instructions, or software. After the instructions are loaded, the computer executes one program instruction after another until the job is complete.

Computer equipment is often referred to as hardware. This equipment consists of input devices, a processor unit, output devices, and auxiliary storage units. Input devices are used to enter data into a computer. The processor unit contains the electronic circuits that cause the processing of data to occur. The processor unit consists of two parts; the central processing unit (CPU) and main memory. The CPU contains a control unit that executes the program instructions and an arithmetic/logic unit (ALU) that performs math and logic operations. Main memory electronically stores data and program instructions when they are being processed. Output devices make information available for use in such forms as printed reports or visual displays. Auxiliary storage units, such as diskette or hard disk drives, store instructions and data when they are not being used by the processor unit. Input devices, output devices, and auxiliary storage units are sometimes referred to as peripheral devices.

Computers can be classified according to their size, speed, processing capabilities, and price into four categories; microcomputers, minicomputers, mainframe computers, and supercomputers. Rapid changes in technology, however, make firm definitions of these categories difficult. Microcomputers, also called personal computers, include desktop, hand-held, notebook, laptop, portable, and supermicrocomputers. Minicomputers support a number of users performing different tasks. Mainframe computers can handle hundreds of users, store large amounts of data, and process transactions at a high rate. Mainframe computers usually require a specialized operating environment. Supercomputers can process hundreds of millions of instructions per second and are used for jobs requiring long, complex calculations.

CHAPTER REVIEW (continued)

Computer software is the key to the productive use of computers and can be categorized into two types; system software and application software.

System software consists of programs that control the operations of the computer equipment. System software called the operating system, tells the computer how to perform functions and is loaded into the computer's main memory each time the computer is turned on. A common microcomputer operating system is the Disk Operating System, usually referred to as DOS.

Application software consists of programs that tell a computer how to produce information. Purchased application software is referred to as application software packages or simply software packages. Some of the most commonly used software packages are word processing, electronic spreadsheet, graphics, and database. Word processing software is used to create and print documents. Electronic spreadsheet software allows the user to add, subtract, and perform user-defined calculations on rows and columns of numbers. Graphics software converts numbers and text into graphic output that visually conveys the relationships of the data. Database software allows the user to enter, retrieve, and update data in an organized and efficient manner.

A useful information system includes more than just software and equipment. It also includes accurate data, trained information systems personnel, knowledgeable users, and documented procedures.

Computers used in business are usually under the control of the information systems department. This group might be called the data processing department or the computer department. Medium and large businesses usually use a multiuser computer that can concurrently process requests from more than one user.

A primary computer input device is a terminal. A terminal is a device consisting of a keyboard and a screen, which is connected through a communications line, or cable, to a computer. The computer processor allocates computer resources, such as memory, to the programs that are being processed.

The most commonly used output devices are printers and terminals. High-speed printers can produce large volumes of printed output and many terminals can display both text and graphics.

The two major types of auxiliary storage for a multiuser computer are magnetic disk and magnetic tape. Magnetic disk records data as a series of magnetic spots on an oxide-coated disk surface. Magnetic tape also stores data as a series of magnetic spots on one-quarter to one-half inch tape on cartridges or reels. A common use of magnetic tape is as backup storage of disk files.

A computer operator monitors the operations of the computer and responds to messages that are displayed on the operator's console. Copies of computer software and data are kept on disks or tapes in a data library. The library is supervised by a data librarian.

Data entry personnel are responsible for entering large volumes of data. Data is usually entered on terminals from source documents such as sales invoices.

Systems analysts review current or proposed applications to determine if the applications should be implemented using a computer. If an application is to be computerized, the systems analyst studies the existing application in detail before designing the new system. The systems analyst works closely with both the people who will be using the new system and the programmers who will be writing the computer programs.

Computer programmers design, write, test, and implement specialized programs that process data on a computer. Whereas the systems analyst specifies what is to be done; the programmer decides how to do it.

The responsibility of the database administrator is to manage the data of an organization. The database administrator must develop procedures to ensure that data is correctly entered into the system, that confidential data is not lost or stolen, that access to company data is restricted to those who need the data, and that data is available when it is needed.

Information systems department management varies depending on the size and complexity of the department. The systems manager oversees the activities in the systems analysis and design area. The programming manager is in charge of all programmers. The operations manager oversees the operational aspects of the department including scheduling, maintenance, and operation of the equipment. The person in charge of the entire department could have the title vice president of information systems, or chief information officer (CIO).

The use of computer technology is widespread in our world. New uses for computers and improvements to existing technology are continually being developed.

Key Terms

ALU (Arithmetic/Logic Unit), *see* **Arithmetic/Logic Unit**

Application software: Programs that tell a computer how to produce information.

Application software packages: Programs purchased from computer stores or software vendors.

Arithmetic/Logic Unit (ALU): The unit of the CPU that performs arithmetic and logic operations.

Arithmetic operations: Numeric calculations performed by the arithmetic/logic unit of the CPU, which include addition, subtraction, multiplication, and division.

Auxiliary storage units: Units that store program instructions and data when they are not being used by the processor unit.

Cathode Ray Tube (CRT), *see* **Screen(s)**

Central Processing Unit (CPU): A processing unit containing a control unit that executes program instructions and an arithmetic/logic unit (ALU) that performs math and logic operations.

Chief Information Officer (CIO): A title sometimes given to the manager of the information systems department.

Computer: An electronic device operating under the control of instructions stored in its own memory unit, that can accept data (input), process data arithmetically and logically, produce output from the processing, and store the results for future use.

Computer department, *see* **Information systems department**

Computer operator: A person who works in the computer room and is responsible for running the computer equipment and monitoring processing operations.

Computer program: The detailed set of instructions that tells the computer exactly what to do, so it can perform the operations in the information processing cycle; also called program instructions, or software.

Computer programmers: Persons that design, write, test, and implement programs that process data on a computer.

Computer software, *see* **Software**

Computer system: The input, processing, output, and auxiliary storage components of computers.

Computer users, *see* **Users**

Control unit: Part of the CPU that executes the program instructions.

CPU, *see* **Central Processing Unit**

CRT, *see* **Cathode Ray Tube**

Data: The raw facts, including numbers and words, that a computer receives during the input operation and processes to produce information.

Data entry personnel: Persons responsible for entering large volumes of data into the computer system.

Data librarian: A person who staffs the data library and catalogues the disk packs and tapes.

Data library: The area where the information systems department keeps the software and data stored on disk packs and tapes when they are not in use.

Data processing, *see* **Information processing**

Data processing department, *see* **Information systems department**

KEY TERMS (continued)

Database administrator (DBA): The person responsible for managing an organization's computerized data and all database activities.

Database software: Software that allows the user to enter, retrieve, and update data in an organized and efficient manner.

Diskettes: Diskettes are used as a principal auxiliary storage medium for personal computers.

Electronic spreadsheet software: Software that allows the user to add, subtract, and perform user-defined calculations on rows and columns of numbers.

End users, *see* **Users**

Graphics software: Software that converts numbers and text into graphic output that visually conveys the relationships of the data.

Hard disks: Auxiliary storage consisting of nonremovable metal disks that provide larger storage capacities than diskettes.

Hardware: Equipment that processes data, consisting of input devices, a processor unit, output devices, and auxiliary storage units.

Information: Data that has been processed into a form that has meaning and is useful.

Information processing: The production of information by processing data on a computer; also called data processing (DP).

Information processing cycle: Input, process, output, and storage operations. Collectively, these operations describe the procedures that a computer performs to process data into information and store it for future use.

Information system: A collection of elements that provides timely and useful information. These elements include: equipment, software, accurate data, trained information systems personnel, knowledgeable users, and documented procedures.

Information systems department: A separate department within an organization that controls the computers; also called data processing department, or computer department.

Input: The process of entering programs and data into main memory. Input can also refer to the media (such as disks, tapes, and documents) that contain these input types.

Input devices: Devices used to enter data into a computer.

Keyboard: An input device that contains alphabetic, numeric, cursor control, and function keys; used to enter data by pressing keys.

Logical operations: Comparisons of data by the arithmetic/logic unit of the central processing unit, to see if one value is greater than, equal to, or less than another.

Magnetic disk: The most widely used storage medium for computers, in which data is recorded on a platter (the disk) as a series of magnetic spots.

Magnetic tape: Tape that stores data as magnetic spots on one-quarter-inch to one-half-inch tape on cartridges or reels. The primary means of backup for most medium and large systems.

Main memory: Memory contained in the processor unit of the computer. It stores the program instructions and data when they are being processed; also called primary storage.

Mainframe: Large systems that can handle hundreds of users, store large amounts of data, and process transactions at a very high rate.

Micro, *see* **Microcomputers**

Microcomputers: The small, desktop-sized systems that are widely used and generally priced under $10,000; also called personal computers, or micros.

Minicomputers: Computers more powerful than microcomputers and can support a number of users performing different tasks.

Monitor, *see* **Screen(s)**

Multiuser computers: Computers that can concurrently process requests from more than one user.

Operating system: One or more programs that manage the operations of a computer. For a computer to operate, an operating system must be stored in the main memory of the computer.

Operations manager: A manager in the information systems department who oversees the operational aspects, such as scheduling, maintenance, and operation of the equipment.

Output: The data that has been processed into a useful form called information that can be used by a person or machine.

Output devices: The most commonly used devices are the printer and the computer screen.

Peripheral devices: The input devices, output devices, and auxiliary storage units that surround the processing unit.

KEY TERMS (continued)

Personal computers, *see* **Microcomputers**

Primary storage, *see* **Main memory**

Printer: An output device.

Process: Part of the information processing cycle; the procedures a computer performs to process data into information.

Processor unit: A unit that contains the electronic circuits that cause the processing of data to occur, divided into two parts, the central processing unit (CPU), and main memory.

Program instruction, *see* **Computer program**

Programming manager: A manager in the information systems department who is in charge of all programmers.

Removable disks: Disk packs that can be taken out of the disk drive.

Screen(s): An output device used to display data on both personal computers and terminals; also called a monitor and a CRT (Cathode Ray Tube).

Software, *see* **Computer program**

Software packages, *see* **Application software packages**

Source document(s): Original documents such as sales invoices from which data can be entered.

Spreadsheet, *see* **Electronic spreadsheet software**

Storage: A computer's electronic storage capability, *see also* **Auxiliary storage; Primary storage**

Supercomputers: Supercomputers are the most powerful category of computers and the most expensive. They can process hundreds of millions of instructions per second.

Systems analysts: Persons who review and design computer applications.

Systems manager: A manager in the information systems department who oversees the activities in the systems analysis and design area.

Systems software: All the programs including the operating system that are related to controlling the operations of the computer equipment, classified into three major categories: operating systems, utilities, and language translators.

User(s): The people who use either the computer directly or the information it provides; also called computer users, or end users.

Vice President of Information Systems: The information systems manager might have this title.

Word processing software: Software used to prepare documents electronically. It allows text to be entered on the computer keyboard in the same manner as on a typewriter. Characters are displayed on a screen and stored in the computer's main memory for ease of editing.

Name _____ Date _____

ClassNotes

Home work chapter 1 & 9

WHAT IS A COMPUTER?

1. A computer is a collection of devices that function together to process *Data or information*

WHAT DOES A COMPUTER DO?

1. List the four general operations that all computers perform.

Input   *PROCESS*

Output   and   *Storage*

2. The listed four general operations combined can be called the *Information Processing cycle*.

3. List three examples of data.

Words   *Numbers*   *raw facts n Picture*

4. List three examples of information.

Letters   *Forecast*   *Presentation*

5. *Information* or *Election data Processing* is the process of converting data into information.

6. Information and data are retained on *Storage* devices.

7. A computer user can also be called a(n) *End User*.

8.–11. Label this diagram, choosing from the following list.

input	storage
processor	main memory
output	user
	printer

8. *Storage*

9. *Output*

10. *Processor*

11. *Input*

CLASSNOTES (continued)

WHY IS A COMPUTER SO POWERFUL?

1. The power of a computer is derived from its capability to perform four primary operations. Identify these operations in their correct order by choosing from the following list.

logic   process   *Input Devices*

input   arithmetic   *Process Unit*

storage   output   *Output*

                 Auxiliary   *Storage Units*

2. A computer is powerful because of the manner in which it executes the information processing cycle. Which three words best describe how the computer executes this cycle?

_____*Speed*_____   _____*Accuracy*_____   _____*Reliable*_____

Quickly

HOW DOES A COMPUTER KNOW WHAT TO DO?

1. A computer follows a detailed set of _____.

2. These instructions can also be called _____, _____

   or ____*Software*____.

THE INFORMATION PROCESSING CYCLE

1.–4. Label the information processing cycle.

1. *Input*

Data

2. *Process*

Information

3. *Output*

4. *Storage*

WHAT ARE THE COMPONENTS OF A COMPUTER?

1. List the computer hardware components.

input Monitor Key   *output*

Processor Unit   *Axll unt*

Monitor

Printer

Cpu

Key Board

CLASSNOTES (continued)

Input Devices

2. Which of the following is an input device? _Key Board_

   printer   plotter   monitor   keyboard   diskette   fixed disk

Processor Unit

3. Identify the arithmetic operations a computer performs, choosing your answers from the following list.

   addition   sine/cosine   square root   subtraction   multiplication   division

   _____   _____

   _____   _____

4. List the logical operations that compare data.

   greater _____   _____   _____

5. Main memory or primary storage electronically stores _Data_ _____

   and _Programme Inst._ _____ currently being used.

Output Devices

6. Give examples of output devices from the following list.

   computer screen   printer   hard disk   scanner   keyboard   diskette

   Printer _____   _Screen_ _____

Auxiliary Storage Units

7. Auxiliary storage stores _Instruction_ and _data_ not currently being used.

8. All components of the computer except the processor unit are called _Peripheral devise_.

CATEGORIES OF COMPUTERS

1. From the following list, identify the four categories of computers.

   maxicomputer   supercomputer   minicomputer   maxiframe computer   hypercomputer

   mainframe computer   hybridcomputer   microcomputer

   _Mi_ _____   _____

   _____   _____

2. From the following list, identify the characteristics common to all computers.

   monitor   speed   size   processing capabilities   price   keyboard   diskette

   _1_   _I_   _3_   _4_

   _____   _____

   _____   _____

3. Computers can be categorized by their price. Fill in the appropriate price ranges for the listed computers.

   Microcomputers: _10,000_ _____

   Minicomputers: _15,000_ _____

   Mainframe computers: _Seven_ _____

   Supercomputers: _Millions of De_ _____

Lelia Heasley

CLASSNOTES (continued)

COMPUTER SOFTWARE

1. What are the four types of instructions?

Input   *logical*

Output   *Arithmetic*

2. The two software categories are *System Software* and *Application Software*
   Operating DOS

3. What are the four commonly used types of application software packages?

Word Processing   *Electronic Spreadsheet*

Graphic   *DataBase*

A TYPICAL BUSINESS APPLICATION

Complete the steps that a user takes when using an application software package. Choose your answers from the following list.

retrieve   load   process   output   save   data   information

1. *Load* the application program.
2. Provide *data* to the application program.
3. Use the application program to *Process* the data.
4. *Output* the information to a printer.
5. *Save* the information on disk.

WHAT ARE THE ELEMENTS OF AN INFORMATION SYSTEM?

1. List the six elements of an information system.

Equipment   *Software*   *Data*

Personnel   *Users*   *Procedures*

A TOUR OF AN INFORMATION SYSTEMS DEPARTMENT

1. A(n) *Multiuser Computer* provides multiple users with computing resources.
2. Multiuser computers are managed by departments within an organization. Typically, the departments will be called the *Information System Department*, *Data Processing Dept*, or *Computer* department.

The Computer Room

3. List two input devices. *KeyBoard*   *Terminal*
4. The *Processor CPU* performs the major processing of data and information.
5. List two output devices. *Printer*   *Monitor*
6. List two auxiliary storage devices. *Magnetic disk*   *Magnetic tape*
7. Magnetic disk devices are both *Fixed* and *Removable*.
8. *Computer operator* run the computer equipment and monitor processing operations.

CLASSNOTES (continued)

Data Library

9. A(n) _Data Library_ holds information in an organized fashion for future reference.

10. The person who is in charge of the data library is the _Data Librarian_

Offices of Information Systems Personnel

11. List the seven types of personnel in an information systems department.

System Analysts Computer Programmer DataBase Administrator
Department Manager System Manager Programming Manager
Chief Information Office

12.–15. Fill in the organization chart.

12. _Information System_   13. _System Manager_

14. _Programming Manager_   15. _Operations Manager_

12. _Information System_

13. _System Manager_   14. _Programming Manager_   15. _Operation Manager_

CLASSNOTES (continued)

THE EVOLUTION OF THE COMPUTER INDUSTRY

1.–18. Identify as many key events as you can without consulting your book.

Dr. Kemeny: BASIC	1951 _____	(1)
IBM 360	_____	(2)
IBM: Software unbundled	1952 _____	(3)
Microsoft Windows 3.0	1957 _____	(4)
FORTRAN	1958 _____	(5)
IBM	1964 _____	(6)
Dr. Hoff: Microprocessor	1965 _____	(7)
DEC Minicomputer	_____	(8)
Jobs and Wozniak: Apple	1969 _____	(9)
Microsoft: MS-DOS	_____	(10)
Intel 80486	1976 _____	(11)
Transistors	1979 _____	(12)
Dr. Hopper	1980 _____	(13)
UNIVAC I	1981 _____	(14)
VisiCalc	1983 _____	(15)
Kapor: Lotus 1-2-3	1987 _____	(16)
IBM PC	1989 _____	(17)
Intel 80386	1990 _____	(18)

CHAPTER ONE—PROJECT TWO

Self-Test
WORKBOOK AND PC VERSIONS

Match the following:

_____ 1. Data Library

_____ 2. Microcomputers

_____ 3. Size

_____ 4. Computer Program

_____ 5. IBM PC

_____ 6. Processor Unit

_____ 7. Information Processing Cycle

_____ 8. Mainframe Computer

1. A factor determining the category of computers
2. Hundreds of thousands to several million dollars
3. Less than $10,000 (portables, laptops)
4. Input, Process, Output, Storage
5. Personal computer developed in 1981
6. Software and data maintained on disks and tapes available for processing
7. Detailed set of instructions telling the computer what to do
8. Magnetic tapes
9. Performs arithmetic and logical operations

You can complete the remainder of Project 2 in two ways—either by marking or filling in your answers in this workbook, or by using the PC version of Project 2. The PC version (available from your instructor) automatically corrects your answers for you. It also calculates the percent of your answers that are correct.

Answer the following questions.

1. A computer is a collection of devices that function together to process _____.
   a. numbers   c. data
   b. words   d. information

2. The information processing cycle is comprised of input, processing, output, and _____.

3. _____ is created from data during the processing phase of the information processing cycle.
   a. Information   c. Input   e. Storage
   b. Output   d. A computer program

4. T F The production of information by processing data on a computer is called information processing or electronic data processing.

5. T F One reason a computer is powerful is due to its storage capability.

6. T F Because computer operations occur at exceptionally fast speeds, the electronic circuits fail on a frequent basis.

7. Instructions that direct the operations of a computer are called _____.

SELF-TEST (continued)

8. Several different forms of _____ can be produced from a single set of data.

    a. input   c. processing   e. information

    b. programs   d. storage

9. T F   The information processing cycle is fundamental to understanding computers and how they process data into information.

10. A keyboard is an example of a(n) _____.

11. All arithmetic and logical processing takes place in the _____.

    a. main memory   c. processor   e. none of the above

    b. controller   d. program

12. Which of the following is part of the CPU?

    a. auxiliary memory   c. secondary memory   e. a peripheral device

    b. main memory   d. the input unit

13. A printer is an example of what type of device?

    a. input device   c. primary memory device   e. none of the above

    b. auxiliary storage device   d. output device

14. T F   Auxiliary storage units are used to store instructions and data when they are not being used by the processor.

15. These computers are the fastest computers available.

    a. supercomputers   c. superminicomputers   e. none of the above

    b. mainframe computers   d. microcomputers

16. T F   At this point in time, minicomputers fall between microcomputers and mainframe computers in price and power.

17. These computers are also called personal computers.

    a. supercomputers   c. minicomputers   e. none of the above

    b. mainframe computers   d. microcomputers

18. T F   A computer program, or software, specifies the sequence of operations that are to be performed.

19. Purchased programs are often referred to as _____ packages.

20. How many elements comprise an information system?

    a. five   c. three   e. eight

    b. six   d. two

21. _____ typically initiate requests to the information systems department.

    a. Database administrators   c. Systems analysts   e. Users

    b. Computer programmers   d. Computer operators

22. The _____ has the responsibility for designing new application systems that will be computerized.

    a. database administrator   c. systems analyst   e. computer programmer

    b. system manager   d. Vice President of Information Systems

23. The _____ has the responsibility of managing the totality of data within an organization.

    a. database administrator   c. systems analyst   e. computer programmer

    b. system manager   d. Vice President of Information Systems

24. T F   The IBM PC was first introduced in 1979.

CHAPTER ONE—PROJECT THREE

Identifying the Components of a Computer System

Instructions: In the space provided, label each component of a computer system.

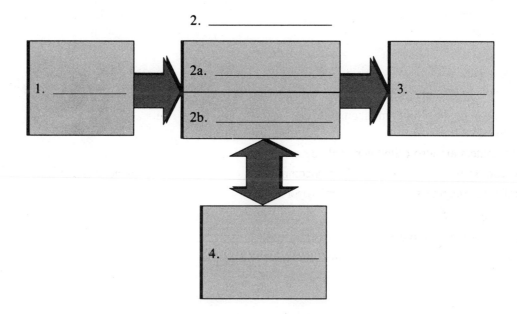

2. _____

1. _____   2a. _____   3. _____

2b. _____

4. _____

Name _____   Date _____

Identifying the Categories of Computers

Instructions: In the space provided, identify the category to which each of the computers in the photos belong.

1. _____

2. _____

3. _____

4. _____

CHAPTER ONE—PROJECT FIVE

Developing Communication Skills

Instructions: Prepare an oral or written report on one or more of the following subjects.

1. Over a period of a week, keep track of the number of times you see computers used or how you, in some way, are affected by the use of computers.
2. Choose a small, medium, and large business in your community. Contact each business and ask how each uses computers in its daily operations.
3. Satisfaction with computer equipment and software varies among users. Contact a user of a large computer at your school or one of the local businesses and ask him or her why or why not he or she is satisfied with the computer equipment and software.
4. Each of the jobs in an information system department requires certain skills. Determine the entry-level skills and knowledge required for: (1) computer operators; (2) systems analysts; and (3) computer programmers.
5. Contact a local computer installation and arrange a tour of its facility. Report on the different categories of computers and how they are being used.
6. Contact a local organization that uses a mainframe computer. Report on the number of people who work in each type of job in the information systems department and describe each job category.
7. Over a period of one week or more, review your local newspaper and national magazines for articles relating to computers. Prepare a report that summarizes each article.

Microcomputer Applications: User Tools

◆ OBJECTIVES

- ◆ Identify the most widely used general microcomputer software applications
- ◆ Describe how each of the applications can help users
- ◆ Explain the key features of each of the major microcomputer applications
- ◆ Explain integrated software and its advantages
- ◆ List and describe six guidelines for purchasing software application packages
- ◆ List and describe learning aids and support tools that help users to use microcomputer applications

◆ CHAPTER OUTLINE

 Chapter 2 provides an introduction to the most commonly used microcomputer applications. A knowledge of these applications is now considered by many educators and employers to be more important than a knowledge of programming and is considered part of being computer literate. General microcomputer applications are useful to a broad range of users and are user friendly, in other words, easy to use.

Commands are instructions that tell the software what you want to do. User interfaces are methods and techniques that make using an application simple. They include function keys, screen prompts, menus, icons, and a device called a mouse. Function keys are a shortcut method of entering a command. Screen prompts are the messages that the program displays to help you while you are using an application. Menus provide a list of processing options. Pull-down menus provide an on-screen list of selections under a category of processing options. Icons refer to pictures instead of words that are displayed on the screen to show you various program options. A graphic user interface (GUI) extensively uses icons to graphically represent files and processing options. A mouse is a small input device used to move the cursor and to input commands. The cursor is a symbol that indicates where you are working on the screen.

Some of the most widely used application software includes: word processing; desktop publishing; electronic spreadsheet; database; graphics; and data communications. These applications are available on computers of all sizes. Word processing is the most widely used general application. Word processing allows you to create, edit (change), format, store, and print documents electronically. The value of word processing is that it reduces the time required to prepare and produce written documents.

Word processing packages often include support features such as a spelling checker and a thesaurus. Grammar checker software is also available for word processors. Spelling checker software allows you to check individual words or an entire document for correct spelling. Additional words can be added to spelling checker dictionaries. Thesaurus software allows you to look up synonyms for words while you are using your word processor. Grammar checker software is used to check for grammar, writing style, and sentence-structure errors. This software can check documents for excessive use of a word or phrase, identify sentences that are too long, and find words that are used out of context.

Word processing terms include: insert, the addition of characters and words to existing text; delete, the removal of characters or words; move, the transfer or removal of text; cut, the removal of text; copy, the duplication of text; and paste, the placement of text that has previously been copied. The capability to easily move text from one location to another is often referred to as cut and paste.

Some word processing packages now incorporate desktop publishing features that allow graphics to be included with the text. Desktop publishing (DTP) software allows users to design and produce professional looking documents that contain both text and graphics. DTP software is frequently used for documents such as newsletters, marketing literature, technical manuals, and annual reports. Using desktop publishing software significantly decreases the cost and time of producing quality documents.

Although most desktop publishing packages have some word processing capabilities, most users create text with a separate word processing package and transfer the text to their desktop publishing document.

CHAPTER REVIEW (continued)

Clip art consists of collections of art that are stored on disks and are designed for use with DTP packages. WYSIWYG is an acronym for What You See Is What You Get. It means that what you see on the computer screen is an exact image of what a printed page will look like.

Electronic spreadsheet software allows you to organize numeric data in a worksheet or table format called an electronic spreadsheet, or spreadsheet. Within a spreadsheet, data is organized horizontally in rows and vertically in columns. The intersection where a row and column meet is called a cell. Cells can contain three types of data: labels (text), values (numbers), and formulas. Formulas perform calculations on the data in the spreadsheet and display the resulting value in the cell containing the formula. One of the most powerful features of the electronic spreadsheet occurs when the data in a spreadsheet changes. The spreadsheets capability to recalculate all formulas when data is changed makes it a valuable tool for decision making.

A database refers to a collection of data that is stored in files. Database software allows you to create a database and to retrieve, manipulate, and update the data that you store in it. Database terms include file, record, and field. A file is a collection of related data that is organized in records. A record contains a collection of related facts called fields.

Information presented in the form of a graph or a chart is commonly referred to as graphics. Studies have shown that information presented as graphics can be understood much faster than information presented in writing. Three common forms of graphics are pie charts, bar charts, and line charts. Many software packages can create graphics, including most spreadsheet packages.

Analytical graphics is widely used by management personnel when they analyze information and when they communicate information to others within their organization.

Presentation graphics goes beyond analytical graphics by offering the user a wide choice of presentation effects such as three-dimensional displays, background patterns, multiple text fonts, and image libraries.

Data communications software is used to transmit data from one computer to another. For two computers to communicate, they each must have data communications equipment, data communications software, and a communications link, such as a telephone line.

Integrated software refers to packages that combine applications such as word processing, electronic spreadsheet, database, graphics, and data communications into a single, easy-to-use set of programs. Integrated packages have a consistent command structure and the capability to easily pass data from one application to another.

Integrated programs frequently use a feature called a window; a rectangular portion of the screen that is used to display information. Many programs today can display multiple windows on the screen at the same time. Each window could contain a different application.

Personal information management (PIM) software helps users keep track of the miscellaneous bits of personal information that each of us deals with everyday. This information might include phone messages, notes, and appointments. PIMs usually offer the following capabilities: appointment calendars, outliners, electronic notepads, data managers, and text retrieval.

Project management software allows users to plan, schedule, track, and analyze the events, resources, and costs of a project. The value of project management software is that it provides a method for managers to control and manage the variables of a project to help ensure that the project will be completed on time and within budget.

Utility software includes a variety or programs to help you manage and maintain the data on your computer system. A valuable utility feature is the capability to recover deleted files. A defragmenter analyzes and reorganizes a disk so that related file information is stored in one continuous area.

To ensure that applications software will meet your needs, you should follow six steps: (1) Read software reviews. (2) Verify that the software performs the task you desire. (3) Verify that the software will run on your computer. (4) Make sure that the software is adequately documented. (5) Purchase software from a reputable software developer or software publisher. (6) Obtain the best value, but keep in mind that value might not mean the lowest price.

Application software learning aids include tutorials, online help, trade books, and keyboard templates. Tutorials are step-by-step instructions using real examples that show you how to use an application. Online help refers to additional instructions that are available within the application. Online help can often be requested by pressing a specific function key. Trade books can help users to learn the features of applications programs and can usually be found where software is sold or in most bookstores. Keyboard templates are plastic sheets that fit around a portion of your keyboard. The keyboard commands to select the various features of the application programs are printed on the template.

Key Terms

Analytical graphics: Graphics used to selectively examine information and to interpret data through a graphic display.

Bar chart: A chart that displays relationships among data with blocks or bars.

Cell: The intersection where a row and column meet on a spreadsheet.

Clip art: Collections of art that are stored on disks and are designed for use with popular desktop publishing packages.

Columns (spreadsheet): Data which is organized vertically on a spreadsheet.

Commands: Key words and phrases that the user inputs to direct the computer to perform certain operations.

Copy (text): A word processing command that makes a copy of the marked text, but leaves the marked text where it was.

Cursor: A symbol such as an underline character or an arrow that indicates where you are working on the screen.

Cut (text): A command that removes text from an area of a word processing document. Text that is cut can be pasted into another area of the document.

Database: A collection of data that is organized in multiple related files.

Database software: Software that allows the user to enter, retrieve, manipulate, and update data in an organized and efficient manner.

Data communications software: Software used to transmit data from one computer to another.

Defragmenter: A defragmenter analyzes and reorganizes a disk so that related file information is stored in one continuous area.

Delete (text): A command that removes text from a word processing document.

Desktop publishing software (DTP): Software that allows users to design and produce professional looking documents that contain both text and graphics.

Documents: Letters or memos created on word processing software.

Edit: Making changes and corrections to electronic text.

Electronic spreadsheet, *see* **Electronic spreadsheet software**

Electronic spreadsheet software: Software that allows the user to add, subtract, and perform user-defined calculations on rows and columns of numbers.

Fields (database): A fact or specific item of information, such as a name or Social Security number, in a record of a database file.

File: A file is a collection of related records, usually stored on an auxiliary storage device.

Formulas (spreadsheet): Formulas perform calculations on the data in a spreadsheet and display the resulting value in the cell containing the formula.

Function keys: A set of numerical keys preceded by an F, included on computer keyboards as a type of user interface. Pressing a function key in an applications program is a shortcut that takes the place of entering a command.

General microcomputer applications: Software that is useful to a broad range of users.

Grammar checker software: Software used to check for grammar, writing style, and sentence-structure errors.

Graphic User Interface (GUI): A user interface that extensively uses on-screen pictures, called icons to represent files and processing options.

KEY TERMS (continued)

Graphics: A type of output used to present information in the form of charts, graphs, or pictures, so it can be quickly and easily understood.

Icons: Icons are on-screen pictures that are used instead of words to show various program options.

Insert (text): Characters and words that are added to existing text in a word processing document.

Integrated software: Software packages that combine applications such as word processing, electronic spreadsheet, database, graphics, and data communications into a single, easy-to-use set of programs.

Keyboard templates: Templates are plastic sheets that fit around a portion of the keyboard. The template details keyboard commands that select various features of the application program.

Label: A label is text that is entered in the cell of a spreadsheet.

Line chart: A graphic chart that indicates a trend by use of a rising or falling line.

Menu(s): A screen display that provides a list of processing options for the user and allows the user to make a selection.

Mouse: A small input device that is used to move the cursor and input commands.

Move (text): A command that enables the user to either cut (remove) or copy a sentence, paragraph, or block of text in a word processing document.

Online help: Instructions within an application showing how to use an application. A function key or special combination of keys are reserved for the help feature.

Paste (text): An option used after performing either the cut or the copy command, where the text is placed elsewhere in a word processing document.

Personal information management (PIM) software: Software that helps users keep track of miscellaneous bits of personal information. Notes to self, phone messages, and appointment scheduling are examples of this type of software.

Pie chart: A graphic representation of proportions depicted as slices of a *pie*.

Presentation graphics: Graphics that offer the user a wide range of presentation effects. These include three-dimensional displays, background patterns, multiple text fonts, and image libraries.

Project management software: Software that allows users to plan, schedule, track, and analyze the events, resources, and costs of a project.

Prompts: Messages to the user that are displayed on screen and provide information or instructions regarding an entry to be made or action to be taken.

Pull-down menu: A menu style wherein the selections are displayed across the screen. As the user makes a selection, the options associated with that selection appear to be pulled down from the top of the screen like a window shade.

Record (database): A collection of related facts or fields.

Rows (spreadsheet): Data which is organized horizontally on a spreadsheet.

Spelling checker software: Software that allows the user to enter a command that tells the software to check individual words or entire documents for correct spelling.

Spreadsheet, *see* **Electronic spreadsheet software**

Thesaurus software: Software that allows the user to look up synonyms for words in a document while the word processor is in use.

Trade books: Books to help users learn to use the features of a microcomputer application package. These books are usually found where software is sold, and are frequently carried in regular bookstores.

Tutorials: Software or manuals that give step-by-step instructions using real examples that show you how to use an application.

User friendly: A system that does not require any special technical skills or ability to use.

User interfaces: Methods and techniques that make using an application simpler. They include function keys, screen prompts, menus, icons, and a device called a mouse.

Utility software: Software that includes a variety of programs to help manage and maintain the data on the computer system.

Values (spreadsheet): Numerical data contained in the cells of a spreadsheet.

Window: A rectangular portion of the screen that is used to display information.

Word processing software: Software used to prepare documents electronically. It allows text to be entered on the computer keyboard in the same manner as on a typewriter. Characters are displayed on a screen and stored in the computer's main memory for ease of editing.

WYSIWYG: An acronym for "What You See Is What You Get." A feature that allows the user to design on screen an exact image of what a printed page will look like.

Name _Lelia Hershey_   Date _10/26/93_

ClassNotes

AN INTRODUCTION TO GENERAL MICROCOMPUTER APPLICATIONS

To answer this question, choose from the following list.   narrow   broad   small

1. For general microcomputer applications there will be a _Broad_ range of users who are computer literate.

2. Applications that are deemed easy to use are typically referred to as _User friendly_.

3. _Commands_ are instructions that tell the software what you want to do.

4. List some of the features of a good user interface, choosing your answers from the following list.
   function keys   menus   interactivity   screen prompts   icons   response time

   Function Keys   _Menus_
   Screen Prompts   _Icons_

5.–7. Label this diagram, choosing your answers from the following list.

   function keys   menus   interactivity   screen prompts   icons   response time

   5. _Icons_

   7. _Screen prompts_

   PLEASE ENTER FILENAME:

   6. _Function Keys_

CLASSNOTES (continued)

WORD PROCESSING SOFTWARE: A DOCUMENT PRODUCTIVITY TOOL

1. Choose from the following list to identify the advantages of word processing software over typewriting.
   spell checking   faster   more accurate   user interface   basic editing   thesaurus
   hardware reliability   grammar checkers   prompt

   Spell Checking _____ *Thesaurus* _____ *Basic editing*
   Faster _____ *More accurate* _____ *Grammar checkers*

2. Which of the items from the list in question 1, allow the user to correct misspelled words?

   Spell Checking _____ *thesaurus* _____ *basic editing*

3. *Spell chickers* _____ perform(s) automatic operations to identify and correct spelling errors.

4. *Thesaurus software* can be used to provide synonyms for identified words within a document and then to substitute that synonym within the text.

5. *Grammar Checkers* _____ will detect and correct grammar mistakes and incorrect sentence structure.

6. Basic editing functions allow users to ____ *Delete* ____ , ____ *Insert* ____ , and ____ *replace* ____ characters.

7. Duplicating blocks of text is often called the ____ *Copy* ____ function.

8. To reorder blocks of text, a user uses the ____ *move* ____ function.

9. Altering the appearance of characters can provide text emphasis. Which of the following are ways in which characters can be altered?
   boldfacing   blinking   using graphics   underlining   changing fonts

   Boldfacing _____ *Underlining* _____ *Changing fonts*

10. The user can indent text or create multiple columns of text in a document. Choosing such operations to change the appearance of a document is referred to as ____ *formatting* ____ the text.

11.–14. The operations performed by a word processor can be categorized into four main features. Write the feature for each list of common items.

11. The following items are examples of the ____ *insert/move* ____ feature.
    insert character   insert word   insert line   move sentence   move paragraphs
    move blocks   merge text

12. The following items are examples of the ____ *delete* ____ feature.
    delete character   delete paragraphs   delete word   delete documents   delete sentence

13. The following items are examples of the ____ *screen Control* ____ feature.
    scroll line up/down   enhance character   scroll page up/down   format display   word wrap

14. The following items are examples of the ____ *printing* ____ feature.
    set page format   auto-paginate   select fonts   print page range   enhance characters
    adjust print size   select spacing

CLASSNOTES (continued)

DESKTOP PUBLISHING SOFTWARE: A DOCUMENT PRESENTATION TOOL

1. Desktop publishing software allows users to design and produce professional looking documents that contain both _Graphics_ and _text_.

2. _Clip Charts_ refers to collections of art that are stored on disks and designed for use with popular desktop publishing packages.

3. The capability to design on the screen an exact image of what a printed page will look like is called _WYSIWYG what you see is what you get_

ELECTRONIC SPREADSHEET SOFTWARE: A NUMBER PRODUCTIVITY TOOL

1. List four advantages of spreadsheet software over the calculator and pencil.

faster   _More accurate_

Easier to use   _More efficient_

2. _Row_, _Columns_, and _cells_ are the major organizational components of the electronic spreadsheet.

3.–5. Label diagrams, choosing your answers from the following list.

row

spreadsheet

column

bar

cell

line

cursor

3. _Row_

4. _Column_

5. _Cells_

CLASSNOTES (continued)

6. Identify the three cell types, choosing your answers from the following list.

   macros   formulas   values   labels   functions   cells

   Labels _____   _values_ _____   _formulas_ _____

7. The process of _recalculation_ _____ occurs when a value is changed and all other values that are affected by this change are updated automatically.

8. _What if ations_ _____ analysis is possible by speculating on changes for certain cells or values, and then observing the effect of the changes on the total spreadsheet. For example, you can change the selling price of a particular product and observe the effect of regional and national sales dollars forecasts.

9.–14. The operations performed by spreadsheet software can be categorized into six main features. Write the feature for each list of common items.

9. The following items are examples of the ___*Work Sheet*___ feature.
   global format   delete column   insert column   delete row   insert row
   set up titles   set up windows

10. The following items are examples of the ___*Range*___ feature.
    format data range   erase cells

11. The following items are examples of the ___*Copy*___ feature.
    copy from cells   copy to cells

12. The following items are examples of the ___*move*___ feature.
    move from cells   move to cells

13. The following items are examples of the ___*Files*___ feature.
    save   erase   retrieve   list

14. The following items are examples of the ___*Print*___ feature.
    set up margins   define print range   define header   define page length   define footer

DATABASE SOFTWARE:
A DATA MANAGEMENT TOOL

1. Identify the three major functions of data management software. Choose your answers from the following list.
   manipulate data   update data   file data   convert data   retrieve data
   Retrieve data   _Manipulate data_   _update data_

2. The concept of a(n) ___*File*___ is equivalent to a manila folder containing data.

3. A(n) ___*record*___ is analogous to a form within the manila folder.

4. A(n) ___*Fields*___ is comparable to an individual piece of data within the form.

5. A(n) ___*data Base*___ compared to file management pertains to multiple related files within a business entity.

6.–9. The operations performed by database software can be categorized into four main features. Write the feature for each list of common items.

6. The following items are examples of the ___*Operations*___ feature.
   copy data   create database   delete data   sort data

CLASSNOTES (continued)

7. The following items are examples of the _Output data_ feature.
   retrieve data   produce a report

8. The following items are examples of the _editing_ feature.
   update data   display data

9. The following items are examples of the _arithmetic_ feature.
   compute the average   sum data fields   count the records

GRAPHICS SOFTWARE:
A DATA PRESENTATION TOOL

1.–3. Label the three common forms of data representation in graphic forms. Choose your answers from the following list.

pie chart   bar chart   spline graph   line graph

1. _Pie Chart_   2. _Bar Charts_   3. _Line Graph_

4. _Analytical Graphics_ graphics is used to deliver concepts and ideas.

5. _Presentation graphics_ goes beyond analytical graphics by offering the user a wide choice of presentation effects.

DATA COMMUNICATIONS SOFTWARE:
A CONNECTIVITY TOOL

1. Data communications software is used to transmit _data_ from one computer to another.

2. For two computers to communicate, they must have _data communication_ software, data communications _equiptment_ , and be connected to a(n) _telephone line_ .

INTEGRATED SOFTWARE:
A COMBINATION PRODUCTIVITY TOOL

1. Integrated software refers to packages that _combine_ applications such as word processing, electronic spreadsheets, database, graphics, and data communications into a single, _easy to use_ set of programs.

2. Integrated programs frequently use _Windows_ .

CLASSNOTES (continued)

OTHER POPULAR MICROCOMPUTER APPLICATIONS
Personal Information Management

1. Personal information management software helps users keep track of the miscellaneous bits of _Personal Information_ that each of us deals with everyday.

2. Some personal information software packages also include communication software capabilities such as _Phone dialers_ and _electronic mail_.

Project Management

3. Project management software allows users to plan, schedule, track, and _Analyze_ the events, resources, and costs of a(n) _project_.

Utilities

4. Utility software includes a variety of programs to help you manage and maintain the _data_ on your computer system.

5. The defragmenter _Analyze_ and _reorganize_ the disk so that related file information is stored in one continuous area.

GUIDELINES FOR PURCHASING MICROCOMPUTER APPLICATIONS SOFTWARE

1.–6. List the six guidelines for purchasing microcomputer applications software.

1. _Read software product reviews_
2. _Verify that the preforms the tasks you desire_
3. _Verify that the software will run on your computer_
4. _make sure that the software is adequately documented_
5. _Purchase software from a reputable software developer_ _or software publishers_
6. _Obtain the best value but keep in mind that value might not mean the lowest price_

LEARNING AIDS AND SUPPORT TOOLS FOR APPLICATION USERS

1. A(n) _Tutorial_ is a computer-based system for teaching the user the basic operations of the application.

2. _Online help_ provides the user with immediate assistance while he or she is utilizing the application software.

3. _Trade book_ provide printed documentation on the various applications.

4. _Key board templates_ provide visual assistance on which keys and key sequences are required for each function.

CHAPTER TWO—PROJECT TWO

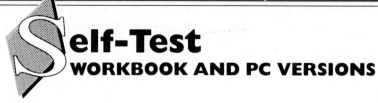

Self-Test
WORKBOOK AND PC VERSIONS

Match the following:

5 1. Database
6 2. Mouse
8 3. Online Help
7 4. Window
2 5. Insert
4 6. User Friendly
1 7. Data Communications
3 8. Documents

1. Transmitting data from one computer to another
2. Adding characters and words to existing text in your document
3. Letters or memos
4. Easy to use
5. Collected data stored in files
6. Small input device that is used to move the cursor and input commands
7. Rectangular portion of the screen that is used to display information
8. Additional instructions available within the application

You can complete the remainder of Project 2 in two ways—either by marking or filling in your answers in this workbook, or by using the PC version of Project 2. The PC version (available from your instructor) automatically corrects your answers for you. It also calculates the percent of your answers that are correct.

Answer the following questions.

1. *User interfaces* _____ are methods and techniques that make using an application simpler.
   a. Windows   c. Function keys
   b. Icons   d. User interfaces

2. T (F) Computer literate is a term used to describe individuals who know how to operate and program computers.

3. T (F) Icons refers to pictures displayed on the screen that are associated with various program options.

4. Four general microcomputer applications are word processing, database, spreadsheet, and *graphics*.
   a. banking   c. marketing
   (b.) graphics   d. games

5. Word processing software is primarily involved with which of the following application areas?
   a. numeric manipulation   d. visual display development
   b. data organization/storage   e. forecasting
   (c.) document preparation

SELF-TEST (continued)

6. (T) F   Thesaurus software allows the user to look up synonyms for words appearing in a word processing document.

7. Which of the following packages provides writing style analysis for word processing documents?
   a. spelling checker
   b. thesaurus
   c. move command
   d. format command
   (e.) grammar checker

8. T (F)   Desktop publishing software combines graphics and text to produce a database system.

9. Electronic spreadsheet software is primarily used to accomplish which of the following tasks?
   a. organize fields, records, and files
   b. develop graphics presentation
   c. spell check a document
   (d.) manage numeric data
   e. document preparation

10. Cells in an electronic spreadsheet can contain three types of data: labels, _Formulas_, and numbers.
    a. cells
    (b.) formulas
    c. forecasts
    d. graphs
    e. balances

11. The capability of an electronic spreadsheet to recalculate when data is changed enables _What if_ testing.

12. A primary way in which database software differs from file management software is that database software works on _Multiple_ files together.

13. A _Record_ is a collection of related data items stored in a computer file.

14. _Analytical_ graphics is widely used by management personnel when reviewing and communicating information.

15. _Data Communication_ software allows data stored on one computer to be transmitted to another computer.

16. Many people consider _Windows_ to be similar to a desktop where the desk has multiple papers lying on it.

17. Personal Information Management (PIM) software includes all of the following except _all of the above_.
    a. outliners
    b. electronic notepads
    c. phone dialers
    d. PIM software includes all of the above

18. Even the best software could be unusable if the _documentation_ does not clearly and completely describe the software.

19. _On line help_ refers to additional instructions that are available on the screen without leaving the application.

20. A(n) _document template_ is a document with the title, headings, footings, spacing, and other features desirable in frequently generated documents.

CHAPTER TWO—PROJECT THREE

Identifying Microcomputer Software Applications

Instructions: In the space provided, identify the microcomputer software applications illustrated below.

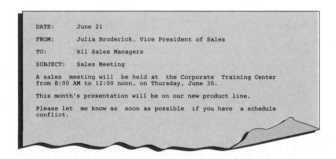

1. _____

2. _____

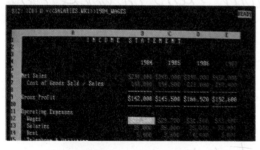

3. _____

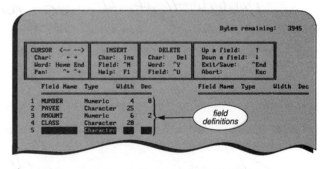

4. _____

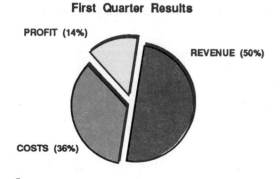

5. _____

6. _____

CHAPTER TWO—PROJECT FOUR

Identifying Software Application Learning Aids

Instructions: In the space provided, identify the software application learning aids illustrated below.

Move

After highlighting the text you want to move, you may choose one of the
following options:

Move/Copy - Move removes the text from the current position in your
    document; copy leaves the text in its current position. The text for
    both options is saved in a buffer (temporary file) and remains there
    until you move or copy again, or until you exit WordPerfect.

Delete - Removes the text from your document. You can restore the deleted
    text by pressing Cancel (press Cancel for more information).

Append - Places the text at the end of the file you specify.

After you select Move or Copy, move the cursor to where the text should be
placed and press Enter. Press Cancel (F1) to avoid retrieving the text.

To retrieve the text again, press Move, select Retrieve (4), then select
the type of text (block, tabular column or rectangle) you want to
retrieve. You may also retrieve a block of text by pressing Retrieve
(Shift-F10) and then pressing Enter.

Selection: 0   (Press ENTER to exit Help)

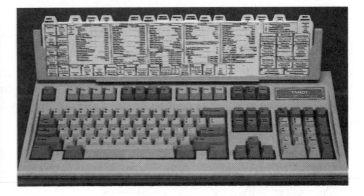

1. _____   2. _____

WordPerfect Beginning Lessons

Introduction	How to use the tutor
Lesson 1	
Lesson 2	**Start**
Lesson 3	Move the highlighted bar in the menu to any lesson and press the Enter key (the ▣ and ▣ keys on the right side of the keyboard move the highlighted bar).
Lesson 4	
Lesson 5	**Exit**
Lesson 6	Highlight EXIT at the bottom of the menu then press Enter ▣.
Advanced Lessons	**Lesson Summary and Estimated Time** Highlight a lesson and press ▣.
EXIT	**Discontinue** Press ▣ anytime during a lesson to return to this menu.

3. _____   4. _____

CHAPTER TWO—PROJECT FIVE

Developing Communication Skills

Instructions: Prepare an oral or written report on one or more of the following subjects.

1. Survey your school or a large organization and identify the different types of general microcomputer applications being used.
2. Interview someone who is now using a general microcomputer application package to perform work that was previously done manually. Ask him or her to comment on his or her level of productivity now as compared with before using the application package.
3. Research one type of general microcomputer application package by reading personal computer magazine articles that review currently available software packages. Prepare a report that summarizes the articles.
4. Research one of the leading grammar checking software packages. Prepare a report on the type of analysis and statistics that the package provides.
5. Interview someone who uses a desktop publishing package to prepare brochures, newsletters, or other documents. Prepare a report on the steps he or she used to create a recent piece of work.
6. Integrated software packages are often used by large businesses and organizations to reduce software costs and provide a standard package for all users. Interview a user of an integrated package and ask how he or she uses the package. Ask if he or she has experience with leading stand-alone packages and whether he or she believes the integrated package is sufficient for his or her needs.
7. Interview a user of a personal information management software package. Prepare a report that describes the way he or she uses the package to schedule appointments.
8. Visit at least two computer stores and ask the sales representatives the steps they suggest a person should use in purchasing software. Prepare a report comparing the sales representatives' suggestions with the guidelines in the textbook.
9. Visit a local bookstore and prepare a report on the number and type of trade books that are available for learning about one of the popular microcomputer application packages.

Input to the Computer

◆ OBJECTIVES

- ◆ Review the four operations of the information processing cycle: input, process, output, and storage
- ◆ Define the four types of input and how the computer uses each type
- ◆ Define data and explain the terms used to describe data: field, record, file, database
- ◆ Describe the standard features of keyboards and explain how to use the cursor control and function keys
- ◆ Explain the three types of terminals and how they are used
- ◆ Describe several input devices other than the keyboard and terminal
- ◆ Explain user interfaces and list the features that a good user interface should have
- ◆ Discuss how data entry differs in interactive and batch processing
- ◆ List and explain the systems and procedures associated with data entry
- ◆ Explain the term ergonomics and describe some of the important features of good equipment design

---

◆ CHAPTER OUTLINE

Chapter Review

Chapter 3 discusses the input operation of the information processing cycle. The nature of data and how it is organized as well as various input devices are also discussed. The information processing cycle consists of four operations: input, processing, output, and storage. Regardless of the size and type of computer, these operations process data into a meaningful form called information.

The input operation must take place before any data can be processed and any information produced and stored. Input refers to the process of entering various types of data such as programs, commands, user responses, and data into main memory. Programs are instructions that direct the computer to perform the necessary operations to process data into information. Commands are key words and phrases that the user inputs to direct the computer to perform certain activities. User responses refer to the data that a user inputs to respond to a question or message from the software.

Data refers to the raw facts, including numbers and words, that a computer receives during the input operation and processes to produce information. Input can also refer to the media (e.g., disks, tapes, documents) that contain these input types. Data must be entered and stored in main memory for processing to occur.

Data is organized into characters, fields, records, files, and databases. Three types of characters include: alphabetic (A–Z), numeric (0–9), and special (all other characters). The raw facts we refer to as data are made up of a combination of these three types of characters. Each fact or unique piece of data is referred to as a data item, data field, or simply a field. Fields are classified as alphabetic, numeric, or alphanumeric based on the type of characters they contain. A record is a collection of related fields and a file is a collection of related records. A database consists of multiple related files.

The keyboard is the most commonly used input device. Keyboards are connected to other devices that have screens, such as a personal computer or a terminal. As the user enters data by pressing keys on the keyboard, the data appears on the screen. To assist the user in entering numeric data, many keyboards are equipped with numeric keypads consisting of numeric keys arranged in an adding machine or calculator format. Cursor control or arrow keys can be used to position the cursor on the screen. Function keys are keys that can be programmed to accomplish certain tasks that will assist the user. Being able to type is required to use the keyboard efficiently.

Terminals, sometimes called display terminals or video display terminals (VDTs), consist of a keyboard and a screen. A dumb terminal consists of a keyboard and a display screen. It has no independent processing capability or auxiliary storage and cannot function as a stand-alone device. An intelligent terminal has built-in processing capabilities and often contains a disk drive and a printer. Intelligent terminals can perform limited processing tasks when they are not communicating directly with the central computer. Intelligent terminals are also known as programmable terminals or smart terminals. Personal computers are frequently used as intelligent terminals.

Point-of-sale (POS) terminals allow data to be entered at the time and place where the transaction with a customer occurs, such as in fast-food restaurants or hotels, for example. Point-of-sale terminals contain features such as specially labeled keys that are uniquely designed for use in a particular industry.

A mouse is a palm-sized device that can be used to control the movement of the cursor on a screen. As the user moves the mouse with his or her hand, a ball on the underside of the mouse translates the movement into

CHAPTER REVIEW (continued)

signals that are used to control the cursor on the screen. Buttons on the top of the mouse can be used to make selections of items on the screen. The mouse is easy to use but does require some desk space and requires the user to remove a hand from the keyboard.

A trackball is similar to a mouse but a larger ball is on top of the device instead of underneath. Rotation of the ball with your fingers or the palm of your hand controls the movement of the cursor on the screen. Because only the ball and not the entire device is moved, the trackball does not require much space.

Touchscreens allow users to touch areas of the screen to enter data. The user enters data by touching words or numbers or locations identified on the screen.

Graphic input devices are used to translate graphic input data, such as photos or drawings, into a form that can be processed on a computer. Three devices that are often used for graphic input are light pens, digitizers, and graphics tablets. A light pen is used to create or modify graphics by touching it on the display screen. An electronic grid on the screen senses the light generated at the tip of the pen. A digitizer converts points, lines, and curves from a sketch, drawing, or photograph to digital impulses and transmits them to a computer. A graphics tablet works in a manner similar to a digitizer, but it also contains unique characters and commands that can be automatically generated by the person using the tablet.

Pen input devices work with hand-held computers and allow the user to input hand-printed letters and numbers to record information.

Voice input allows the user to enter data and issue commands to the computer with spoken words. Most voice systems require the user to train the system to recognize his or her voice.

Scanners include a variety of devices that read printed codes, characters, or images and convert them into a digitized form that can be processed by the computer. A page scanner is an input device that can electronically capture an entire page of text or images such as photographs or art work. Smaller hand-held scanners work in a similar manner but can scan only a portion of a page at one time. Image processing systems use software and special equipment, including scanners, to input and store an actual image of a source document such as an insurance claim form with a signature. Laser scanners, also called bar code readers, use a laser beam to scan and read the special bar code printed on products. Optical character recognition (OCR) devices are scanners that read typewritten, computer-printed, and in some cases hand-printed characters from ordinary documents. The most widespread use of OCR is for reading turn-around documents. A turn-around document is designed to be returned to the organization in which it was originally issued. The remittance portion of a credit card bill is an example of a turn-around document. An optical mark reader (OMR) is a scanning device that can read carefully placed pencil marks on specially designed documents. OMR devices are frequently used to score tests.

MICR (magnetic ink character recognition) devices are used by the banking industry to read special characters encoded on checks.

Data collection devices are designed and used for obtaining data at the site where the transaction or event being reported takes place.

A user interface is the combination of hardware and software that allows a user to communicate with a computer system. Two commonly found user-interface techniques are prompts and menus. A prompt is a message to the user that appears on the screen and provides helpful information or instructions regarding an entry to be made or an action to be taken. A menu is a screen display that provides a list of processing options and allows the user to make a selection.

Four common menu selection techniques are: (1) sequential number; (2) alphabetic selection; (3) cursor positioning; and (4) reverse or inverse video. A submenu further defines the processing options that are listed on a higher level menu. Advantages of using menus are that the user does not have to remember special commands, he or she can become productive with minimal training, and he or she is guided through the application. A disadvantage of using menus is that they can be slow and restrictive because they force the user to proceed step by step through the possible operations that can be performed.

A graphic user interface (GUI) uses on-screen pictures, called icons, to represent data or processing options. Rather than typing a command, a GUI allows the user to use a mouse to select one of the icons and initiate processing. The advantages of a graphic user interface (GUI) include ease of use, shorter learning time, and quicker execution of commands.

A good user interface should include the following features: meaningful responses to the user, good screen design, simple user responses, error recovery procedures, and control and security.

Many multiuser computer systems require users to *sign-on* to the computer by entering identification such as a name or an account number followed by a password. A password is a value, such as a word or number, that identifies the user.

CHAPTER REVIEW (continued)

The most common type of input is data. Two methods of processing data on a computer are interactive processing and batch processing. Interactive processing means that data is processed immediately as it is entered. In batch processing, data is collected and, at some later time, all the data that has been gathered is processed as a group, or batch.

Online data entry used with interactive processing means that the device from which the data is being entered is connected directly to the computer. Offline data entry used with batch processing means that the device from which the data is being entered is not connected to the computer that will process it.

When large amounts of data are entered by a terminal operator whose only job is to enter the data, the data entry function is called production data entry.

Comparing a total value of all input documents to a total that was determined prior to processing the documents is called batch control.

Data can be entered into the system in various ways. In a centralized data entry operation, the data is input by trained operators from source documents. In distributed data entry, data is entered from various locations in an organization. Source data collection is the process of entering data at the location where the transaction occurs.

A transcription error occurs when an error is made in copying the values from a source document. A transposition error happens when the data entry operator switches two numbers during data entry.

Ergonomics is the study of the design and arrangement of equipment so that people will interact with the equipment in a healthy, comfortable, and efficient manner.

CHAPTER THREE

Key Terms

Alphabetic characters: The elements that comprise data; specifically, characters A–Z.

Alphabetic field: A field that contains only alphabetic characters.

Alphanumeric fields: Fields that contain a combination of character types, including alphabetic, numeric, and special characters.

Arrow keys: Keys on a keyboard that move the cursor up, down, left, or right on the screen.

Bar code reader, *see* **Laser scanner**

Batch control: During batch processing, batch control balances to a predetermined total to ensure the accuracy and reliability of data and processing techniques.

Batch processing: Data is collected and, at some later time, all the data that has been gathered is processed as a group, or *batch*.

Centralized data entry: The data is input by trained operators from source documents.

Character(s): The elements that comprise data, including alphabetic characters (A–Z), numeric characters (0–9), and special characters (punctuation).

Commands: Key words and phrases that the user inputs to direct the computer to perform certain operations.

Cursor: A symbol such as an underline character or an arrow that indicates where you are working on the screen.

Cursor control keys, *see* **Arrow keys**

Data: The raw facts, including numbers and words, that a computer receives during the input operation and processes to produce information.

Database: A collection of data that is organized in multiple related files.

Data collection devices: Input devices designed and used for obtaining data at the site where the transaction or event being reported takes place.

Data editing: Software that has the capability to check data as it is input for proper format and acceptable values.

Data field: A fact or unique piece of data.

Data item: A fact or unique piece of data.

Digitizer: A digitizer converts points, lines, and curves from a sketch, drawing, or photograph to digital impulses and transmits them to a computer.

Display terminals: Terminals that consist of a keyboard and a screen and fall into three basic categories: dumb terminals, intelligent terminals, and special-purpose terminals.

Distributed data entry: Data entry from various locations in an organization, often at the site where the data is generated.

Dumb terminal: A keyboard and a display screen that can be used to enter and transmit data to, or receive and display data from a computer to which it is connected. A dumb terminal has no independent processing capability or auxiliary storage.

Ergonomics: The study of the design and arrangement of equipment so that people will interact with the equipment in a healthy, comfortable, and efficient manner.

Field, *see* **Data field**

File: A collection of related records, usually stored on an auxiliary storage device.

KEY TERMS (continued)

Function keys: A set of numerical keys preceded by an F, included on computer keyboards as a type of user interface. Function keys can be programmed to accomplish certain tasks that will assist the user.

Graphic input devices: Devices used to translate graphic input data, such as photos or drawings, into a form that can be processed on a computer.

Graphic User Interface (GUI): A user interface that uses on-screen pictures, called icons, to represent data and processing options.

Graphics tablet: A graphics tablet converts points, lines, and curves from a sketch, drawing, or photograph to digital impulses and transmits them to a computer. It also contains unique characters and commands that can be automatically generated by the person using the tablet.

Icons: Icons are on-screen pictures that represent data or processing options.

Image processing systems: Systems that use software and special equipment, including scanners, to input and store an actual image of the source document. These systems are like electronic filing cabinets.

Input: The process of entering programs, commands, user responses, and data into main memory. Input can also refer to the media (such as disks, tapes, and documents) that contain these input types.

Intelligent terminal: A terminal that contains not only a keyboard and a screen, but also has built-in processing capabilities, disk drives, and printers.

Interactive processing: Data is processed immediately as it is entered.

Inverse video, *see* **Reverse video**

Keyboard: The most common input device, used to enter data by pressing alphabetic, numeric, cursor control, and function keys.

Laser scanner: A scanner that uses a laser beam to scan and read the special bar code printed on products.

Light pen: A light-emitting pen; used to create or modify graphics by touching it to a screen with an electronic grid.

Magnetic ink character recognition, *see* **MICR (magnetic ink character recognition) readers**

Menu(s): A screen display that provides a list of processing options for the user and allows the user to make a selection.

MICR (magnetic ink character recognition) readers: A type of input device that reads characters encoded with a special magnetized ink.

Mouse: A small input device that is used to move the cursor and input commands.

Numeric characters: The elements that comprise data; specifically, the numerals 0–9.

Numeric field: A field that contains numeric characters and some special characters.

Numeric keypad: Numeric keys arranged in an adding machine or calculator format to aid the user with numeric data entry.

Offline data entry: The device from which the data is being entered is not connected to the computer that will process it; used for batch processing.

Online data entry: Data entry for interactive processing; the device from which the data is being entered is connected directly to the computer.

Optical character recognition (OCR): Scanners that read typewritten, computer printed, and in some cases handprinted characters from ordinary documents. These devices range from large machines that can automatically read thousands of documents per minute to hand-held wands.

Optical mark reader (OMR): A scanning device that can read carefully placed pencil marks on specially designed documents.

Page scanner: An input device that can electronically capture an entire page of text or images such as photographs or art work. The scanner converts the text or image on the original document into digital information that can be stored, printed, or displayed.

Password: A value, such as a word or number, which identifies the user. In multiuser operating systems, the password must be entered correctly before a user is allowed to use an application program. The password is usually confidential.

Pen input devices: Allows the user to input hand-printed letters and numbers to record information.

Point-of-sale (POS) terminals: Terminals that allow data to be entered at the time and place where the transaction with the consumer occurs, such as in fast-food restaurants or hotels.

Production data entry: Large amounts of data are entered by a terminal operator whose only job is to enter the data.

Programmable terminals, *see* **Intelligent terminals**

KEY TERMS (continued)

Programs: Instructions that direct the computer to perform the necessary operations to process data into information.

Prompts: Messages to the user that are displayed on-screen and provide information or instructions regarding an entry to be made or an action to be taken.

Record: A collection of related fields.

Reverse video: A screen feature used to emphasize characters in which the normal display on the screen is reversed, such as a dark background with light characters; also called inverse video.

Scanners: Scanners include a variety of devices that read printed codes, characters, or images and convert them into a form that can be processed by the computer.

Smart terminals, *see* **Intelligent terminals**

Source data collection: Data that is entered as the event or transaction is occurring and at the location where it is occurring.

Special characters: All characters other than A–Z and 0–9; specifically, punctuation and symbols.

Submenus: Menus that are used to further define the processing options that are available.

Touch screens: Screens that allow users to touch areas of the screen to enter data. They let the user interact with the computer by the touch of a finger rather than typing on a keyboard or moving a mouse.

Trackball: A graphic pointing device like a mouse. To move the cursor with a trackball, the user simply rotates the top mounted ball in the desired direction.

Transcription error: During data entry, an operator error made in copying the values from a source document.

Transposition error: During data entry, an operator error made by switching two characters.

Turn-around document: A document designed to be returned to the organization in which is was originally issued. When it is returned (turned around), the data on it is read by an OCR device.

User interface: A combination of hardware and software that allows a user to communicate with a computer system.

User responses: The data that a user inputs to respond to a question or message from the software.

Video display terminals (VDT), *see* **Display terminals**

Voice input: Input that allows the user to enter data and issue commands to the computer with spoken words.

CHAPTER THREE—PROJECT ONE

ClassNotes

OVERVIEW OF THE INFORMATION PROCESSING CYCLE

1.–4. Fill in the four operations of the information processing cycle in this diagram.

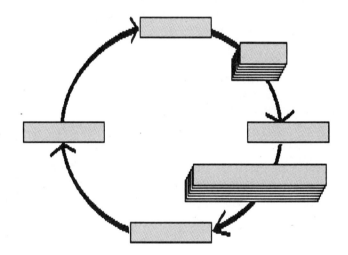

5.–7. Give examples of the following information processing cycle operations. Choose your answers from the following list.

fixed disk   diskette   keyboard   printer   computer screen

5. Input: _Keyboard_

6. Output: _Printer Computer Screen_

7. Auxiliary storage: _Fixed disk diskette_

WHAT IS INPUT?

1. Identify the four types of input, choosing your answers from the following list.

information   programs   user responses   commands   data   documents

Programs _____   _Commands_ _____

User responses _____   _data_ _____

CLASSNOTES (continued)

2.–7. Fill in the blanks in the questions, choosing your answers from the following list. Some answers might be used more than once.

auxiliary storage　　processor　　keyboard　　file　　command　　monitor
user responses　　main memory　　printers

2. All input is processed in _Main Memory_.

3. Computer programs are typically entered via _keyboard_ input and saved on _____.

4. After saving computer programs on auxiliary storage, they can typically be recalled or transferred back into main memory by a(n) _____.

5. Commands can be entered via _____ input.

6. A(n) _____ is the data a user inputs to respond to a question or message from the software.

7. Data entered to an application is routed to the computer's _____.

HOW IS DATA ORGANIZED?

1. Name the three types of character data.

_____　　_____　　_____

2. Name the three types of fields.

_____　　_____　　_____

3. A(n) _Field_ is an individual data item.

A(n) _Record_ is a collection of related fields.

A(n) _File_ is a collection of related records.

4.–6. Circle a field, place a check mark next to a record, and draw a box around a file in this diagram.

```
1250 Smith  (Clerk)     2540 01-Dec-87 1,250.00   500.00     10
1050 Wang   Salesman    2300 15-Apr-85 3,600.00               20
2300 Juarez Manager     3510 01-Jan-80 4,200.00 1,500.00     20
1520 Adami  Salesman    2300 15-Jul-83 2,500.00   250.00     20
0010 Benito President   0000 01-Aug-65 6,500.00               30
```

7. A(n) _Key Field_ can be used to arrange the contents of a file into a specific order.

8. A collection of related files is called a(n) _Data Base_.

THE KEYBOARD

Fill in the blanks in the question, choosing your answers from the following list.

terminal　　personal computer　　printer　　scanner

1. A user can input data by using a keyboard attached to a(n) _Terminal_, which is in turn attached to a mainframe and/or a(n) _Printer_.

CLASSNOTES (continued)

2.–7. These questions pertain to the typical personal computer keyboard. Choose your answers from the following list.

function keys   Insert key   Delete key   cursor control keys   number keys   Shift key

numeric keypad   arrow keys   special characters   Spacebar   Control key   Escape key

2. _____ are located above the alphabetic keys and can be used to type in numeric data.

3. _____ are keys that are not numeric and not alphabetic but are required in almost all applications.

4. The _____ is a collection of number keys, the + and – signs, and the decimal point. It is designed for fast input of numeric data.

5. _____ or _____ are used to control the movement of the cursor.

6. By using the _____ and the _____, you can add or remove characters from a series of characters.

7. The _____ can be used for special-purpose actions. These keys are typically found at the left of the keyboard or at the top of the keyboard.

TERMINALS

1. Identify the three types of terminals. Choose your answers from the following list.

special-purpose   engineering   scientific   dumb   intelligent   CAD/CAM

_____   _____   _____

2.–5. Fill in the blanks about the three types of terminals. Choose your answers from the following list.

downloading   independent   processing   printing   dependent

programmable   point-of-sale   special-purpose   uploading

2. A dumb terminal does not perform _____ processing, as all the processing takes place in an external processor.

3. Intelligent terminals contain _____ capabilities and are sometimes called

_____ terminals or _____ terminals.

4. When data moves from an intelligent terminal to an external processing capability, this activity is called data

_____.

5. A _____terminal maintains sales records, updates inventory, calculates sales tax, verifies credit, and performs other sales transaction activities.

CLASSNOTES (continued)

OTHER INPUT DEVICES

1. The input device below is a _____.

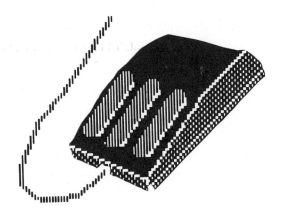

2. An advantage of the mouse is _____.

3. The disadvantages of the mouse include _____ and _____.

4. To move the cursor with a trackball, all you have to do is _____ the ball in the desired direction.

5. The main advantage of a trackball is that it doesn't require the clear _____ that a mouse does.

6. Screens that use infrared light beams to identify an input point are called _____.

7. Touch screens have two advantages. They are a _____ method and provide

   _____.

8. The disadvantages of touch screens include _____ and _____.

9.–11. Identify these graphic input devices. Choose your answers from the following list.

   scanner   light pen   graphics tablet   touch screen   digitizer   mouse

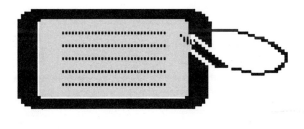

9. _____

10. _____

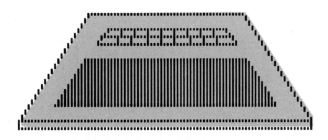

11. _____

CLASSNOTES (continued)

12. Pen input devices allow the user to enter _____ letters and numbers to record

    _____.

13. _____ input allows the user to speak directly to the application using verbal commands and responses.

14. One advantage of voice input is _____.

INPUT DEVICES DESIGNED FOR SPECIFIC PURPOSES

1.–7. These questions pertain to different types of scanners and other input devices. Choose your answers from the following list.

scanners   page scanners   image processing   laser scanners   optical character readers

optical mark readers   MICR readers   data collection devices

1. _____ are scanners that read typewritten, computer-printed and in some cases hand-printed characters from ordinary documents.

2. _____ are scanning devices that can read carefully placed pencil marks on specially designed documents.

3. A scanning device often used by modern grocery stores at checkout counters is a _____.

4. A(n) _____ is an input device that can electronically capture an entire page of text or images, such as photographs or art work.

5. _____ systems use software and special equipment, including scanners, to input and store an actual image of a document.

6. _____ are used in the banking industry for processing checks.

7. _____ are designed and used for obtaining data at the site where the transaction or event being reported takes place.

USER INTERFACES

1. A user interface is the combination of _____ and _____

   that allows a user to _____ with a computer system.

2.–4. Fill in the blanks, choosing your answers from the following list.

saturate   control   respond to   process   information   data

Through a user interface, users are able to input values that:

2. _____ messages from the computer.

3. _____ the computer.

4. request _____ from the computer.

5. A prompt is a _____ to the user that appears on the screen and provides helpful

   _____ or _____ regarding an entry to be made or action to be taken.

6. _____ is the capability to check the data for proper format and acceptable values.

CLASSNOTES (continued)

7.–18. Look at this menu and fill in the blanks, choosing your answers from the following list.

```
HyperGraphics: Object   Selection
───────────────────────────────────────
      Box
      Circle
      Arc
      Line
      Draw
      Fill
      Text
      Animation
      Cut
      End
───────────────────────────────────────
Enter Selection:___
```

menu prompt	alphabetic
menu title	sequential number
reverse video	menu selection
icon	alphanumeric
mobile	cursor positioning

7. The portion of the menu above the first line is called the _____.

8. The portion of the menu between the two lines is called the _____.

9. The portion of the menu below the bottom line is called the _____.

10. If the menu selection portion of the menu is labeled with numeric items, the selection approach is called

_____ selection.

11. If the menu selection portion of the menu is labeled with alphabetic labels, the selection approach is called

_____ selection.

12. If the menu selection portion of the menu has a movable cursor, the selection approach is called

_____ selection.

13. If you use a movable reverse image to make a selection, the selection approach is called

_____ selection.

14. A submenu further defines the processing _____ that are available.

15. The user does not have to remember _____.

16. The user can become productive with minimum _____.

17. The user is _____ through the application.

18. The disadvantage most often associated with menus is that they can be _____

and _____.

GRAPHIC USER INTERFACE

1. A graphic user interface uses on-screen pictures called _____ to represent data or processing optionns.

2. The user uses a _____, not the keyboard to select one of the graphic images on the screen.

CLASSNOTES (continued)

FEATURES OF A USER INTERFACE

1. Match the following features of a user interface in the left column with the characteristics in the right column.

_____ system responses to the user   a. password

_____ screen design   b. uncluttered

_____ user responses   c. simple

_____ error recovery   d. user told how to recover

_____ control and security   e. response time

DATA ENTRY

1. The most common type of input is _____.

DATA ENTRY FOR INTERACTIVE AND BATCH PROCESSING

Fill in the blanks, choosing your answers from the following list.

online   input   offline data entry   output   online data entry   offline production   data entry

1. Data entered in the interactive processing mode generates immediate _____.

2. Data entry for interactive processing is said to be _____.

3. When large amounts of data are entered by a terminal operator whose only job is to enter the data, the data entry function is called _____.

4. Data batch processing can be entered in either an _____ or an _____ manner.

5.–7. Consider the screen and answer these questions. Choose your answers from the following list.

protected fields

prompt

input field

record

unprotected field

```
04/05                    ** ENTER ORDERS **
                           - SCREEN 1 -

CUSTOMER NUMBER:
ORDER NUMBER:

BILL TO:                                 SHIP TO:


ORDER DATE:
TERMS:
SALESPERSON:
DISCOUNT %:
```

5. CUSTOMER NUMBER: is an example of a(n) _____.

6. The box to the right of ORDER DATE: is an example of a(n) _____.

7. The fields to the right of ORDER NUMBER:, BILL TO:, and SHIP TO: are called _____.

CLASSNOTES (continued)

DATA ENTRY PROCEDURES

1.–8. List the eight questions that must be answered to successfully implement a data entry application.

1. _____

2. _____

3. _____

4. _____

5. _____

6. _____

7. _____

8. _____

ERGONOMICS

1. Match the following ergonomic considerations in the left column with the appropriate characteristic in the right column.

_____ screen angle   a. 80 to 120 degrees

_____ screen   b. 20 to 60 inches

_____ viewing angle   c. antiglare

_____ viewing distance   d. plus or minus 7 degrees

_____ elbow angle   e. 10 to 20 degrees

CHAPTER THREE—PROJECT TWO
Self-Test
WORKBOOK AND PC VERSIONS

Match the following:

_____ 1. Commands

_____ 2. OMR

_____ 3. Record

_____ 4. Menus

_____ 5. MICR

_____ 6. Function Keys

_____ 7. Prompts

_____ 8. File

1. Magnetic ink character recognition
2. Collection of related fields
3. Collection of records
4. One of the first steps in improving the user interface
5. Optical character reader
6. Key words or phrases entered by the user
7. Optical mark reader
8. Provides the user with a list of choices
9. Can be programmed to perform specific operations

You can complete the remainder of Project 2 in two ways—either by marking or filling in your answers in this workbook, or by using the PC version of Project 2. The PC version (available from your instructor) automatically corrects your answers for you. It also calculates the percent of your answers that are correct.

Answer the following questions.

1. Which of the following is(are) part of the information processing cycle?
   a. equipment
   b. input
   c. procedures
   d. telecommunication
   e. personnel

2. The information processing cycle is comprised of input, processing, output, and _____.
   a. computing
   b. information
   c. storage
   d. arithmetic operations
   e. data

3. The operations in the information processing cycle are carried out by computer hardware and _____.
   a. peripherals
   b. storage
   c. software
   d. logic

4. When input is entered into the computer it is placed initially into _____.
   a. auxiliary storage
   b. main memory
   c. the CRT
   d. computer tapes
   e. an output buffer

SELF-TEST (continued)

5. Commands are key words and phrases that are entered by the _____.
   a. computer hardware   c. user   e. computer program
   b. main memory   d. auxiliary storage

6. User responses refer to the data that a user inputs in response to a question or message from the

   _____.
   a. input device   c. main memory   e. computer program
   b. output device   d. source document

7. The field 01/31/90 is called a(n) _____ field.
   a. numeric   c. alphanumeric
   b. character   d. data

8. A _____ is a collection of related fields.
   a. file   c. relational field
   b. program   d. record

9. A collection of records is called a _____.
   a. database   c. field
   b. file   d. bit

10. The _____ field is used to arrange records in a specific order.
    a. key   c. last
    b. first   d. organization

11. In a(n) _____ file organization records are not arranged in any particular order.
    a. sequential   c. random
    b. normal   d. unfixed

12. A _____ implies that a relationship has been established among multiple files.
    a. field   c. record
    b. file   d. database

13. A _____ is a symbol that indicates where on the screen the next character entered
    will be displayed.
    a. cursor   c. control character   e. rectangle
    b. tab   d. caret

14. Keys that move the cursor symbol on the computer screen are called cursor control keys

    or _____.
    a. movement keys   c. numeric keys   e. pointer keys
    b. function keys   d. arrow keys

15. _____ are keys that can be programmed to accomplish certain tasks that will assist
    the user.
    a. Help keys   c. Arrow keys   e. Function keys
    b. Assist keys   d. Control keys

16. T F   A dumb terminal has no independent processing capability.

SELF-TEST (continued)

17. Intelligent terminals are also known as _____ terminals.
    a. processing   c. data   e. programmable
    b. control   d. intellectual

18. A _____ terminal allows data to be entered at the time and place a transaction with a customer occurs.
    a. dynamic   c. point-of-sale   e. portable
    b. graphics   d. end user

19. T   F   The only function of a mouse is to move the cursor quickly on the terminal screen.

20. A major disadvantage of a touch screen is that the _____ of the touching area is not precise.
    a. resolution   c. depth   e. coordination
    b. color   d. instrumentation

21. Light pens, digitizers, and graphics tablets are examples of _____ input devices.
    a. inexpensive   c. expensive   e. point-of-sale
    b. portable   d. graphic

22. Voice input is achieved by creating _____ patterns for words and storing these patterns in auxiliary storage.
    a. repeated   c. audio   e. video
    b. several   d. digital

23. The magnetic ink character recognition (MICR) input device is used almost exclusively in the _____ industry.
    a. automobile   c. manufacturing   e. computer
    b. banking   d. retail

24. Scanners are devices that read _____ codes, characters, or images and convert them into a computer format.
    a. printed   c. alphabetic   e. medical
    b. nonnumeric   d. raised

25. OCR stands for _____.
    a. optical card reader   c. optical cash register   e. optical character reader
    b. our computer reader   d. octal character recognition

26. Optical mark readers (OMR) are frequently used in which of the following applications?
    a. desktop publishing input   c. capturing customer data   e. commercial real estate
    b. test scoring   d. banking transactions

27. A laser scanner is often used by modern _____ to scan and read special bar codes.
    a. automobile dealerships   c. restaurants   e. computer dealers
    b. grocery stores   d. manufacturing plants

28. Desktop publishing systems will frequently use _____ to convert images into computer format.
    a. laser scanners   c. image processors   e. OCR devices
    b. page scanners   d. matrix printers

SELF-TEST (continued)

29. When an actual image of a document is required to be captured, _____ will be used.
    a. image processing systems   c. optical imaging   e. digital/video readers(D/VR)
    b. filing systems   d. laser adapted optics

30. _____ devices are designed to obtain data at the site of the transaction.
    a. Data collection   c. Magnetic recording   e. Offline collection
    b. External collection   d. Video collection

31. A _____ provides the means for communication between an information system and the user.
    a. CPU   c. modem   e. graphics terminal
    b. disk drive   d. user interface

32. In most instances the _____ determines the ultimate quality of the user interface.
    a. computer size   c. number of colors   e. software
    b. terminal quality   d. computer speed

33. One of the first steps in improving the user interface was the utilization of _____ on the screen.
    a. prompts   c. extensive directions   e. commands
    b. terse imperatives   d. graphical images

34. _____ were implemented to assist the end user with the selection of alternatives.
    a. Choices   c. Directories   e. Menus
    b. Prompts   d. Options

35. Sequential number, alphabetic selection, cursor positioning, and reverse video are examples of

    _____.
    a. prompt selection alternatives   c. user alternatives   e. menu directions
    b. menu selection alternatives   d. menu headers

36. When icon selection is used for identifying a user alternative, the choice is identified by a _____.
    a. special function key   c. graphic image   e. menu of menus
    b. textual prompt   d. character alternative

37. _____ are those messages and actions taken by the computer when a user enters data into the computer.
    a. System responses   c. User alternatives   e. Menu directions
    b. Menu selection alternatives   d. Menu headers

38. _____ is the elapsed time between the instant a user enters data and the instant the computer responds.
    a. Time between prompts   c. Data entry time   e. System selection time
    b. Menu selection time   d. Response time

39. A _____ is a value, such as a word or number, that identifies a user to the information system.
    a. character ID   c. password   e. system tag
    b. unique identifier   d. user program

40. The most common type of input is _____.
    a. program   c. user responses
    b. commands   d. data

SELF-TEST (continued)

41. T   F   In offline data entry, the device that stores the data that is entered is not connected to the computer.

42. A common method for data entry is to use _____ to identify input fields to the data entry operator.

    a. prompt characters   c. reverse video   e. touch screens

    b. numeric codes   d. windowing

43. Entering data from various locations in an organization is called _____.

    a. external data entry   c. centralized data entry   e. production data entry

    b. remote data entry   d. distributed data entry

44. Which of the following would be of concern if you were considering the ergonomics of a given situation?

    a. screen height   c. menu type

    b. user responses   d. response time

45. _____ is the amount of data entered for a given time period.

    a. Data entry speed   c. Flow of data   e. Data flow processing

    b. Transaction volume   d. Transaction processing

46. A _____ error occurs when an error is made in copying the values from a source document.

    a. transposition   c. critical   e. computer

    b. numeric   d. transcription

CHAPTER THREE—PROJECT THREE

Identifying Information Processing Cycle Operations and Devices

Instructions: In the space provided, identify the four information processing cycle operations and the six computer devices illustrated below.

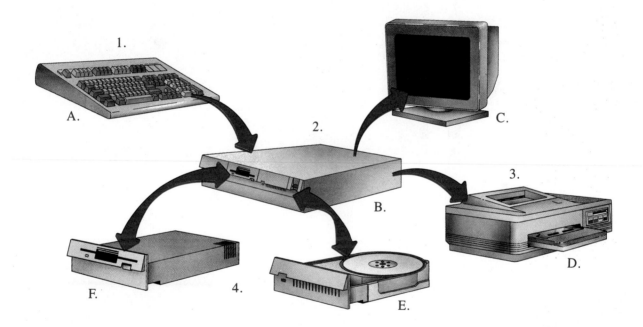

INFORMATION PROCESSING CYCLE OPERATIONS

1. _____

2. _____

3. _____

4. _____

COMPUTER DEVICES

A. _____

B. _____

C. _____

D. _____

E. _____

F. _____

Name _____ Date _____

Identifying Computer Input Devices

Instructions: In the space provided, identify the computer input devices shown below.

1. _____

2. _____

3. _____

4. _____

5. _____

6. _____

CHAPTER THREE—PROJECT FIVE

Developing Communication Skills

Instructions: Prepare an oral or written report on one or more of the following subjects.

1. Visit your school's computer center and determine the types of input devices that are used.
2. Contact a local bank computer center and prepare a report on how checks are processed. Be sure to include information on how magnetic ink character recognition (MICR) equipment is used.
3. Contact a local grocery store and prepare a report on how laser scanners are used at check-out counters.
4. Visit an engineering firm that uses computer-aided design (CAD) equipment and software to design its products. Report on how the equipment and software are used.
5. Visit a restaurant where a point-of-sale terminal is used. Prepare a report on the special features of the terminal.
6. Prepare a report that compares the use of a mouse versus the use of a trackball. Interview users of both input devices.
7. Prepare a report on existing and possible future uses of voice input.
8. Interview a person who uses a graphic user interface (GUI) such as the Macintosh operating system or Microsoft Windows. Ask him or her to demonstrate what he or she likes or dislikes about the interface.
9. Interview the office manager of a medium or large organization. Ask him or her what he or she does to make the workplace healthy, comfortable, and efficient for the employees.

CHAPTER FOUR

The Processor Unit

◆ OBJECTIVES

- ◆ Identify the components of the processor unit and describe their use
- ◆ Define a bit and describe how a series of bits in a byte is used to represent characters
- ◆ Discuss how the ASCII and EBCDIC codes represent characters
- ◆ Describe why the binary and hexadecimal numbering systems are used with computer systems
- ◆ List and describe the four steps in a machine cycle
- ◆ Discuss the three primary factors that affect the speed of the processor unit
- ◆ Describe the characteristics of RAM and ROM memory, and list several other types of memory
- ◆ Describe the process of manufacturing integrated circuits

◆ CHAPTER OUTLINE

What Is the Processor Unit?
    The Central Processing Unit
    Main Memory
**How Programs and Data Are Represented
in Memory**
    The ASCII Code
    The EBCDIC Code
    Binary Representation of Numbers
Parity
Number Systems
    The Decimal Number System
    The Binary Number System
    The Hexadecimal Number System
    Summary of Number Systems
**How the Processor Unit Executes Programs
and Manipulates Data**
    Machine Language Instructions

    The Machine Cycle
Processor Speeds
    System Clock
    Buses
    Word Size
Architecture of Processor Units
    Microprocessors
    Coprocessors
    Parallel Processing
    RISC Technology
Types of Memory
    RAM Memory
    ROM Memory
    Other Types of Memory
Summary
Making a Chip

 Chapter 4 examines the components of the processor unit, describes how main memory stores programs and data, and discusses the sequence of operations that occurs when instructions are executed on a computer. It is in the processor unit that the computer programs are executed and the data is manipulated. The main components of the processor unit are the central processing unit (CPU) and main memory.

The central processing unit (CPU) contains the control unit and the arithmetic/logic unit (ALU). The control unit can be thought of as the brain of the computer because it controls the computer. The control unit operates by repeating the following four operations: fetching, decoding, executing, and storing. Fetching means obtaining the next instruction. Decoding is translating the program instruction into the commands the computer can process. Executing refers to the actual processing of the computer commands. Storing takes place when the result of the instruction is written to main memory. The arithmetic/logic unit (ALU) contains the electronic circuitry necessary to perform arithmetic and logical operations on data. Arithmetic operations include addition, subtraction, multiplication, and division. Logical operations include comparing one data item to another to determine if the first data item is greater than, equal to, or less than the other. Both the control unit and the ALU contain registers, temporary storage locations for specific types of data.

Main memory, also called primary storage, stores three types of items: the operating system, application programs, and data.

Each memory storage location is called a byte. Generally speaking, a byte can store one character. Each byte has a unique memory address that indicates its location and can be used to reference the byte. Memory is usually measured in kilobytes. A kilobyte (abbreviated as K or KB) is equal to 1,024 bytes. When memory exceeds 1,000K, or one million bytes, it is referred to in megabytes, abbreviated MB.

A byte contains eight bits. A bit is an element of a byte that can represent one of two values; either off or on. Each alphabetic, numeric, or special character can be represented by a unique combination of off and on bits. The binary number system (base 2) represents quantities by using only two symbols, 0 and 1. The binary number system is used in computers because the 0 and 1 symbols can be represented by the off and on condition of bits. Two popular codes that use combinations of zeros and ones to represent characters in memory and on auxiliary storage are the ASCII and EBCDIC codes. The American Standard Code for Information Interchange (ASCII) is the most widely used coding system to represent data and is widely used on personal computers and many minicomputers. The Extended Binary Coded Decimal Interchange Code (EBCDIC) is a common coding scheme used primarily on mainframe computers.

For each byte of memory, most computers have at least one extra bit, called a parity bit, that is used by the computer for error checking. For computers with odd parity, the total number of on bits in the byte (including the parity bit) must be an odd number. For even parity computers, the on bits must total an even number.

A hexadecimal (base 16) number system represents the decimal numbers 10 through 15 by using the letters A through F. Hexadecimal is used to represent binary in a more compact form.

A machine language instruction is one that the electronic circuits in the CPU can interpret and convert into one or more of the commands in the computer's instruction set.

CHAPTER REVIEW (continued)

The instruction set contains commands that the computer's circuits can directly perform. A machine language instruction is usually composed of three parts: an operation code; values that indicate the number of characters to be processed by the instruction; and the addresses in main memory of the data to be used in the execution of the instruction. The operation code indicates which operation is to be performed.

An instruction register is an area of memory within the control unit that can store a single instruction at a time.

The instruction cycle includes the fetch and decode steps. The execution cycle includes the execute and store steps. Together, these four steps are called the machine cycle.

The processing speed of computers is often measured in MIPS—millions of instructions per second. The speed at which a computer can execute the machine cycle is influenced by three factors: the system clock, the buses, and the word size. The control unit utilizes the system clock to synchronize, or control the timing of, all computer operations. The system clock generates electronic pulses at a fixed rate, measured in megahertz. One megahertz equals one million pulses per second. Data is transmitted between computer components via electrical pathways called buses. Bus size is the number of bits the computer can transmit at one time. The word size is the number of bits that the CPU can process at one time. The larger the word size of the processor, the faster the capability of the computer to process data.

A microprocessor is a single integrated circuit that contains the CPU and sometimes memory. An integrated circuit, also called an IC, chip, or microchip, is a complete electronic circuit that has been etched on a small chip of nonconducting material such as silicon.

The main circuit board of a personal computer is called a motherboard.

A coprocessor is a special microprocessor chip or circuit board designed to perform a specific task such as perform mathematical calculations.

Most computers use serial processing; the execution of one instruction at a time. Some computers have multiple CPUs and can perform parallel processing where more than one instruction is being processed at the same time.

Reduced instruction set computers (RISC) use a smaller number of instructions to increase the throughput of the system.

Core memory consisted of small, ring-shaped pieces of material that could be magnetized, or polarized, in one of two directions. The polarity could be read to determine if the memory location was off or on.

Semiconductor memory is an integrated circuit containing thousands of transistors that can be either off or on and represent a bit in memory.

Memory access speeds are measured in microseconds and nanoseconds. A microsecond is one millionth of a second. A nanosecond is one billionth of a second.

RAM, ROM, PROM, EPROM, and EEPROM are all types of semiconductor memory chips used in computers. Random access memory, or RAM, chips are the semiconductor chips used for main memory. Dynamic RAM (DRAM) chips require a periodic electrical charge to retain stored data. Static RAM chips do not require a periodic electrical charge but are larger and more complicated that DRAM chips. High-speed RAM memory used to store the most frequently used instructions is called cache memory. Ram memory is said to be volatile because the programs and data stored in RAM are erased when the power to the computer is turned off.

Read only memory (ROM) has its data permanently recorded when it is manufactured and retains its contents even when the power is turned off. Program instructions that are stored in ROM are called firmware or micro-code.

Programmable read only memory (PROM) is similar to ROM but can be loaded with instructions or data after it is manufactured but before it is installed in a computer.

Erasable programmable read only memory (EPROM) is similar to PROM with the additional feature of being able to be erased so that new programs or data can be loaded in the memory. EPROM is erased through the use of special ultraviolet light devices that destroy the bit settings within the memory.

Electronically erasable programmable read only memory (EEPROM) allows the stored data or programs to be erased electronically without having to remove the memory from the computer.

CHAPTER FOUR

Key Terms

American Standard Code for Information Interchange (ASCII): The most widely used coding system to represent data, primarily on personal computers and many minicomputers.

Arithmetic/Logic Unit (ALU): The unit of the CPU that performs arithmetic and logic operations.

Arithmetic operations: Numeric calculations performed by the arithmetic/logic unit of the CPU, which include addition, subtraction, multiplication, and division.

ASCII code, *see* **American Standard Code for Information Interchange**

Binary (base 2): A number system which represents quantities by using only two symbols, 0 and 1, used to represent the electronic status of bits inside the processor unit, and also for addressing the memory locations.

Bit: An element of a byte that can represent one of two values, on or off. There are eight bits in a byte.

Bus: Any line that transmits bits between memory and the input/output devices and between memory and the CPU.

Byte: A byte is each storage location within main memory, identified by a memory address.

Cache memory: Cache memory is high-speed RAM memory between the CPU and main memory that increases processing efficiency.

Chip, *see* **Integrated circuit**

Control unit: The unit of the CPU that directs and coordinates all the activities on the computer, consisting of four operations: fetching, decoding, executing, and storing.

Coprocessor: A special microprocessor chip or circuit board designed to perform a specific task, such as numeric calculations.

Core memory: An old style memory that was small, ring-shaped pieces of material that could be magnetized, or polarized, in one of two directions. The polarity indicated whether the core was on or off.

Decoding: A control unit operation that translates the program instruction into the commands that the computer can process.

Dynamic RAM (DRAM) chips: A type of RAM memory chip that is small and simple in design, in which the current, or charge, on the chip is periodically regenerated by special regenerator circuits.

EBCDIC, *see* **Extended Binary Coded Decimal Interchange Code**

EEPROM, *see* **Electronically erasable programmable read only memory**

Electronically erasable programmable read only memory (EEPROM): A type of EPROM in which the data or programs can be erased electronically without being removed from the computer.

EPROM, *see* **Erasable programmable read only memory**

Erasable programmable read only memory (EPROM): A variation of PROM that allows the user to erase the data stored in memory and to store new data or programs in the memory. EPROM is erased with special ultraviolet light devices that destroy the bit settings within the memory.

Even parity: A mechanism used by the computer for error checking, the total number of on bits in the byte (including the parity bit) must be an even number.

Executing: A control unit operation that processes the computer commands.

KEY TERMS (continued)

Execution cycle (E-cycle): Steps in the machine cycle that include the execution of the instruction and the storage of the processing results.

Extended Binary Coded Decimal Interchange Code (EBCDIC): A coding system used to represent data, primarily on mainframes.

Fetching: A control unit operation that obtains the next program instruction from main memory.

Firmware: Instructions that are stored in ROM memory; also called microcode.

Hexadecimal (base 16): A number system which represents binary in a more compact form. Hexadecimal is used to represent the electronic status of bits in main memory, and addressing the memory locations.

IC, *see* **Integrated circuit**

Instruction cycle (I-cycle): Steps in the machine cycle that include fetching the next program instruction and the decoding of that instruction.

Instruction register: An area of memory within the control unit of the CPU that can store a single instruction at a time.

Instruction set: The collection of commands, such as ADD or MOVE, that the computer's circuits can directly perform.

Integrated circuit (IC): A complete electronic circuit that has been etched on a small chip of nonconducting material such as silicon; also called chip, or microchip.

K, *see* **Kilobyte**

KB, *see* **Kilobyte**

Kilobyte (K, or **KB):** A measure of memory equal to 1,024 bytes.

Logical operations: Comparisons of data by the arithmetic/logic unit of the central processing unit, to see if one value is greater than, equal to, or less than another.

Machine cycle: The four steps which the CPU carries out for each machine language instruction: fetch, decode, execute, and store.

Machine language instructions: Program instructions that the electronic circuits in the CPU can interpret and convert into one or more of the commands in the computer's instruction set.

Main memory: Memory contained in the processor unit of the computer that stores the operating system, application programs, and data; also called primary storage.

MB, *see* **Megabyte**

Megabyte (MB): A measure of memory equal to one million bytes.

Megahertz: A measurement used to describe the speed of the system clock; it is equal to one million cycles (or pulses) per second.

Memory address: The location of a byte in memory.

Microchip, *see* **Integrated circuit**

Microcode, *see* **Firmware**

Microprocessor: The smallest processor, which is a single integrated circuit that contains the CPU and sometimes memory.

Microsecond: A measure of time equal to one millionth of a second.

MIPS (million instructions per second): A measure of the processing speed of computers.

Motherboard: The main circuit board of a personal computer.

Nanosecond: A measure of time equal to one billionth of a second.

Odd parity: A mechanism used by the computer for error checking. The total number of on bits in the byte (including the parity bit) must be an odd number.

Operation code: A unique value typically stored in the first byte in a machine language instruction that indicates which operation is to be performed.

Parallel processing: The use of multiple CPUs, each with its own memory, that work on their assigned portions of a problem simultaneously.

Parity bit: One extra bit for each byte that is used by the computer for error checking.

Primary storage, *see* **Main memory**

Programmable read only memory (PROM): Acts the same as ROM except the data can be stored into the PROM memory prior to being installed in the computer.

PROM, *see* **Programmable read only memory**

RAM, *see* **Random access memory**

Random access memory (RAM): The name given to integrated circuits, or chips, that are used for main memory.

KEY TERMS (continued)

Read only memory (ROM): Memory in which data or programs are written to it once at the time of manufacture, and always retained thereafter, even when the computer's power is turned off.

Registers: Storage locations in the CPU that temporarily store specific data such as the address of the next instruction.

RISC (reduced instruction set computing): Technology that involves reducing the computer's instruction set to only those instructions that are most frequently used, which allows the computer to operate faster.

ROM, *see* **Read only memory**

Semiconductor memory: A type of memory used in virtually all computers, consisting of an integrated circuit containing thousands of transistors etched into a semiconductor material such as silicon.

Serial processing: Computers that contain one CPU that processes a single instruction at a time.

Static RAM: A type of RAM memory chip that is larger and more complicated than dynamic RAM and does not require the current to be periodically regenerated.

Storing: A control unit operation that takes place when the result of the instruction is written to main memory.

System clock: The clock used by the control unit to synchronize, or control the timing of, all computer operations, generating electronic pulses at a fixed rate, measured in megahertz.

Transistor: An electronic component etched into a semiconductor material such as silicon. The transistor can be either on or off and represents a bit in memory.

Volatile: RAM memory is said to be volatile because the programs and data stored in RAM are erased when the power to the computer is turned off.

Word size: The number of bits that the CPU can process at one time.

CHAPTER FOUR—PROJECT ONE

ClassNotes

WHAT IS THE PROCESSOR UNIT?

1.–2. In the following illustration of a processor unit, identify which part represents the memory and which part represents the central processing unit.

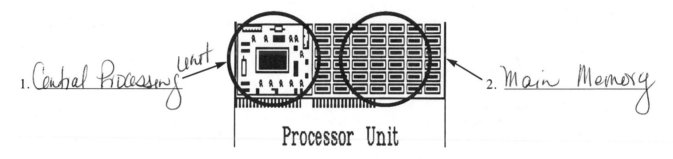

1. _Central Processing unit_

2. _Main Memory_

Processor Unit

The Central Processing Unit

3.–4. Complete the statements, choosing your answers from the following list.

control unit   main memory   arithmetic/logic unit   central processing unit

3. The brain within a human being is analogous to the _Central Processing Unit_ within the computer system.

4. The two major subunits within the CPU are the _Control Unit/_ and _arithmetic logic unit_

5.–11. Fill in the major functions of the control unit and the arithmetic/logic unit in this illustration.

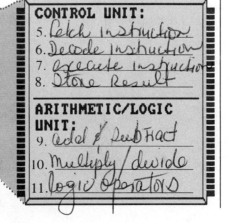

CONTROL UNIT:
5. _Fetch Instruction_
6. _Decode Instruction_
7. _Execute Instruction_
8. _Store Result_

ARITHMETIC/LOGIC UNIT:
9. _add & subtract_
10. _Multiply / divide_
11. _logic Operators_

4.7

CLASSNOTES (continued)

Main Memory

12.–14. Complete the following illustration of main memory within the processor unit.

Main Memory

OPERATING SYSTEM	APPLICATION PROGRAM	
		Data
	12. _Code_	13. _Working_ 14. _I/O_

15.–18. Complete the statements, choosing your answers from the following list.

     megabyte   value   byte   address   512   nibble   640   nanobyte   gibabyte   1024

15. Each location within main memory has a(n) _Address_.

16. One _Byte_ can be stored or retained at each location in main memory.

17. One kilobyte (KB) equals _1024_ bytes.

18. One thousand KB equal a(n) _Megabyte_, and one million KB equal a(n) _Gigabyte_.

HOW PROGRAMS AND DATA ARE REPRESENTED IN MEMORY

1.–2. Complete the statements about data in memory.

1. The three classifications of characters are alphabetic, _Numeric_, and _Special_.

2. Within memory, a character equals one _Byte_.

3.–4. Show how the following characters would be represented in memory locations.

3. John Doe

4. $123.69

5.–11. Complete the statements about binary numbers and character representations within memory.

5. A byte is equal to _____ binary digits.

6. Binary digits is another way of saying _____.

7. A bit can be either ◯ = _____ or ⬤ = _____.

CLASSNOTES (continued)

8. The number 0101001 is called a _____ number.

9. American Standard Code for Information Interchange, abbreviated as _____, is a method for representing characters in memory.

10. EBCDIC is another method for representing _____ in memory.

11. Binary representation is restricted to the representation of powers of the number _____.

PARITY

1.–6. Complete the statements about parity, choosing your answers from the following list.

   data   error   transmission   left   odd   right   even   information

1. The parity bit is an additional bit that is added to the _____ end of a memory location or byte.

2. _____ parity implies that the sum of the bits (including the parity bit) that are on will equal an odd number.

3. _____ parity implies that the sum of the bits (including the parity bit) that are on will equal an even number.

4. Parity is typically used for _____ detection during the movement or transmission of bytes of data.

5. In this example the parity bits are the same, both off, and the parity is _____.

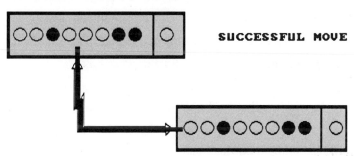

6. In this example, a(n) _____ error has occurred, and the parity bit from the original location disagrees with the parity bit of the destination location.

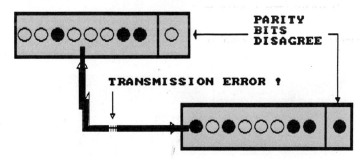

CLASSNOTES (continued)

NUMBER SYSTEMS

Complete the following statements.

1. In the decimal number system there is(are) _____ symbol(s).

2. In the binary number system there is(are) _____ symbol(s).

3. In the hexadecimal number system there is(are) _____ symbol(s).

4. Fill in the following table for these three number systems.

NUMBER SYSTEM	BASE	SYMBOLS USED
DECIMAL		
BINARY		
HEXADECIMAL		

5. In the decimal system, the positional value for the first position to the left of the decimal point represents 10 raised to the _____ power.

6. In the decimal system, the positional value for the fourth position to the left of the decimal point represents 10 raised to the _____ power.

7. Number systems make use of _____ to represent different quantities.

8. The number of symbols used in a system determines the _____ of that system.

9. The value of a digit depends upon the value of the symbol itself and its _____ value within the number.

10. The first position of a binary integer number represents 2 raised to the _____ power.

11. The third position of a binary integer number represents a value of _____.

12. What is the decimal equivalent of the following binary number? 10110 = _____.

13. The second position of a hexadecimal integer number represents 16 raised to the _____ power.

14. What is the decimal equivalent of the following hexadecimal number? 1 2 A C F =

_____.

15. In converting from binary to hexadecimal and hexadecimal to binary, each hexadecimal digit is represented by _____ binary digits.

16. Fill in the equivalent numbers.

	EQUIVALENT BASE 2 NUMBER		EQUIVALENT BASE 16 NUMBER
5		1100	
A		1011	

17. Convert the following binary number to hexadecimal. 10101100 = _____.

CLASSNOTES (continued)

HOW THE PROCESSOR UNIT EXECUTES PROGRAMS AND MANIPULATES DATA

1. _____ instructions are the instructions that the processor unit executes.

2. The _____ of the instruction specifies the operation that the instruction is to perform.

3.–4. Fill in the missing portions of a typical machine language instruction.

OPERATION CODE	3. _____	VALUE 1 ADDRESS	4. _____

Complete the statements about the machine cycle.

5. List the four parts of the machine cycle.

_____   _____

_____   _____

6. The fetch and decode phase of the machine cycle is called the _____ cycle.

7. The execute and store phase of the machine cycle is called the _____ cycle.

PROCESSOR SPEEDS

1.–6. Complete the statements, choosing your answers from the following list.

kilohertz   MIPS   megahertz   length   bus   width   port   system clock

1. The control unit utilizes the _____ to synchronize, or control the timing, of all computer operations.

2. The unit of measurement for the processor speed is _____.

3. The execution rate of instructions is measured in _____.

4. The _____ is the transmission path for data flow among the various components of the computer system.

5. The _____ of the bus determines how much data can flow among the various components.

6. Fill in the number of transfers in the table below.

Buses:

BUS WIDTH	TRANSFER SIZE (IN BITS)		
	8	16	32
8			
16			
32			

NUMBER OF TRANSFERS

CLASSNOTES (continued)

7.–13. Complete the statements regarding various processor capabilities, choosing your answers from the following list.

twelve   640   one   two   sixteen   four   512   word size

7. An eight-bit processor can operate on _____ byte(s) of data at a time.

8. A 16-bit processor can operate on _____ byte(s) of data at the same time.

9. A 32-bit processor can operate on _____ byte(s) of data at the same time.

10. An eight-bit processor can address up to _____ KB of memory.

11. A 16-bit processor can address up to _____ MB of memory.

12. A 32-bit processor can address up to _____ MB of memory.

13. The _____ is the number of bits that the CPU can process at one time.

ARCHITECTURE OF PROCESSOR UNITS

1. Silicon is an example of a(n) _____.

2. The main circuit board of a personal computer is called the _____.

3. The design of the processor can range from a single board to _____ boards.

4. Two special purposes that a coprocessor can have are _____ and

   _____.

5. In _____ processing, several program instructions can be executed at the same time in multiple processing units.

6. In _____ technology, there is a subset of instructions that are frequently used that comprise the instruction set.

TYPES OF MEMORY

1.–7. Complete the statements, choosing your answers from the following list.

EEPROM   transistors   ROM   vacuum tubes   PROM   core   RAM   semiconductor   EPROM

1. _____ were the earliest physical devices used for memory operations.

2. With _____ memory the speed of computers reached the microsecond range, while

   _____ memory took the speed to the nanosecond range.

3. In _____, memory is erased when power is removed.

4. In _____ no data is lost when power is removed.

5. _____ can be loaded with specially selected data or programs prior to installing it in a computer.

6. _____ stands for erasable programmable read only memory.

7. _____ allows the data to be stored or programs to be erased electronically.

Name _____ Date _____

CHAPTER FOUR—PROJECT TWO

Self-Test
WORKBOOK AND PC VERSIONS

Match the following:

_____ 1. Control Unit

_____ 2. System Clock

_____ 3. Binary Number System

_____ 4. MB

_____ 5. Coprocessor

_____ 6. Parity Bit

_____ 7. ASCII

_____ 8. Operation Code

1. Synchronizes or controls timing of all computer operations
2. Most widely used coding system to represent data
3. 1,000K
4. Used by computer for error checking
5. Fetches, decodes, executes, and stores
6. Unique value typically stored in the first byte of instruction
7. Circuit board designed to perform a specific task
8. Reduced instruction set
9. Base 2; represents electronic status of bits in main memory

You can complete the remainder of Project 2 in two ways—either by marking or filling in your answers in this workbook, or by using the PC version of Project 2. The PC version (available from your instructor) automatically corrects your answers for you. It also calculates the percent of your answers that are correct.

Answer the following questions.

1. The central processing unit (CPU) is comprised of two primary units, the arithmetic/logic unit and the

   _____ unit.

   a. memory   c. operating   e. function

   b. control   d. files

2. In addition to the central processing unit (CPU), the processor also contains the computer's

   _____.

   a. brain   c. input devices   e. disk drives

   b. main memory   d. output devices

3. Sixteen kilobytes (16KB) is approximately how many bytes?

   a. 1.6 million   c. 166,000   e. 1.6 billion

   b. 16   d. 16,000

4. How many bytes would be required to represent the following series of symbols (numbers/special characters)?

   a. 6   c. 8   e. 10

   b. 7   d. 9

SELF-TEST (continued)

5. If ● represents an OFF condition and ○ represents an ON condition, what is the binary equivalent of the following storage locations?

    a. 10100110   c. 01011001   e. 01011010
    b. 01101001   d. 10100101

6. _____ is the most widely used character coding system for microcomputers.
    a. ASCII   c. Packed decimal   e. Decimal
    b. EBCDIC   d. Hexadecimal

7. T F   The ASCII coding scheme is primarily used on mainframes.

8. For an odd parity system, what is the value of the parity bit for 01101001?
    a. 1   c. 5   e. none of the above
    b. 0   d. 4

9. T F   A parity bit can detect if one of the bits in a byte has been inadvertently changed.

10. The _____ of a number system indicates how many symbols are used in it.
    a. position   c. digit   e. sum
    b. exponent   d. base

11. In a binary number system, what is the value of the indicated position? 0<u>1</u>10
    a. 8   c. 2   e. 0
    b. 4   d. 1

12. In the hexadecimal number system a 16-bit binary number can be represented by _____ hexadecimal digits.
    a. 8   c. 3   e. 6
    b. 2   d. 4

13. A machine language instruction usually consists of three parts: the _____, the data length(s), and the memory addresses of the data.
    a. CPU address   c. instruction set   e. none of the above
    b. operation code   d. CPU data

14. Collectively, the steps fetch instruction, execute instruction, decode instruction, and store results are called the _____.
    a. execution cycle   c. machir.e cycle   e. none of the above
    b. instruction cycle   d. information cycle

15. The processing speed of computers is often compared in _____.
    a. chips   c. address range   e. none of the above
    b. bus width   d. MIPS

16. For a computer incorporating a 16-bit bus, how many data transfers are required to move 8 bytes of memory?
    a. 4   c. 2   e. 16
    b. 1   d. 8

SELF-TEST (continued)

17. The amount of memory that a CPU can efficiently access is primarily determined by the

    _____.

    a. system clock   c. word size   e. character codes
    b. bus width   d. processor speed

18. T   F   The processing speed of computers is often measured in MIPS.

19. A specialized processor designed to perform a specific task (such as numeric processing) in conjunction with

    the CPU is called a _____.

    a. RISC processor   c. coprocessor   e. none of the above
    b. bus processor   d. perpendicular processor

20. Currently, the most prevalent technology used to implement primary memory is _____.

    a. RISC   c. vacuum tube   e. semiconductor
    b. core   d. EPROM

21. T   F   Integrated circuits are circuit boards designed to perform a specific task.

22. RAM is said to be _____, because the programs and data stored are erased when
    power to the computer is turned off.

    a. volatile   c. erasable   e. read only
    b. static   d. programmable

CHAPTER FOUR—PROJECT THREE

Identifying the Types of Items Stored in Main Memory

Instructions: In the space provided, identify the types of programs and data that can be stored in main memory.

MEMORY USAGE

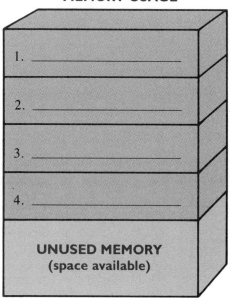

1. _____

2. _____

3. _____

4. _____

UNUSED MEMORY
(space available)

CHAPTER FOUR—PROJECT FOUR

Representing Data in Memory

Instructions: Convert each of the following binary EBCDIC codes into its character symbol (alphabetic, numeric, or special) and its hexadecimal representation.

	EBCDIC	CHARACTER SYMBOL	HEXADECIMAL
Example	11010010	K	D2*
1.	11110010	_____	_____
2.	01011011	_____	_____
3.	01111110	_____	_____
4.	11000011	_____	_____
5.	11010101	_____	_____
6.	11101001	_____	_____
7.	10000101	_____	_____
8.	10010111	_____	_____
9.	10100011	_____	_____
10.	01101111	_____	_____

* How to convert a binary number to hexadecimal.

1. Divide the binary number (11010010) into two groups of four digits.

   1101   0010

2. Using the positional value, calculate the decimal value of each four-digit group.

   <u>8421</u>   <u>8421</u>
   1101   0010
   8+4+0+1   0+0+2+0
   13   2

3. Change any two-digit decimal value (10 through 15) to the corresponding hexadecimal symbol (A through F).

   D   2

4. Combine the results into a hexadecimal number.

   D2

Developing Communication Skills

Instructions: Prepare an oral or written report on one or more of the following subjects.

1. Prepare a report on the history of computer memory. Include information on vacuum tubes, magnetic core, and semiconductor.
2. Discuss the production processes used to manufacture semiconductor memory.
3. Research the history and origin of the ASCII code.
4. Research the history and origin of the EBCDIC code.
5. Prepare a report on the next generation of microprocessor chips currently under development.
6. Report on the development and future of parallel processor computers.
7. Prepare a report on the current use of reduced instruction set computers (RISC).
8. Obtain a current and a one-year-old copy of a personal computer magazine. Prepare a report that compares the type of computer systems and components, such as memory, that are being sold today with those being sold one year ago.
9. Prepare a report that discusses the environmental concerns of manufacturing semiconductor chips.

Output from the Computer

◆ OBJECTIVES

- ◆ Define the term output
- ◆ List the common types of reports that are used for output
- ◆ Describe multimedia
- ◆ Describe the features and classification of printers
- ◆ Identify and explain impact printers
- ◆ Identify and explain nonimpact printers
- ◆ Describe the types of screens available and list common screen features
- ◆ List and describe other types of output devices used with computers

---

◆ CHAPTER OUTLINE

What Is Output?
Types of Output
    Reports
    Graphics
    Multimedia
Printers
    Printer Features
       Speed
       Paper Types and Sizes
       Print Quality
       Typefaces
       Other Printer Features
    How Are Printers Classified?
Impact Printers
    Dot Matrix Printers
    Daisy Wheel Printers
    Chain Printers
    Band Printers
Nonimpact Printers
    Ink Jet Printers
    Thermal Printers
    Page Printers

Considerations in Choosing a Printer
Screens
    Screen Features
       Size
       Resolution
       Color
       Cursor
       Scrolling
       Other Screen Features
    Types Of Screens
    How Images Are Displayed on a CRT Screen
       How Color Is Produced
       How Flat Panel Displays Work
Other Output Devices
    Data Projectors
    Plotters
    Computer Output Microfilm
    Voice Output
Summary of Output from the Computer

CHAPTER FIVE

Chapter Review

 Chapter 5 discusses the types of output and the devices computers use to produce output. Output is data that has been processed into a useful form called information that can be used by a person or a machine. Output that is printed is called hard copy and output that is displayed on a screen is called soft copy.

A report is information presented in an organized form and includes items displayed on a screen as well as items printed on paper. An internal report is used within an organization by individuals in the performance of their jobs. An external report is one used outside an organization. Four common types of reports are narrative reports, detail reports, summary reports, and exception reports. Narrative reports can contain graphic or numeric information but are primarily text-based reports. A detail report usually contains one report line for each input record that has been read and processed. A summary report contains summary information regarding detail records. An exception report contains information that is outside of normal user-specified values or conditions, called the exception criteria. Periodic reports, also called scheduled reports, are produced on a regular basis such as daily, weekly, or monthly. On-demand reports are created for information that is not required on a scheduled basis, but only when it is requested.

Computer graphics display information in the form of charts, graphs, or pictures so that the information can be understood easily and quickly. Multimedia is the mixing of text, graphics, video (pictures) and audio (sound) output on a screen.

The key to the more widespread use of full motion on computers is video compression that will enable large amounts of data to take up less storage space. Digital video interactive (DVI) is a compression technique that can reduce storage requirements by a factor of 100 or more.

The main feature choices for printers include speed, paper types and sizes, print quality, and typefaces. Other features include the capability to print color, printer size, and the type of printer interface. Printers can be rated as low speed, medium speed, high speed and very high speed. Low-speed printers print one character at a time and are sometimes called character printers. The rate of printing for low-speed printers is expressed in characters per second (cps). Medium-speed and high-speed printers are called line printers because they can print multiple characters on a line at the same time. Line printer speed is expressed in the number of lines per minute (lpm) that can be printed. The speed of very-high speed printers is rated in pages per minute (ppm).

Pages of continuous-form paper are connected together so they can continue to flow through the printer.

Letter-quality (LQ) print means that the character is a fully formed, solid character like those made by a typewriter. Near letter-quality (NLQ) printers cannot make fully formed characters but still offer good print quality.

Draft-quality printers provide output that a business would use for internal purposes but not for correspondence.

A typeface is a set of letters, numbers, and special characters that have a similar design. Typefaces can be printed in different styles, such as italics or bold and different sizes, measured in points which are 1/72 of one inch. A font is a complete set of characters in the same typeface, style, and size.

The footprint is the amount of desk space a printer requires.

CHAPTER REVIEW (continued)

With a serial interface, data is sent to the printer a single bit at a time. With a parallel interface, an entire byte (eight bits) is sent to the printer at the same time.

Impact printers transfer the image onto paper by some type of printing mechanism striking the paper, ribbon, and character together. Nonimpact printing means that printing occurs without having a mechanism strike the paper.

A dot matrix printer uses a series of small pins to print closely spaced dots that form the character. Overlapping the dots results in the appearance of a solid character. Some dot matrix printers can print color by repeatedly striking a red, yellow, blue, and black ribbon.

Bidirectional printing increases the speed of the printer by printing both left to right and right to left.

Tractor feed mechanisms transport continuous-form paper through the printer by using sprockets, small protruding prongs of plastic or metal, which fit into holes on each side of the paper. Friction feed mechanisms use pressure on the paper, in a manner similar to a typewriter, to move the paper through the printer.

A daisy wheel printer is an impact printer that uses a rotating type wheel that resembles the structure of a flower, with many long, thin petals. Each petal has a raised character at the tip.

Chain and band printers both use a horizontal, rotating series of characters that are struck by hammers located at each print position behind the paper and ribbon.

Ink jet, thermal, and page printers (including laser printers) are examples of nonimpact printers. An ink jet printer uses a nozzle to shoot electronically charged droplets of ink onto the page. Thermal printers use heat to produce fully formed characters and graphic images on special chemically treated paper. A page printer is a nonimpact printer that operates similar to a copying machine.

Page printers use several methods to direct light to a photosensitive drum and create the text or image that will be transferred to the paper. These methods include a laser beam (hence the name laser printers), light emitting diode (LED) arrays, and liquid crystal shutters (LCS). High-speed page printers can produce printed output at the rate of several hundred pages per minute.

Factors that affect the choice of a printer include; how much output will be produced, who will use the output, where the output will be produced, and if multiple copies are required.

The screen, also called the monitor, CRT (cathode ray tube), or VDT (video display terminal) is another important output device. Although smaller and larger sizes exist, most screens are between 12 and 16 inches measured diagonally from corner to corner. Screens usually display 25 lines of 80 characters but can display more if the character size is reduced. The resolution, or clarity, of a screen depends on how many dots, or picture elements, called pixels, can be displayed. Dot-addressable or bit-mapped displays are monitors used for graphics. CGA (color graphics adapter), EGA (enhanced graphics adapter), VGA (video graphics array), super VGA, and 1024 are all different graphics standards. Types of screens used with computers include monochrome, color, plasma, and LCD. Plasma and LCD screens, which do not use the conventional cathode ray tube technology, are sometimes called flat panel display screens. Monochrome screens display a single color such as white, green, or amber on a black background or black characters on a white background.

The dots, or pixels, on a screen are coated with phosphor that glow when struck by an electron beam. Color screens use three dots (red, green, and blue) for each pixel. A composite video color monitor uses a single electron signal to turn on the color phosphors with the pixel. An RGB monitor uses three separate signals, one for each color, to turn on the red, green, and blue phosphors within each pixel.

A plasma screen uses a grid of connectors to activate neon/argon gas to create an image. An LCD screen creates an image when the liquid crystals are aligned when exposed to an electrical current.

Projection panels using liquid crystal display (LCD) technology can be placed on top of overhead projectors to project a screen image.

Plotters can create high-quality, large-scale (up to 40 by 48 inches) line drawings. Pen plotters create images on a sheet of paper by moving one or more pens over the surface of the paper or by moving the paper under the tip of the pens. Two different kinds of pen plotters are flatbed plotters and drum plotters.

Computer output microfilm (COM) is an output technique that records output from a computer as microscopic images on roll or sheet film. The sheet film is called microfiche. Computer-assisted retrieval (CAR) is the use of a microfilm reader and an attached computer to quickly locate microfilm records.

Voice output consists of spoken words that are conveyed to the user from the computer. A voice synthesizer can transform words stored in main memory into speech and make it sound as though a person were speaking.

Band printers: Impact printers that use a horizontal, rotating band and can print in the range of 300 to 2,000 lines per minute.

Bidirectional: A printing method of dot matrix printers in which the print head can print while moving in either direction.

Bit-mapped displays, *see* **Dot-addressable displays**

Blinking: A screen feature used for emphasis in which characters or words on a screen blink.

Bold: A screen feature used for emphasis in which characters are displayed at a greater brightness level than the surrounding text.

Chain printer: A high-speed impact printer that uses a rotating chain to print up to 3,000 lines per minute of good print quality.

Character per second (cps): The rating of printing speed for low-speed printers.

Color screens: Screens that display information in color and are used because they enable users to more easily read and understand the information on the screen; more expensive than monochrome.

Composite video monitor: A color screen that uses a single electron signal to turn on the color phosphors within the pixel.

Computer-assisted retrieval (CAR): A process in which microfilm readers perform automatic data lookup.

Computer graphics: A type of output used to present information in the form of charts, graphs, or pictures, so it can be quickly and easily understood.

Computer-output microfilm (COM): An output technique that records output from a computer as microscopic images on roll or sheet film.

Continuous-form paper: A type of paper that is connected together for a continuous flow through the printer.

CRT (cathode ray tube), *see* **Screens**

Cursor: A symbol such as an underline character or an arrow that indicates where you are working on the screen.

Daisy wheel printer: An impact printer that can print high-quality text, but not graphics. The daisy wheel type element rotates during printing, and a hammer strikes the selected character against the ribbon and paper. Printing speeds range from 20 to 80 characters per second.

Detail report: A report in which each line usually corresponds to one input record.

Digital video interactive (DVI): A video compression technique that can reduce storage requirements by a factor of 100 or more.

Dot-addressable displays: Screens that are used for graphics in which the number of addressable locations corresponds to the number of dots (pixels) that can be illuminated; also called bit-mapped displays.

Dot matrix printer: An impact printer in which the print head consists of a series of small tubes containing pins that, when pressed against a ribbon and paper, print small dots closely together to form characters.

Draft quality: Printer output that a business would use for internal purposes and not for correspondence.

Drum plotter: A plotter that uses a rotating drum, or cylinder, over which drawing pens are mounted.

Electrostatic plotter: A plotter in which the paper moves under a row of wires (styli) that can be turned on to create an electrostatic charge on the paper.

KEY TERMS (continued)

Exception report: A report that contains information that is outside the normal user-specified values or conditions and will help users to focus on situations that might require immediate decisions or specific actions.

External report: A report used outside the organization.

Flatbed plotter: A plotter in which the pens are instructed by the software to move to the down position so the pen contacts the flat surface of the paper.

Flat panel display screens: Plasma and LCD screens which do not use the conventional cathode ray tube technology, and are relatively flat.

Font: A complete set of characters in the same typeface, style, and size.

Friction feed mechanisms: Printing mechanisms that move paper through a printer by pressure between the paper and the carriage.

Hard copy: Output that is printed.

High-speed page printers: Nonimpact printers that can produce output at the rate of several hundred pages per minute and use a dedicated computer and tape drive to maximize printing speed.

Impact printers: Printers that transfer the image onto paper by some type of printing mechanism striking the paper, ribbon, and character together.

Ink jet printer: A nonimpact printer that forms characters by using a nozzle that shoots electronically charged droplets of ink onto the page, producing high-quality print and graphics.

Internal report: A report used by individuals in the performance of their jobs and only by personnel within an organization.

Inverse video, *see* **Reverse video**

Laser printers: Nonimpact page printers that use a laser beam aimed at a photosensitive drum to create the image to be transferred to paper.

Letter quality (LQ): High-quality printer output in which the printed character is a fully formed, solid character like those made by a typewriter, used for business or legal correspondence.

Line printers: Medium- and high-speed printers that print multiple characters on a line at the same time.

Lines per minute (lpm): A measurement for the rate of printing of line printers.

Liquid crystal displays (LCD): Flat screens often used with portable computers.

Microfiche: The sheet film used by computer output microfilm.

Monitor, *see* **Screen(s)**

Monochrome screens: Screens that display a single color such as white, green, or amber characters on a black background, or black characters on a white background.

Multimedia: The mixing of text, graphics, video (pictures), and audio (sound) output on a screen.

Narrative reports: Reports that are primarily text-based, but can contain some graphic or numeric information.

Near letter quality (NLQ): Printer output that is not fully formed characters, but still offers good print quality.

Nonimpact printing: Printing that occurs without having a mechanism striking against a sheet of paper.

On-demand reports: Reports created for information that is not required on a scheduled basis, but only when it is requested.

Output: The data that has been processed into a useful form called information that can be used by a person or machine.

Page printer: A nonimpact printer that operates similar to a copying machine to produce high-quality text and graphic output.

Pages per minute (ppm): A measure of the speed of printers that can produce an entire page at one time.

Parallel interface: The computer communication with the printer, in which an entire byte (eight bits) is sent at the same time.

Pen plotters: Plotters that are used to create images on a sheet of paper by moving one or more pens over the surface.

Periodic reports: Reports that are produced on a regular basis such as daily, weekly, or monthly; also called scheduled reports.

Picture element, *see* **Pixels**

Pixel (picture element): On screens, each dot that can be illuminated.

Plasma screens: Flat screens that are often used with portable computers.

Plotter: An output device used to produce high-quality line drawings and diagrams.

Projection panels: The projection of the computer screen image that can be clearly seen by a room full of people, using liquid crystal display technology, and designed to be placed on top of an overhead projector.

Report: Information that is presented in an organized form.

KEY TERMS (continued)

Resolution: The measure of a screen's image clarity that depends on the number of individual dots displayed, called pixels, that can be illuminated.

Reverse video: A screen feature used to emphasize characters in which the normal display on the screen is reversed, such as a dark background with light characters; also called inverse video.

RGB (red, green, blue) monitor: A color screen that uses three signals, one for each color, red, green, and blue, to turn on the required phosphors.

Scheduled reports, *see* **Periodic reports**

Screen(s): An output device used to display data on both personal computers and terminals; also called a monitor, CRT (cathode ray tube), or VDT (video display terminal).

Scrolling: The movement of screen data up or down one line or one screen at a time.

Serial interface: The computer communication with the printer in which data is sent to the printer a single bit at a time.

Soft copy: Output that is displayed on a screen.

Summary report: A report which summarizes data, containing totals from detailed input data.

Thermal printers: Nonimpact printers that use heat to produce fully formed characters and graphics on chemically treated paper.

Thermal transfer printers: Thermal printers used for color printing.

Tractor feed mechanisms: Printer mechanisms that transport continuous-form paper by using sprockets inserted into holes on the sides of the paper.

Typeface: A set of letters, numbers, and special characters that have a similar design.

Underlining: A screen feature for emphasis that allows characters, words, lines, or paragraphs to be underlined.

VDT (video display terminal), *see* **Screen(s)**

Video compression: The key to use of full-motion video in multimedia, that makes large amounts of data take up less storage space.

Voice output: Spoken words that are conveyed to the user from the computer.

Voice synthesizer: A type of voice generation that can transform words stored in main memory into speech.

CHAPTER FIVE—PROJECT ONE
ClassNotes

WHAT IS OUTPUT?

1. Output is data that has been processed into a useful form called _____.

TYPES OF OUTPUT

1.–2. Correctly label the form of output at which the people are looking in the two diagrams below. Choose your answers from the following list.

terminal   hard copy   soft copy   printing reports

1. _____

2. _____

3.–5. Complete the statements regarding reports, choosing your answers from the following list.

Information   Internal reports   External reports   Reports   Documents

3. _____ represent information presented in an organized form.

4. _____ are those reports used by individuals within an organization.

5. _____ are those reports used by individuals outside the organization.

CLASSNOTES (continued)

6.–8. Classify the three examples of reports below.

UNITS SOLD REPORT				
				QTY
DEPT	DEPT NAME	ITEM	DESCRIPTION	SOLD
10	MENS FURNISHINGS	105	T-SHIRT	3
10	MENS FURNISHINGS	109	SOCKS	127
12	SLEEPWEAR	199	ROBE	6

SALES BY DEPARTMENT			
		UNITS	
DEPT	DEPT NAME	SOLD	SALES $
10	MENS FURNISHINGS	130	653.35
12	SLEEPWEAR	6	189.70
14	MENS ACCESSORIES	4	98.00

INVENTORY EXCEPTION REPORT		
ITEM	ITEM	QUANTITY
NO.	DESCRIPTION	ON HAND
105	T-SHIRT	24
125	SCARF	3
126	BELT	17

6. _____   7. _____   8. _____

9. _____ output displays information in the form of charts, graphs, or pictures, assisting in analyzing and understanding data quickly and easily.

10.–12. Label the three types of graphics displayed below.

10. _____   11. _____   12. _____

13. _____ is the mixing of text, graphics, video (pictures), and audio (sound) output on a screen.

14. _____ makes the large amounts of data take up less storage space.

15. One compression technique currently being developed is _____.

PRINTERS

1.–4. Fill in the following table.

SPEED CLASSIFICATION OF PRINTER	
SPEED TYPE	**SPEED DESCRIPTION**
1.	Prints one character at a time (15-600 characters per second)
2.	Prints a line at a time (300-600 lines per minute)
3.	Prints a line at a time (300-3,000 lines per minute)
4.	Prints a page at a time (3,000-20,000 lines per minute)

CLASSNOTES (continued)

5. The two types of feed mechanisms for printers are _____ feed and _____ feed.

6. _____ allows a continuous flow through the printer.

7. The term _____ means that the printed character is a fully formed, solid character like those made by a typewriter.

8. A(n) _____ is a set of letters, numbers, and special characters that have a similar design.

9. The two types of impact printers are _____ striking and _____ striking printers.

10. _____ printing occurs without having a mechanism strike the paper.

IMPACT PRINTERS

1. Label the printer pictured below. Choose your answers from the following list.

   laser   daisy wheel   dot matrix   chain

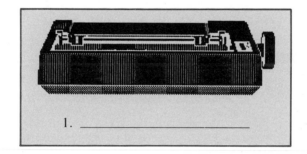

1. _____

2.–4. Label the components in the figure below. Choose your answers from the following list.

   printing head   printing chain   paper   ribbon   laser

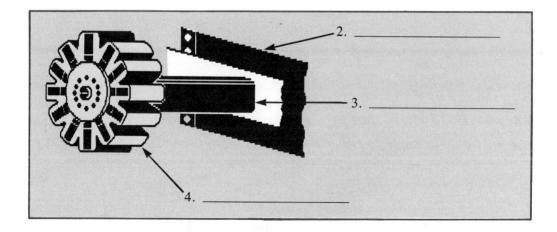

2. _____

3. _____

4. _____

5. The least number of pins a dot matrix printer can have is _____ pins.

CLASSNOTES (continued)

To complete this statement, choose your answer from the following list.

bold   standard   italicized

6. The letter E in the figure at the right is in _____ print.

To complete this statement, choose your answer from the following list.

bold   condensed   enlarged

7. The letter E in the figure at the right is in _____ print.

8. A _____ printer can print in both directions.

9. The standard carriage size for printers is 8 1/2 inches, or _____ characters per line.

10. The wide carriage is 14 inches, or _____ characters per line.

11. Dot matrix printers can print text and _____.

12. The diagram below represents a _____ printer.

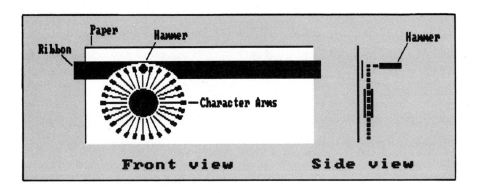

13.–17. Label the components of the chain printer in the figure below. Choose your answers from the following list.

chain   hammers   paper   ribbon   drive gear   printer   slug   daisy wheel

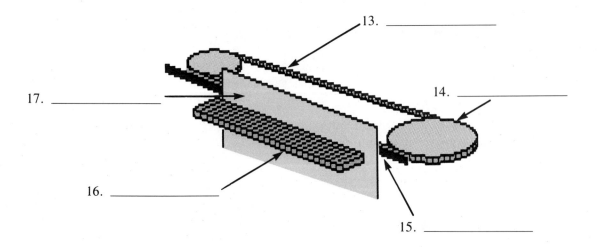

13. _____

17. _____

16. _____

14. _____

15. _____

CLASSNOTES (continued)

18.–22. Label the diagram of the chain and band printers below. Choose your answers from the following list.

chain band   printer slug   hammer   scalloped steel   print band   paper   ribbon   magnet

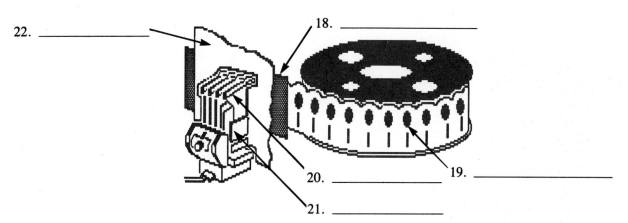

22. _____

18. _____

20. _____

19. _____

21. _____

NONIMPACT PRINTERS

1. The _____ printer is designed to achieve substantial output speed.

2. The _____ printer uses heat to produce output.

3. The _____ printer works like a photocopy machine and supports desktop publishing.

CONSIDERATIONS IN CHOOSING A PRINTER

Fill in the blanks in the questions, choosing your answers from the following list.

When   How much   Who   Where   Why

1. _____ output will be produced?

2. _____ will use the output?

3. _____ will the output be produced?

SCREENS

1. The output screen can be called a(n) _____, a(n) _____, or a(n) _____.

2.–14. Complete the statements about screens, choosing your answers from the following list.

pixels   dot-addressable displays   color   medium resolution   underline
cursor   80   VGA   blinking   LCD   scroll   CGA   higher resolution
monochrome   EGA   bit-mapped displays

2. The typical output screen has a capacity of 25 lines of _____ characters.

CLASSNOTES (continued)

3. Each screen is composed of many small units that can be illuminated, which are called

   _____.

4. _____ screens have smaller pixels and, therefore, have higher quality graphic output.

5. Screens used for graphics are called _____, or sometimes

   _____.

6. _____ has 16 available colors.

7. _____ was developed in 1986 and has 256 colors that can be displayed.

8. The _____ is a marker on the screen that identifies where on the screen the next character will be entered.

9. A cursor can appear as a(n) _____, a(n) _____,

   or a(n) _____.

10. As a line of data is placed on the last line of the screen, the topmost line will _____ off of the screen.

11. Characteristics of most screens include reverse video, underlining, bold, _____, and double size.

12. Screens will generally be either monochrome or _____.

13. Both the plasma and _____ screens are associated with laptop microcomputers.

14. _____ screens use three electron guns to produce color output.

OTHER OUTPUT DEVICES

1. Smaller, lower cost units, called _____, use liquid crystal display (LCD) technology designed to be placed on top of an overhead projector.

2. Label the output device shown below.

2. _____

3. List three types of plotters.

   _____   _____   _____

4. _____ can record information on microfiche or 16mm, 35mm, or 105mm roll film.

5. _____ can be recorded, stored, and played back to produce audio output.

6. A(n) _____ can transform words stored in main memory into human speech.

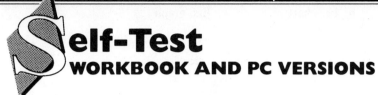

Self-Test
WORKBOOK AND PC VERSIONS

Match the following:

_____ 1. Laser Printer

_____ 2. VGA

_____ 3. Letter Quality

_____ 4. Narrative Reports

_____ 5. Dot Matrix Printer

_____ 6. CRT

_____ 7. EGA

_____ 8. Draft Quality

1. Memos, letters, and sales proposals are examples
2. Nonimpact page printer
3. Cathode ray tube
4. Suitable for internal purposes
5. Video graphics adapter
6. Enhanced graphics adapter
7. Suitable for business or legal correspondence
8. Impact printer that forms characters by placing dots on paper
9. Video graphics array

You can complete the remainder of Project 2 in two ways—either by marking or filling in your answers in this workbook, or by using the PC version of Project 2. The PC version (available from your instructor) automatically corrects your answers for you. It also calculates the percent of your answers that are correct.

Answer the following questions.

1. _____ is data that has been processed into a useful form called information.
   - a. A computer program
   - b. Printed reports
   - c. Output
   - d. Graphics

2. The two most common types of output are _____.
   - a. reports and graphics
   - b. computer screens and printers
   - c. hard copy and soft copy
   - d. computer programs and computer screens

3. A(n) _____ report should have a high-quality print output because it is used by individuals outside the organization.
   - a. internal
   - b. external

4. Each line on a(n) _____ report usually corresponds to one input record.
   - a. summary
   - b. detail
   - c. exception

5. Computer _____ is(are) used to present information so it can be quickly and easily understood.
   - a. screens
   - b. output
   - c. graphics
   - d. reports

SELF-TEST (continued)

6. The following graphic is an example of a _____.

    a. pie chart   b. bar chart   c. line graph

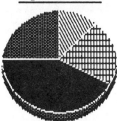

Regional Sales

7. The following graphic is an example of a _____.

    a. pie chart   b. bar chart   c. line graph

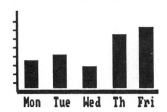

Sales - 7/11-7/15

8. Printers are classified as being either _____.

    a. low speed or high speed   c. impact or nonimpact

    b. small or large   d. graphic or letter quality

9. The printing rate for medium-speed and high-speed printers is stated as the number of _____ per minute.

    a. characters   c. lines

    b. pages   d. forms

10. Printer features include _____.

    a. speed   c. print quality

    b. paper types   d. all of the above

11. The standard carriage size is _____ inches.

12. Two types of printer feed mechanisms are _____.

    a. tractor feed and continuous flow   c. tractor feed and friction feed

    b. continuous flow and sprockets   d. none of the above

13. _____ printers have small pins that are contained in a print head.

    a. Daisy wheel   c. Band

    b. Dot matrix   d. Chain

14. The _____ printer prints fully formed characters for letter-quality output.

    a. daisy wheel   c. band

    b. dot matrix   d. ink jet

SELF-TEST (continued)

15. Thermal printers use _____ to produce fully formed characters.

16. A(n) _____ printer is a nonimpact printer that operates in a manner similar to a copying machine.

    a. ink jet   c. chain

    b. laser   d. band

17. _____ printers have interchangeable bands with many different styles of fonts.

18. Large, high-speed printers are often called _____ printers.

    a. super   c. page

    b. fast   d. chain

19. T F   Who will use the output is not an important consideration when choosing a printer.

20. Which of the following is not a type of screen?

    a. color   c. scrolling   e. LCD

    b. monochrome   d. plasma

21. Laptop computers use a special display device called _____, using a polarizing material to form images on the screen.

    a. CRT—cathode ray tube   c. COM—computer output microfilm

    b. LCD—liquid cystal display   d. VDT—video display terminal

22. Which output device would most likely be used in an architectural, engineering, or design firm?

    a. chain printer   c. plotter

    b. daisy wheel printer d. microfiche

23. T F   Computer output microfilm (COM) records microscopic images on roll or sheet film.

CHAPTER FIVE—PROJECT THREE

Identifying Types of Reports

Instructions: From the illustrations below, identify the report as either a detail report, summary report, or exception report.

Part #	Description	Reorder Point	Quantity On Hand
1001	claw hammer	2,000	1,495
1075	gas welder	40	31

1. Type of report _____

Part #	Description	Quantity On Hand
1001	claw hammer	1,495
1049	pipe wrench	725
1075	gas welder	31

2. Type of report _____

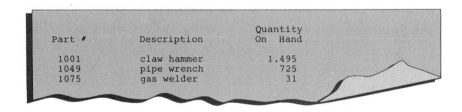

Part #	Description	Location	Quantity On Hand
1001	claw hammer	W1	1,000
1001	claw hammer	W2	420
1001	claw hammer	W3	75
1049	pipe wrench	W2	725
1075	gas welder	W1	13
1075	gas welder	W2	7
1075	gas welder	W4	11

3. Type of report _____

CHAPTER FIVE—PROJECT FOUR

Identifying Types of Printers

Instructions: In the space provided, identify each printer shown as either an impact printer or a nonimpact printer.

dot matrix

_____

laser

_____

chain

_____

thermal

_____

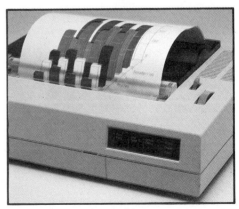

ink jet

_____

CHAPTER FIVE—PROJECT FIVE

Developing Communication Skills

Instructions: Prepare an oral or written report on one or more of the following subjects.

1. Survey the different types of printers used at your school or where you work. For each printer, record the printing method used, number of pages printed each day, and the cost of the printer.
2. Obtain copies of detail, summary, and exception reports dealing with the same subject, such as inventory or accounts receivable. Prepare a report that discusses how each report is used.
3. Report on the type of information that is currently available in multimedia.
4. Prepare a report on page printers that can be purchased for less than $1,000.
5. Prepare a report on page printer technology. Include information on laser, light emitting diode, and liquid crystal shutter methods.
6. Discuss the types of screens used for notebook computers.
7. Make a presentation on current and future applications of voice output.
8. Interview someone who regularly uses computer graphics in his or her job. Obtain samples of the graphics produced and report on how they are used.
9. Visit your school or public library and prepare a report on the different types of information that are available on microfiche or microfilm. Estimate how much storage space is saved by the microfilmed documents.
10. Visit an architect or engineer that uses a plotter. Report on how the plotter is used.

CHAPTER SIX

Auxiliary Storage

◆ OBJECTIVES

- ◆ Define auxiliary storage
- ◆ Identify the primary devices used for computer auxiliary storage
- ◆ Explain how data is stored on diskettes and hard disks
- ◆ Describe how data stored on magnetic disks can be protected
- ◆ Explain how magnetic tape storage is used with computers
- ◆ Describe three other forms of auxiliary storage: optical disks, solid-state devices, and mass storage devices
- ◆ Describe how special-purpose storage devices such as smart cards are used

◆ CHAPTER OUTLINE

CHAPTER SIX

Chapter Review

 Chapter 6 discusses storage operations and the various types of auxiliary storage devices that are used with computers. Auxiliary storage, also called secondary storage, stores programs and data when they are not being processed, just as a filing cabinet is used in an office to store records. Unlike main memory, most auxiliary storage devices are nonvolatile, that is, data and programs stored on auxiliary storage devices are retained when the power is turned off. Auxiliary storage devices can be used as both input and output devices.

Magnetic disk offers high storage capacity, reliability, and the capability to directly access stored data. It is the most widely used storage medium for all types of computers. Diskettes are the principal auxiliary storage medium for personal computers. Early diskettes were thin and flexible and were called floppies. The most common diskette sizes today are 5 1/4" and 3 1/2". A diskette consists of a circular piece of thin mylar plastic (the actual disk), which is coated with an oxide material similar to that used on recording tape. The disk is enclosed in a protective jacket or cover.

The formatting process prepares the diskette so that it can store data and includes defining the tracks, cylinders, and sectors on the surfaces of the diskette. A track is a narrow recording band forming a full circle around the diskette. A cylinder is all tracks of the same number. A sector is a pie-shaped section of the disk and is also used to refer to a section of a track. The amount of data that can be stored on a diskette depends on three factors: (1) the number of sides of the diskette used; (2) the recording density of the bits on a track; and (3) the number of tracks on the diskette. Single-sided drives record data on only one side of the diskette. Double-sided drives record and read data on both sides of the diskette.

Recording density is the number of bits that can be recorded on one inch of the innermost track on the diskette. Recording density is measured in bits per inch (bpi). Tracks per inch (tpi) is a measure of how many tracks onto which data can be recorded. Low-density diskettes can store 360K on a 5 1/4" diskette and 720K on a 3 1/2" diskette. High-density diskettes (sometimes abbreviated as HD) can store 1.2 megabytes (million characters) on a 5 1/4" diskette and 1.44 megabytes on a 3 1/2" diskette.

An opening in the diskette jacket or cover allows the read/write head of the disk drive to rest on the diskette surface and generate electronic impulses that record data. The electronic impulses change the surface polarity, or alignment, of magnetic spots along a track on the diskette. The plus or minus polarity can be read as either on or off to represent the 1 or 0 bits that are used to record data.

Data stored on a diskette must first be retrieved and placed in main memory before it can be processed. The time required to access and retrieve data from a disk is called access time. Access time depends on four factors: (1) seek time; (2) rotational delay or latency; (3) settling time; and (4) the data transfer rate. In handling diskettes, you should take care to avoid exposing them to heat, magnetic fields, and contaminated environments such as dust, smoke, or salt air.

Hard disks consist of one or more rigid metal platters coated with an oxide material that allows data to be magnetically recorded on the surface of the platters.

On minicomputers and mainframes, hard disks are sometimes referred to as fixed disks or direct-access storage devices (DASD). Some disk drives used on large computers can store over a billion bytes, called a gigabyte, of data.

CHAPTER REVIEW (continued)

Storing data on hard disks is similar to the method used on diskettes. Read/write heads at the end of access arms, or actuators, float on a thin cushion of air as the disk surface rotates at approximately 3,600 revolutions per minute (RPM). On diskettes, the read/write heads actually touch the disk surface which rotates at approximately 300 RPM. The access arms move the heads over the track to be read or recorded on. A head crash is when the read/write heads scratch the surface of the disk and cause a loss of data.

Data is physically organized on a disk using two methods; the sector method and the cylinder method. Using the sector method, data is organized by disk surface, track, and sector. Each sector can contain a specified number of bytes. Using the cylinder method, all tracks of the same number on each recording surface are considered part of the same cylinder. By using the cylinder method to record data down the disk surfaces, movement of the read/write heads is reduced during both reading and writing.

Advantages of using a hard disk drive on a personal computer include increased storage capacity, faster access time, and the online availability of applications and data. Removable disk devices consist of the drive unit, which is usually in its own cabinet, and the removable recording media, called a disk pack. The advantage of removable disk packs is that the data on a disk drive can be quickly changed by removing one pack and replacing it with another.

A hard card is a circuit board that has a hard disk built onto it. Hard cards provide an easy way to expand the storage capacity of a personal computer because they can be installed into an expansion slot of the computer. A disk cartridge offers the fast access and storage features of a hard drive with the portability of diskettes. The disk cartridge can be easily removed from the computer for data transfer or security reasons.

Data and programs stored on a diskette can be protected from accidental removal by using the write-protect feature. On 5 1/4" diskettes, if a small notch in the corner of the diskette is covered by a piece of removable tape, data cannot be written to the disk. On 3 1/2" diskettes, if a small window in the corner of the diskette is open, data cannot be written to the disk. Back-up storage means creating a copy of important programs and data. Diskettes are usually copied onto other diskettes. However, magnetic tape, another form of auxiliary storage, is commonly used to backup data stored on large-capacity hard disk drives.

Magnetic tape consists of a thin ribbon of plastic, coated on one side with a material that can be magnetized to record the bit patterns that represent data. Reel-to-reel tape devices use two reels: a supply reel to hold the tape that will be read or written on, and the take-up reel to temporarily hold portions of the supply reel tape as it is being processed. Cartridge tape is enclosed in a plastic case. Cartridge tape is frequently used for backup on personal computers and is increasingly replacing reel-to-reel devices on minicomputers and mainframes. Tape is considered a sequential storage media because the computer must record and read tape records one after another. Tape density is the number of bits that can be stored on an inch of tape and is expressed in bits per inch, or bpi. Data is recorded on tape in blocks which usually consist of two or more records. The individual records are referred to as logical records. The group of records making up the block is referred to as a physical record. To allow room for the tape to slow down and stop after each block has been read, in between each block is a gap of approximately .6 inches called an interblock gap (IBG) or an interrecord gap (IRG). In the streaming mode, the tape drive records data in exactly the same byte-by-byte order that it appears on the hard disk. Although the streaming mode is faster than the normal recording method, it cannot be used to selectively record or restore an individual file. Digital audio tape (DAT) uses helical scan technology to write data at much higher densities across the tape at an angle instead of down the length of the tape.

Large quantities of data can be stored on optical disks that use high powered laser beams to burn microscopic holes in the surface of a hard plastic disk. Low powered laser beams read the intensity of reflected light on the disk to determine if the bit read is a 1 or 0. Smooth, unpitted areas of the disk reflect the light and are read as 1s or on bits. Holes that have been burned by the laser do not reflect the light and are read as 0s or off bits.

A 14-inch optical disk can store 6.8 billion bytes of information. Automated disk library systems can hold 150 such disks totaling over one trillion bytes (called a terabyte) of online storage. Smaller 5-inch disks called CDROM (compact disk read only memory) can store over 800 million characters, or approximately 1,100 times the data that can be stored on a standard density 3 1/2" diskette. That's approximately 400,000 pages of data. Most optical disks are prerecorded and cannot be modified by the user. Write once read many (WORM) devices allow the user to record data. Magneto-optical technology allows for writable and erasable optical disk by changing the polarity of a spot on the disk that has been heated by a laser.

Solid-state storage devices use the latest in random access memory (RAM) technology to provide high-speed data access and retrieval. Mass storage devices provide automated retrieval of data from a library of storage media such as tape or data cartridges. Smart cards are the same size and thickness of a credit card and contain a thin microprocessor capable of storing recorded information. Optical cards can store up to 800 pages of text or images on a device the size of a credit card.

Key Terms

Access arm: The access arm contains the read/write heads and moves the heads across the surface of the disk.

Access time: The time required to access and retrieve data stored in sectors on a diskette.

Actuator, *see* **Access arm**

Auxiliary storage: The storage of programs and data that is not being processed; also called secondary storage.

Bits per inch (bpi): A measure of the recording density of disk and tape.

Blocks: Data that is recorded on tape in blocks.

Cartridge tape: Tape that is frequently used for backup on personal computers.

CDROM (compact disk read-only memory): A small optical disk that uses the same laser technology as audio compact disks.

Cylinder: All the tracks on a diskette or hard disk that have the same number.

Cylinder method: The physical organization of data on a disk where the data is stored *down* the disk surfaces reducing the movement of the read/write head during both reading and writing operations.

Data transfer rate: The time required to transfer data from disk to main memory.

Digital audio tape (DAT): A method of storing large amounts of data on tape that uses helical scan technology to write data at much higher densities across the tape at an angle instead of down the length of the tape.

Direct-access storage devices (DASD), *see* **Fixed disks**

Disk cartridges: Disk storage available for use with personal computers, which can be inserted and removed, and offer the storage and fast access features of hard disks and the portability of diskettes.

Diskettes: Diskettes are used as a principal auxiliary storage medium for personal computers.

Disk pack: A removable recording media, consisting of five to eleven metal platters that are used on both sides for recording data, used on medium and large computers.

Double-sided diskettes: Diskettes on which data can be read and written on both sides.

Double-sided drives: Disk drives that can read and write data on both sides of a diskette.

Fixed disks: Hard disks on minicomputers and mainframes; also called direct-access storage devices.

Floppy disks, *see* **Diskettes**

Formatting: A process that prepares a diskette so that it can store data, and includes defining the tracks, cylinders, and sectors on the surfaces of the diskette.

Gigabyte (GB): A measurement of memory space, equal to a billion bytes.

Hard card: A circuit board that has a hard disk built onto it. The board can be installed into an expansion slot of a personal computer.

Hard disks: Auxiliary storage consisting of one or more rigid metal platters coated with an oxide material that allows data to be magnetically recorded on the surface of the platters. These disks are permanently mounted inside the computer.

Head crash: The disk head collides with and damages the surface of a hard disk, causing a loss of data. The collision is caused if some form of contamination is introduced, or if the alignment of the read/write heads is altered.

Helical scan technology: Technology used by digital audio tape to write data at high densities across the tape at an angle instead of down the length of the tape.

High-density (HD) diskettes: Diskettes that can store 1.2 megabytes on a 5 1/4" diskette and 1.44 megabytes on a 3 1/2" diskette.

KEY TERMS (continued)

Interblock gap (IBG): A gap of approximately .6 inches that separates the blocks stored on tape; also called interrecord gap.

Interrecord gap (IRG), *see* **Interblock gap**

Latency, *see* **Rotational delay**

Logical records: Data is recorded on magnetic tape in blocks which usually consist of two or more records. The individual records are referred to as logical records.

Low-density diskettes: Diskettes that can store 360K on a 5 1/4" diskette and 720K on a 3 1/2" diskette.

Magnetic disk: The most widely used storage medium for computers, in which data is recorded on a platter (the disk) as a series of magnetic spots. Magnetic disks offer high storage capacity, reliability, and the capability to directly access stored data.

Magnetic tape: A thin ribbon of plastic coated on one side with a material that can be magnetized to record the bit patterns that represent data. The primary means of backup for most medium and large systems.

Magneto-optical technology: Technology used by erasable optical disk drives, in which a magnetic field changes the polarity of a spot on the disk that is heated by a laser.

Mass storage: Storage devices that provide automated retrieval of data from a library of storage media such as tape or data cartridges.

Nonvolatile: Data and programs are retained when the power is turned off. Most auxiliary storage devices provide *nonvolatile* storage.

Optical cards: Special-purpose storage devices that store up to 800 pages of text or images on a device the size of a credit card.

Optical disks: A storage medium that uses lasers to burn microscopic holes on the surface of a hard plastic disk; capable of storing enormous quantities of information.

Physical record: The group of records making up a block of data recorded on tape.

Read/write head: A recording mechanism in the drive that rests on or floats above the surface of the rotating disk, generating electronic impulses to record bits, or reading bits previously recorded.

Recording density: The number of bits that can be recorded on one inch of the innermost track on a disk, referred to as bits per inch.

Reel-to-reel: Tape devices that use two reels: a supply reel to hold the tape that will be read or written on, and the take-up reel to temporarily hold portions of the supply reel tape as it is being processed. As the tape moves from one reel to another, it passes over a read/write head.

Removable disk: A unit consisting of the drive, which is usually in its own cabinet, and the removable recording media, called a disk pack.

Rotational delay: The time it takes for the sector containing the data to rotate under the read/write head; also called latency.

Secondary storage, *see* **Auxiliary storage**

Sector: A pie-shaped section of the disk; also a section of a track.

Sector method: The physical organization and addressing of data stored on disk which divides each track on the disk surface into individual storage areas called sectors.

Seek time: The time it takes to position the read/write head over the proper track.

Sequential storage: Magnetic tape is considered a sequential storage media because the computer must record and read tape records one after another.

Settling time: The time required for the read/write head to be placed in contact with the disk.

Single-sided diskettes: Diskettes on which data can be read and written on only one side.

Single-sided drives: Disk drives that can read and write data on only one side.

Smart cards: Special-purpose storage devices about the same size and thickness of a credit card that contain a thin microprocessor capable of storing recorded information.

Solid-state storage: Storage that uses RAM chips to provide fast data access and retrieval. These devices are volatile.

Streaming mode: The magnetic tape records data in exactly the same byte-by-byte order that it appears on the hard disk; used to backup and restore hard disk drives.

Tape density: The number of bits that can be stored on one inch of tape. Commonly used densities are 800, 1,600, 3,200, and 6,250 bpi.

Terabyte: A terabyte is one trillion bytes.

Track: A narrow recording band forming a full circle around the disk.

Tracks per inch (tpi): A measure of the amount of data that can be stored on a disk.

WORM (write once, read many): Optical disk devices that provide for one-time recording.

CHAPTER SIX—PROJECT ONE

ClassNotes

WHAT IS AUXILIARY STORAGE?

1. To answer this question, choose from the following list.

   volatile   nonvolatile   static   dynamic

   Auxiliary storage is _____ program and data storage.

2. Name two auxiliary storage devices.

   _____   _____

3. Auxiliary storage is a(n) _____ device capable of receiving output from the computer and/or sending input to the computer.

4. Fill in the typical storage requirements of these entities, choosing your answers from the following list.

   gigabytes   magnabytes   kilobytes   megabytes   nanobytes

   Personal User _____

   Small Business _____

   Large Business _____

MAGNETIC DISK STORAGE

Diskettes

1. Name three characteristics of diskette auxiliary storage.

   _____   _____   _____

2. Choose from the following list to identify the physical dimensions of the two most commonly used diskettes.

   8   3 1/4   5 1/4   3 1/2   5 1/2

   _____ inches   _____ inches

CLASSNOTES (continued)

3.–4. Label the 5 1/4" disk below, providing the names of the material of which the disk is made and with which it is coated.

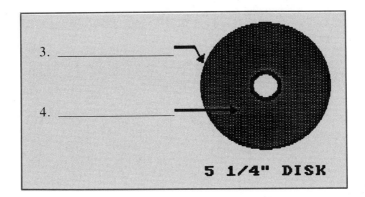

3. _____

4. _____

5 1/4" DISK

5. The 5 1/4" disk fits into a _____.

6. Name two parts of the disk jacket.

_____   _____

7. The 3 1/2" disk has a(n) _____ cover.

8. When you format a diskette you are defining the disk's _____ and

_____.

9.–10. Label the diskette below, specifying which is a track and which is a sector.

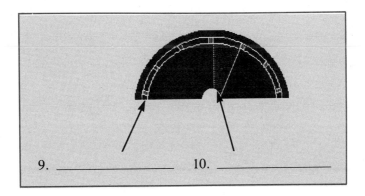

9. _____   10. _____

11. Fill in the following table on formatting diskettes.

DISKETTE TYPE	TRACKS PER DISK	SECTORS PER TRACK	TRACK NUMBERING
5 1/4"			
3 1/2"			

12. Name the three factors that determine the storage capacity of the diskette.

_____   _____   _____

13. To record and read a double-sided disk, the physical mechanism must have _____ read/write heads.

CLASSNOTES (continued)

14. The recording density of the diskette is measured in _____ per inch.

15. The storage capacity for a low density 5 1/4" diskette is _____ and for a low density 3 1/2" diskette it is _____ .

16. List the four factors that determine access time.

    _____   _____

    _____   _____

17. List five Don'ts when caring for the diskette.

    _____

    _____

    _____

    _____

    _____

18. List two Do's when caring for the diskette.

    _____   _____

Hard Disks

19. The hard disk consists of several _____ of disks.

20. The hard disk when compared to the diskette is typically _____ and _____ .

21. The fixed disk is permanently _____ in a(n) _____ case.

22. _____ is used as an abbreviation for direct-access storage device.

23. The access time for the 5 1/4" hard disk ranges from _____ milliseconds to _____ milliseconds.

24. Name three advantages of the hard disk auxiliary storage device, choosing your answers from the following list.

    easily backed up   online storage   large capacity   faster access   more reliable

    _____   _____   _____

25. Label the following fixed disk type.

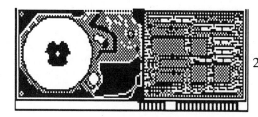

25. _____

CLASSNOTES (continued)

26.–29. Label this diagram of a hard disk. Choose your answers from the following list.

actuators   sectors   plates   spindle   platters   read/write heads   rotator arms

28. _____   26. _____

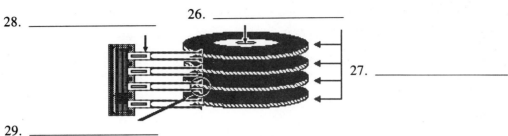

27. _____

29. _____

30. The disk head clearance on the hard disk is one _____ of one inch.

31. When the disk head collides with and damages the disk surface, causing the loss of data on the fixed disk, we say that we have a _____.

32. The capacity range for the 5 1/4" hard disk drive is from _____ MB to _____ MB.

33. Name four characteristics of the disk cartridge, choosing your answers from the following list.

portable   easily backed up   easily secured   more reliable   fast access   high capacity   cost

_____   _____

_____   _____

Protecting Data Stored on a Disk

34. Circle the write-protect notch on the following disk.

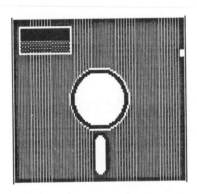

35. On a 5 1/4" disk, when the write-protect notch is _____, data can be written, and when it is _____, data cannot be written.

36. A _____ copy is a copy of an original disk that protects the data stored on the original disk.

CLASSNOTES (continued)

MAGNETIC TAPE

1. Name two primary uses of magnetic tape.

_____   _____

2. The magnetic tape reel lengths range from _____ feet up to

_____ feet.

3. One magnetic tape reel can contain up to _____ MB of data or information.

4.–7. Label the reel-to-reel tape device shown below.

4. _____   5. _____

6. _____

7. _____

8. Data is stored on the magnetic tape using the _____ coding method and using
_____ channels on the tape.

9. The recording density of the magnetic tape ranges from _____ bpi to
_____ bpi.

10. The newer cartridges can hold up to _____ bpi.

11. The space between records on a magnetic tape is referred to as a(n) _____ gap.

12. Blocked records means that several _____ records are grouped into one block.

13. Each block in the blocked record format is referred to as a(n) _____ record.

14. A Digital Audio Tape (DAT) uses _____ technology.

OTHER FORMS OF AUXILIARY STORAGE

1.–2. Complete the statements about optical storage technology, choosing your answers from the following list.

    trillion   laser   WORM   billion   CDROM   EPROM

1. Optical storage technology uses a 12-inch optical disk capable of storing several _____
characters of data and utilizes lasers to burn microscopic holes on the disk.

2. The two major types of optical storage technology are _____ and

_____.

3. Two other forms of auxiliary storage devices include _____ storage devices

and _____ storage devices.

elf-Test
WORKBOOK AND PC VERSIONS

Match the following:

_____ 1. Removable Disk

_____ 2. Cylinder

_____ 3. Cartridge Tape

_____ 4. Read/Write Head

_____ 5. Diskettes

_____ 6. Access Time

_____ 7. Hard Card

_____ 8. DASD

1. Time required to access and receive data
2. Principal auxiliary storage medium for personal computers
3. Consists of a thin plastic ribbon
4. Consists of a drive unit and disk pack
5. All types of hard disks
6. All tracks on a diskette that have the same number
7. Recording mechanism in the drive that generates electronic impulses
8. Used for a backup on a PC
9. A circuit board that has a hard disk built in

You can complete the remainder of Project 2 in two ways—either by marking or filling in your answers in this workbook, or by using the PC version of Project 2. The PC version (available from your instructor) automatically corrects your answers for you. It also calculates the percent of your answers that are correct.

Answer the following questions.

1. Auxiliary storage is also known as _____.
   a. primary storage
   b. main storage
   c. secondary storage
   d. read-only storage

2. T F   Auxiliary storage is a volatile storage medium.

3. A small business would have storage requirements of _____.

4. The _____ inch diskette holds more data than the _____ inch diskette.
   a. 5 1/4, 3 1/2
   b. 3 1/2, 5 1/4
   c. 5 1/2 , 3 1/2
   d. 3 1/2 , 5 1/2

5. Formatting a diskette involves _____.
   a. labelling the diskette
   b. defining the capacity of the diskette
   c. labelling the tracks on the diskette surface
   d. defining the tracks and sectors on the diskette surface

SELF-TEST (continued)

6. T F   The number of sectors on a soft-sectored diskette is determined when a disk is formatted.

7. Which of the following does NOT contribute to the storage capacity of a diskette?

   a. the number of sectors on the disk

   b. the recording density of the bits on a track

   c. the number of tracks on the disk

   d. the number of sides of the disk

8. Recording density refers to the number of _____.

   a. characters recorded   c. bits recorded per inch per inch

   b. sectors on a track   d. tracks on a disk

9. Access time is comprised of seek time, _____, settling time, and data transfer rate.

10. Seek time is the time required _____.

   a. to position the read/write head over the desired record

   b. to position the read/write head over the proper track

   c. to place the read/write head in contact with the disk

   d. for the sector to rotate under the read/write head

11. T F   Hard disks are called fixed disks because the read/write heads do not move; only the platters rotate.

12. T F   Hard disks have slower access time than diskettes because hard disks store larger volumes of data.

13. Disk cartridges provide _____.

   a. storage and access features of diskettes

   b. less security than hard disks

   c. storage features of a hard disk

   d. the portability of a hard disk

14. Protection of data on a hard drive is accomplished by _____.

   a. backing up data onto a cartridge tape

   b. covering the write-protect notch

   c. opening the write-protect window

   d. all of the above

15. Which of the following would you NOT expect to find as auxiliary storage on a large computer system?

   a. fixed disks   c. magnetic tape

   b. removable disks   d. hard card

16. The _____ method of organizing data is more efficient because it reduces movement of the read/write heads.

   a. sector   c. track

   b. cylinder   d. sectional

17. T F   The primary uses of magnetic tape are data transfer and backup.

18. Which of the following has the greatest storage capacity?

   a. magnetic tape   c. cartridge tape

   b. 5 1/4 inch diskette   d. hard card

SELF-TEST (continued)

19. A program processes _____; auxiliary storage transfers
    _____.

    a. physical records, logical records
    b. physical records, physical records
    c. logical records, physical records
    d. logical records, logical records

20. Blocking refers to the _____.

    a. gaps between each block (IBG)
    b. gaps between each record (IRG)
    c. grouping of physical records
    d. grouping of logical records

21. A disadvantage of CDROM is its _____.

    a. limited storage capacity   c. volatility
    b. inability to be reused   d. use of second-generation technology

22. T F   Solid-state storage devices contain no moving parts and provide faster access than conventional disk drives.

23. T F   Mass storage devices are NOT useful in large database environments.

24. T F   A smart card is about the same size as a credit card.

CHAPTER SIX—PROJECT THREE

Identifying Parts of a Diskette

Instructions: In the space provided, label each part of the 3 1/2" diskette illustrated below.

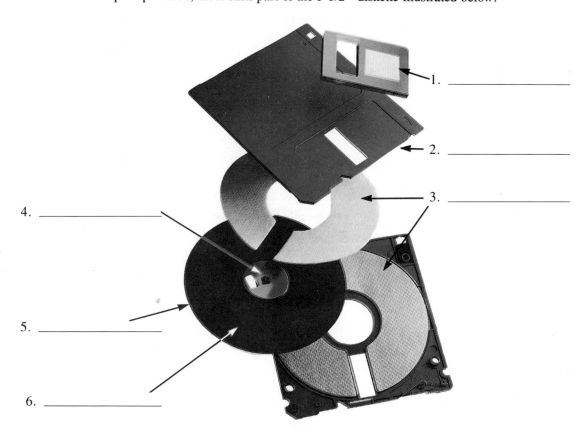

1. _____

2. _____

3. _____

4. _____

5. _____

6. _____

CHAPTER SIX—PROJECT FOUR

Identifying Auxiliary Storage Devices

Instructions: In the space provided, identify each of the auxiliary storage devices illustrated below.

1. _____

2. _____

3. _____

4. _____

5. _____

6. _____

Name _____ Date _____

CHAPTER SIX—PROJECT FIVE

Developing Communication Skills

Instructions: Prepare an oral or written report on one or more of the following subjects.

1. Visit your local computer store and obtain information about the smallest and largest capacity hard disk drives available. Prepare a report comparing their cost, speed, storage capacity, and cost per megabyte of storage.
2. Prepare a report on the advantages and disadvantages of using a removable disk cartridge.
3. Discuss the types and cost of magnetic tape storage devices available for personal computers.
4. Prepare a report on magneto-optical technology used for optical disks.
5. Report on the type of information that is available for personal computers on CDROM disks.
6. Contact a manufacturer or distributor of solid-state storage devices. Prepare a paper on why you do or do not think solid-state devices will eventually replace rotating magnetic devices.
7. Prepare a report on the current and potential future uses of smart cards.
8. Report on why a disk needs to be formatted and what happens when the formatting process takes place.
9. Prepare a paper on the history of the diskette. Include information on high-capacity diskettes currently under development but not yet available for sale.

CHAPTER SEVEN

File and Database Management

◆ OBJECTIVES

- ◆ Discuss data management and explain why it is needed
- ◆ Describe sequential files, indexed files, and direct (or relative) files
- ◆ Explain the difference between sequential retrieval and random retrieval of records from a file
- ◆ Describe the data maintenance procedures for updating data including adding, changing, and deleting
- ◆ Discuss the advantages of a database management system (DBMS)
- ◆ Describe hierarchical, network, and relational database systems
- ◆ Explain the use of a query language
- ◆ Describe the responsibilities of a database administrator
- ◆ Discuss personal computer database systems

◆ CHAPTER OUTLINE

Data Management
    Data Accuracy
    Data Security
    Data Maintenance
    Summary of Data Management
What Is a File?
Types of File Organization
    Sequential File Organization
    Indexed File Organization
    Direct or Relative File Organization
    Summary of File Organization Concepts
How Is Data in Files Maintained?
    Adding Records
    Changing Records
    Deleting Records
    Summary of How Data Is Maintained
**Databases: A Better Way to Manage and
  Organize Data**

What Is a Database?
Why Use a Database?
Types of Database Organization
    Hierarchical Database
    Network Database
    Relational Database
Database Management Systems
Query Languages: Access to the Database
    A Query Example
    Structured Query Language
Database Administration
    The Database Administrator
    The Responsibility of the User in a Database
      Management System
Personal Computer Database Systems
Summary of File and Database Management

CHAPTER SEVEN

Chapter Review

Chapter 7 explains the need for data management, how files on auxiliary storage are organized and maintained (kept current), and the advantages, organization, and use of databases.

Data management refers to procedures that are used to keep data accurate and timely and provide for the security and maintenance of data. Data accuracy, sometimes called data integrity, means that the source of the data is reliable and the data is correctly reported and entered. Accurate data must also be timely. Data security refers to protecting data to keep it from being misused or lost. One way to protect data is to make a backup copy so that if data is lost or destroyed, a timely recovery can be made and processing can continue. Data maintenance refers to procedures used to keep data current. Maintaining or updating data includes adding new data, changing existing information, and deleting obsolete information.

A file is a collection of related records. A record is a collection of related fields and a field, also called a data item or data element, is a fact.

Three types of file organization are used on auxiliary storage devices; sequential, indexed, and direct, or relative, file organization.

Sequential file organization means that records are stored one after the other, normally in ascending or descending order, based on a value in each record called the key. The key is a field that contains unique data, such as a Social Security number, that is used to identify the records in a file. Files stored on tape are processed as sequential files. Files on disk can be sequential, indexed, or direct.

Sequential retrieval, also called sequential access, means that the records in a file are retrieved one record after another in the same order that the records are stored. A disadvantage of sequential retrieval is that the only way the system can retrieve a record is to read all the preceding records first.

An indexed file contains an index which itself is a file. The index contains the values of a key field and the corresponding disk address for each record in the file.

Random retrieval, also called random access or direct access, means the system can go directly to a record without having to read the preceding records. To directly access a record in an indexed file, the index is searched until the key of the record to be retrieved is found. The associated disk address is then used to directly access the record.

A direct file or relative file (sometimes called a random file) uses the key value of a record to determine the location on the disk where the record is or will be stored. These locations are sometimes called buckets. The process of using a formula and performing a calculation to determine the location of a record is called hashing. One hashing method, called the division/remainder method, uses a prime number close to but not greater than the number of records to be stored in the file. If the hashing process generates the same location from different keys, they are called synonyms and the result is called a collision. Often, the next available storage location is used. Relative file records can be retrieved either randomly or sequentially.

CHAPTER REVIEW (continued)

Data maintenance is adding, changing, and deleting data stored on auxiliary storage.

Next to the skills of their employees, data (and the information it represents) is one of a company's most valuable assets.

In a database, data is organized in multiple related files. Because these files are related, users can access multiple files at one time. A database management system (DBMS) is the software that allows the user to create, maintain, and report the data and file relationships. In a file management system is software that allows the user to create, maintain, and access one file at time. Advantages of database systems over file management systems include: reduced data redundancy, improved data integrity, integrated files, improved data security, and reduced development time.

There are three major types of database organization: hierarchal, network, and relational. In a hierarchical database, data is organized in a series like a family tree or organization chart (the term hierarchy means an organized series). Like a family tree, the hierarchical database has branches made up of parent and child records. Each parent record can have multiple child records. However, each child record can have only one parent. The parent record at the top of the database is referred to as the root record. All accesses to the database must be made through parent-child relationships that are established when the database is created in a separate process that is sometimes called generating the database.

A network database is similar to a hierarchical database except that each child record can have more than one parent. In network database terminology, a child record is referred to as a member and a parent record is referred to as an owner. Unlike the hierarchal database, the network database is capable of establishing relationships between different branches of the data and thus offers increased access capability for the user. However, like the hierarchical database, these data relationships must be established prior to the use of the database and must be redefined if fields are added or modified.

The relational database structure is the most recently developed of the three methods and takes advantage of large-capacity, direct-access storage devices that were not available when the hierarchical and network methods were developed. In a relational database, data is organized in tables that in database terminology are called relations. The tables are further divided into rows (called tuples) and fields (called attributes). The tables can be thought of as files and the rows as records. The range of values that an attribute can have is called a domain.

An important advantage of a relational database is that the data relationships do not have to be predefined. The relational database needs only a common field in both data files to make a relationship between them.

Common database management system features include: a data dictionary, utility programs, security to control user access privileges, and a query language to allow the user to retrieve information. A query language is a simple English-like language that allows users to specify the data they want to see on a report or screen display.

In a relational database, the user can use three relational operations (select, project, and join) to manipulate the data from one or more files to create a unique view, or subset, of the total data. The select relational operation selects certain records (rows or tuples) based on user-supplied criteria. The project relational operation specifies the fields (attributes) that appear on the query output. The join relational operation is used to combine two files (relations or tables).

One of the most widely used query languages is Structured Query Language, often referred to as SQL or sequel. Most database vendors have incorporated SQL into their products.

The centralization of an organizations's data into a database requires a great deal of cooperation and coordination. The role of coordinating the use of the database belongs to the database administrator, or DBA. The job of DBA usually includes the following responsibilities: database design, user coordination, backup and recovery, system security, and database performance monitoring.

Database responsibilities of the user include becoming familiar with the data in the existing database and playing an active role in specifying additions to the database.

Popular database packages for personal computers include dBASE III PLUS, dBASE IV, Paradox, Rbase, and Foxpro.

Key Terms

Adding (data): The updating of data, such as creating a record for a new employee to include in a file or database.

Attributes: Fields in a relational database.

Backup: Procedures that provide for maintaining copies of program and data files so that in the event the files are lost or destroyed, they can be recovered.

Buckets: The location on a disk where records in a direct file can be stored.

Changing (data): The updating of data, such as posting a change of address to an existing record.

Child record: In a hierarchical database, a record that is below the parent record. Each child record can have only one parent.

Collision: A collision occurs with direct files when a hashing operation generates the same disk location (called synonyms) for records with different key values.

Data accuracy: The source of the data is reliable and the data is correctly reported and entered; also called data integrity.

Data dictionary: The data dictionary defines each data field, or element, to be used in the database.

Data integrity, *see* **Data accuracy**

Data maintenance: The procedures used to keep data current, called updating.

Data management: Procedures that are used to keep data accurate and timely and provide for the security and maintenance of data.

Data security: The protection of data to keep it from being misused or lost.

Database: A collection of data that is organized in multiple related files.

Database administrator (DBA): The person responsible for managing an organization's computerized data and all database activities.

Database management system (DBMS): The software that allows the user to create, maintain, and report the data and file relationships.

Deleting (data): An update procedure for getting rid of obsolete information, such as removing inactive records.

Direct access, *see* **Random retrieval**

Direct file: File organization that uses the key value of a record to determine the location on the disk where the record is or will be stored; also called relative file, or random file.

Domain: The range of values an attribute can have in a relational database.

File management system: Software that allows the user to create, maintain, and access one file at a time.

Hashing: The program managing the disk uses a formula or performs a calculation to determine the location (position) where a record will be placed on a disk.

Hierarchical database: A database in which data is organized in a top-to-bottom series like a family tree or organization chart, having branches made up of parent and child records.

Index: A file that consists of a list containing the key field and the corresponding disk address for each record in a file.

KEY TERMS (continued)

Indexed file organization: Records are stored on disk in an indexed file in ascending or descending sequence based on a key field. An index is used to retrieve records.

Join relational operation: In a relational database query, join is used to combine two files (relations or tables).

Key: A field that contains unique data, such as a Social Security number, that is used to identify the records in a file.

Member: A lower level record in a network database that is related to one or more higher level (owner) records.

Network database: A database similar to a hierarchical database except that each member can have more than one owner.

Owner: The higher level record in a network database.

Parent record: In a hierarchical database, a record that has one or more child records.

Prime number: A number divisible by only itself and 1. Prime numbers are used in hashing operations.

Project relational operation: In a relational database query, specifies the fields (attributes) that appear on the query output.

Query language: A simple, English-like language that allows users to retrieve information from the database based on the criteria and in the format specified by the user.

Random access, *see* **Random retrieval**

Random retrieval: A retrieval method in which the system can go directly to a record without having to read the preceding records; also called random access, or direct access.

Relational database: A database in which data is organized in tables called relations.

Relational operations: When a user queries a relational database, the three relational operations are select, project, and join.

Relations: Tables in a relational database.

Relative file, *see* **Direct file**

Root record: In a hierarchical database, the parent record at the top of the hierarchy.

Security: In a DBMS, the control of access to data. Usually the user can specify different levels of user access privileges.

Select relational operation: In a relational database query, selects certain records (rows or tuples) based on user-supplied criteria.

Sequential access, *see* **Sequential retrieval**

Sequential file organization: A file organization process in which records are stored one after the other, normally in ascending or descending order, based on a value in each record called the key.

Sequential retrieval: The records on a tape or disk are retrieved (accessed) one after another in the same order that the records are stored; also called sequential access.

Structured Query Language (SQL): A widely used query language.

Synonyms: Synonyms are the same disk location for records with different key values, in a hashing operation for a direct file.

Tuples: Rows in a relational database.

Updating: Data maintenance procedures used for adding new data, changing existing information, and deleting obsolete information.

Utilities: In a DBMS, programs that provide for a number of maintenance tasks including creating files and dictionaries, monitoring performance, copying data, and deleting unwanted records.

View: In a relational database, the data from one or more files that the user manipulates for a query.

CHAPTER SEVEN—PROJECT ONE

ClassNotes

DATA MANAGEMENT

1. Data management can be described as _____ used to keep data

   _____ and _____.

2. Data management also provides for _____ and _____ of data.

3. The purpose of data management is to ensure that data for an application is available in correct

   _____ and the proper _____.

WHAT IS A FILE?

Complete the following statements, choosing your answers from the following list.

database   file   fields   data item   header   field

1. A _____ is a collection of related records.

2. A record is a collection of _____.

3. A _____ is a data item or data element.

TYPES OF FILE ORGANIZATION

1. Name the three major types of file organization.

   _____   _____   _____

Sequential File Organization

2. Choosing from the following list, identify two applications for which sequential organization is useful.

   database   applications   printing   backup   payroll

   _____   _____

CLASSNOTES (continued)

3. In the following illustration of records organized as a sequential file, how many records would you have to read in order to access the data in record 56? _____

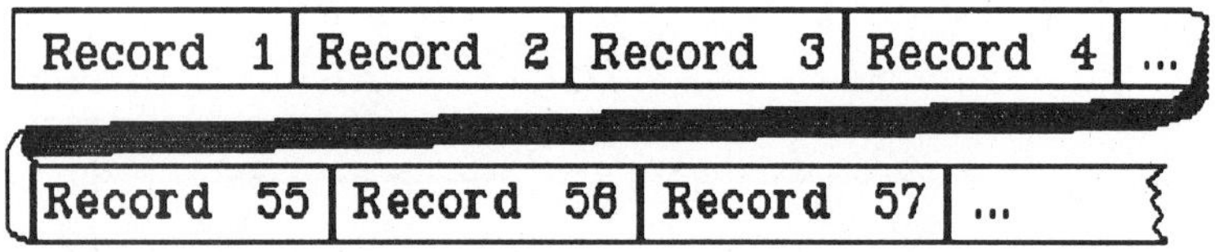

| Record 1 | Record 2 | Record 3 | Record 4 | ... |

| Record 55 | Record 56 | Record 57 | ... |

Indexed File Organization

4. In indexed file organization, the index to the file uses which two items to identify a particular record? Choose your answers from the following list.

   key field   hash function   disk address   relative record number

   _____   _____

5. Using indexed organization you can access a file in either a sequential manner or a _____ manner.

Direct or Relative File Organization

6. In direct file organization you can access a file using direct disk address or using the file's _____ position within the file.

7. Another approach for retrieval in direct or relative file organization is the use of a _____ formula to produce the relative position number within the file.

Summary of File Organization Concepts

8. Fill in the following table, which summarizes the file processing characteristics of the three file types. For those file types that have multiple access methods, place an asterisk next to the primary access method.

FILE TYPE	TYPE OF STORAGE	ACCESS METHOD
SEQUENTIAL		
INDEXED		
DIRECT (RELATIVE)		

HOW IS DATA IN FILES MAINTAINED?

1. To keep data current, you need to perform three operations on records. Name these three operations.

   _____   _____   _____

CLASSNOTES (continued)

DATABASES: A BETTER WAY TO MANAGE AND ORGANIZE DATA

1.–2. Consider the two illustrations below. One illustrates multiple separate files—that is, maintaining separate files for multiple applications. The other illustrates a database—that is, integrated files. Label the two illustrations.

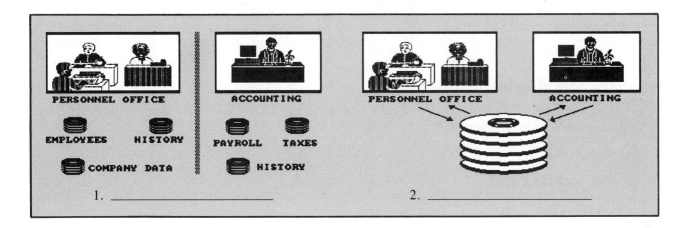

1. _____

2. _____

3. In your own words, list advantages and disadvantages of each approach.

_____

_____

_____

WHAT IS A DATABASE?

1. In each illustration below, place asterisks above those data items that are redundant or duplicated.

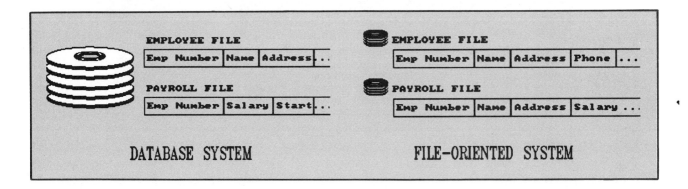

2. The software used to create, maintain, and extract information in the multiple related files of a database is called a(n) _____.

3. The software used to create, maintain, and extract information from a single file at a time is called a(n) _____.

WHY USE A DATABASE?

1. Choose from the following list to identify four reasons why you would use a database over a file approach.

    easier to print   improved data integrity   improved data security   faster access time

    reduced data redundancy   integrated files

    _____   _____

    _____   _____

TYPES OF DATABASE ORGANIZATION

1. Name the three types of databases, choosing your answers from the following list.

    network   random   communication   relational   hierarchical   integrated

    _____   _____   _____

Hierarchical Database

2. The topmost record in a hierarchical database is called the _____ record.

3. One method of discussing the relationship of records in a hierarchical database is to use the family relation-

    ship approach of _____.

4.–6. In the illustration below, label the records as to their relationship to each other. That is, label which are the parent records and which are the children records.

ABC CORPORATION 4. _____

DEPT 20 5. _____   DEPT 30 6. _____

7369 Smith 7566 Gomez 7788 Chung   7499 Allen 7564 Martin 7844 Dolske

7. In the hierarchical approach, each child will have only one _____.

8. List two disadvantages of the hierarchical approach.

    _____   _____

Network Database

9. In the network approach, we use the terminology of owner records and _____ records.

10. Each member record can have multiple _____ records.

11. In both the network and hierarchical approaches, all relationships (parent-child in the hierarchical approach and owner-member in the network approach) must be defined when you _____ or generate the database.

12. Name a disadvantage of the network approach. _____

CLASSNOTES (continued)

Relational Database

13.–17. Complete the statements about the relational approach, choosing your answers from the following list.

gate   field .   data item   link   record   file   domain   range

13. A table or relation is analogous to the concept of a _____.

14. A row or tuple is analogous to the concept of _____.

15. An attribute is analogous to the concept of a _____.

16. The field label, or title (e.g., EMPLOYEE NUMBER), is called a _____ in the relational approach.

17. A field that is common to more than one relational file is called a _____.

18. List two advantages of the relational approach.

_____   _____

DATABASE MANAGEMENT SYSTEMS

Label the descriptions about database management systems, choosing your answers from the following list.

query language   utility   data dictionary   linker   security   hierarchy   database

1. _____ holds the characteristics of the database, items such as field names, field sizes, field descriptions, types of data, and relationships.

2. _____ creates files and dictionaries, monitors performance, copies data, and deletes records.

3. _____ specifies the type of access to each data field in the database for each user.

4. _____ allows the user to retrieve information with user-specified criteria as well as output information in a user-specified format.

QUERY LANGUAGES: ACCESS TO THE DATABASE

1. Name the three major relational database operations, choosing your answers from the following list.

combine   select   collect   project   join   search   retrieve

_____   _____   _____

2. _____ is the emerging relational database management system query language and is implemented on systems ranging from microcomputers to supercomputers.

DATABASE ADMINISTRATION

1. The _____ coordinates all database activities, which include database design, user coordination, backup and recovery, system security, and performance monitoring.

PERSONAL COMPUTER DATABASE SYSTEMS

1. One advantage of a package that supports SQL on the personal computer is that it can directly query _____ databases that also support SQL.

CHAPTER SEVEN—PROJECT TWO

Self-Test
WORKBOOK AND PC VERSIONS

Match the following:

___8___ 1. Database Administrator

___4___ 2. File Management System

___5___ 3. Field

___7___ 4. Query Language

___1___ 5. Data Management

___3___ 6. File

___9___ 7. Data Maintenance

___2___ 8. Database Management System

1. Provide for security and maintenance of data
2. Software to create, maintain, and extract information in a database
3. Collection of related records
4. To create, maintain, and extract information in a single file
5. Data item or data element
6. Magnetic tapes
7. Allows users to retrieve information with user-specified criteria
8. Coordinates all database activities
9. Updating, adding, changing, deleting

You can complete the remainder of Project 2 in two ways—either by marking or filling in your answers in this workbook, or by using the PC version of Project 2. The PC version (available from your instructor) automatically corrects your answers for you. It also calculates the percent of your answers that are correct.

Answer the following questions.

1. T (F) Data professionals are solely responsible for data management.
2. Data maintenance refers to ___all of the above x___.
   a. deleting   c. changing   (e.) all of the above
   b. updating   d. adding
3. A file is a collection of related ___Records x___.
   a. fields   c. data
   b. information d. records
4. (T) F   A field is also called a data item or data element.
5. A collection of related fields or data elements is called a ___Records xx___.
   a. data item   (c.) record
   b. file   d. database
6. Files are usually stored on a(n) ___auxiliary storage x___ device.
7. Files that are stored on tape are always organized as ___sequentials___ xx files.

7.11

SELF-TEST (continued)

8. A major disadvantage of retrieving a record from the middle of a sequential file is that
   access speed is slow *

   a. space is required for data
   c. access speed is slow
   b. key values must be allocated
   d. it requires tapes

9. A key is a field or combination of fields that contain data used to _sequence_ records in a sequential file.

   a. unlock
   c. organize
   b. lock
   d. sequence *

10. An index is a list holding the values of a key field and the associated _disk_ address for each record in the file.

    a. memory
    c. disk *
    b. tape
    d. input

11. (T) F   Random retrieval means that any record can be directly retrieved regardless of its position in the file.

12. A relative file contains records that are stored and retrieved according to their _position_ * within the file.

13. The process of using a formula and performing calculations to determine the location of a record is called _hashing_ *   indexing

    a. indexing
    c. hashing
    b. accessing
    d. collision

14. When two keys produce the exact same position or address, it is called a _collision_ *.

    a. duplicate
    c. crash
    b. merger
    d. collision

15. Adding records to a file, changing records within the file, and deleting records from the file are all examples of _updating_.

    a. purging
    c. file sustenance
    b. merging
    d. updating *

16. (T) F   Data maintenance is another term used in the same manner as file updating.

17. In a database the data is organized in _multiple_ * related files.

    a. uniform
    c. multiple
    b. direct
    d. indexed sequential

18. _Database Management_ * software allows the user to create, maintain, and extract data and file relationships.

    a. Application
    c. File management
    b. Operating system
    d. Database management

19. _File Management_ * software allows the user to create, maintain, and access only a single file at a time.

    a. Database management
    c. Operating system
    b. File management
    d. Application

20. Which of the following is NOT an advantage of database systems over file-oriented systems?

    a. reduced data redundancy
    c. reduced data integrity *
    b. improved data security
    d. integrated files

SELF-TEST (continued)

21. A database in which the data is organized as a collection of tables is called a _relational_ database.
    - a. relational
    - b. hierarchical
    - c. network
    - d. random

22. In a relational database the various tables are related by a common field called a(n) _link_.
    - a. attribute
    - b. domain
    - c. link
    - d. key

23. One important advantage of the relational database approach is _flexibility_.
    - a. speed
    - b. flexibility
    - c. data storage savings
    - d. appearance

24. In a _hierarchial_ database, data is organized in a series like a family tree or organization chart.

25. The parent record at the top of a hierarchical database is referred to as the _root_.
    - a. heir
    - b. father
    - c. root
    - d. origin

26. Due to the predefined nature of relationships within hierarchical databases, access is very _fast_.
    - a. unreliable
    - b. slow
    - c. fast
    - d. reliable

27. In a network database, each member can have _multiple_ owners.
    - a. exactly one
    - b. multiple
    - c. no
    - d. infinite

28. (T) F   In hierarchical and network databases, data relationships must be defined prior to use within the database.

29. A query language is a simple _Englishlike_ language allowing users to specify the data they want to retrieve.
    - a. algebraic
    - b. Englishlike
    - c. programming
    - d. procedural

30. The select operator is directed to the _rows_ of a table or relation.
    - a. rows
    - b. columns
    - c. domains
    - d. attributes

31. The project relational operator is directed to the _field_ of a relation.
    - a. keys
    - b. rows
    - c. domains
    - d. fields

32. SQL is one of the two most widely used query languages. It is used strictly with the _relational_ database approach.
    - a. hierarchical
    - b. network
    - c. relational
    - d. single file

33. The role of coordinating the use of the database belongs to the _data Base administrator_

SELF-TEST (continued)

34. (T) F   System security is NOT a responsibility of the database administrator.

35. The first widely used database system for personal computers was _dBase_____ .
    a. NOMAD   c. SQL
    (b) dBASE   d. Ask Sam

36. Databases provide a better way of organizing data by relating items in _Multiple_____ files.
    a. numeric   c. unrelated
    b. information   (d.) multiple

Name _____   Date _____

Random Retrieval Using an Indexed File

Instructions: The following diagram illustrates random retrieval using an indexed file. Analyze the diagram and briefly explain each of the steps in the procedure as identified by the numbers 1 through 6.

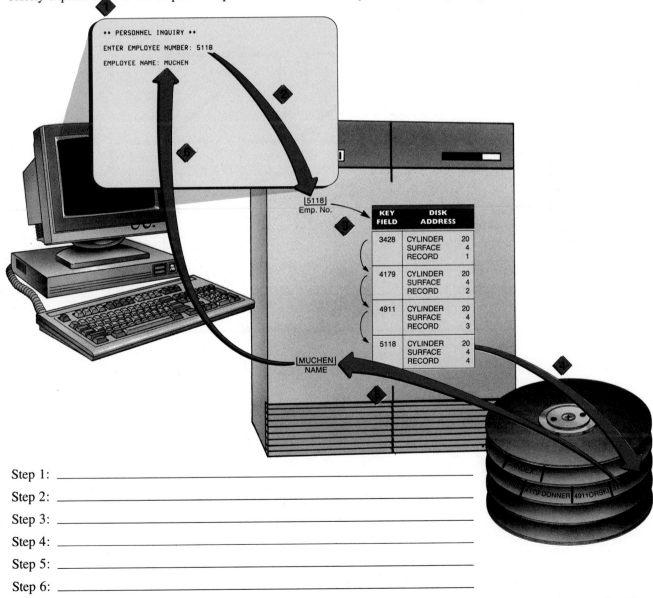

Step 1: _____

Step 2: _____

Step 3: _____

Step 4: _____

Step 5: _____

Step 6: _____

CHAPTER SEVEN—PROJECT FOUR

Identifying Types of Database Organization

Instructions: The following diagrams illustrate two types of database organization. Identify each type in the space provided below the diagram.

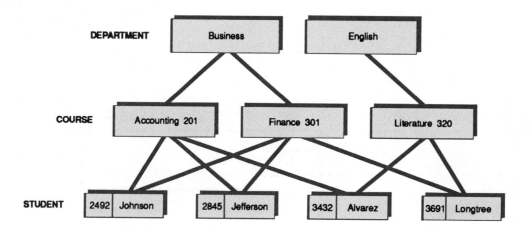

1. Type of database organization _____

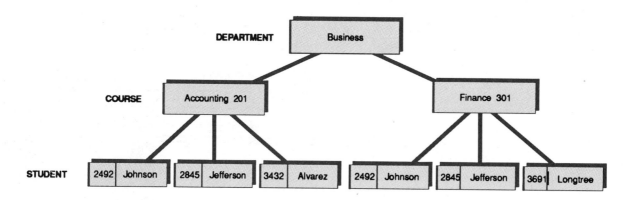

2. Type of database organization _____

CHAPTER SEVEN—PROJECT FIVE

Developing Communication Skills

Instructions: Prepare an oral or written report on one or more of the following subjects.

1. Contact an organization that has recently (within a year) begun using a relational database management package. Ask a knowledgeable user to comment on the changes that have taken place.
2. Interview someone at your school who is responsible for maintaining computerized student or personnel records. Ask him or her what measures are taken to safeguard the data from unauthorized access or use.
3. Research and prepare a report on the different hashing methods that can be used to locate data shared on a disk.
4. Prepare a report on the history of relational database systems.
5. Interview someone at your school or place of work who works in the personnel department, and prepare a report on the computer and paper records produced when a new employee is hired.
6. Prepare a report on the development and current status of structured query language (SQL).
7. Interview a database administrator (DBA) and describe his or her background and job responsibilities.
8. Interview a user who has recently (within the last year) participated in the development of a new computer application. Ask him or her to comment on his or her participation in the design of the database.
9. Review recent articles on microcomputer database packages. Comment on which package you think would be most appropriate for personal use, for a small organization, and for a medium business.

CHAPTER EIGHT

Communications

◆ OBJECTIVES

- ◆ Define the term communications
- ◆ Describe the basic components of a communications system
- ◆ Describe the various transmission media used for communications channels
- ◆ Describe the different types of line configurations
- ◆ Describe how data is transmitted
- ◆ Identify and explain the communications equipment used in a communications system
- ◆ Describe the functions performed by communications software
- ◆ Explain the two major categories of networks and describe three common network configurations
- ◆ Describe how bridges and gateways are used to connect networks

---

◆ CHAPTER OUTLINE

What Is Communications?
A Communications System Model
Communications Channels
    Twisted Pair Wire
    Coaxial Cable
    Fiber Optics
    Microwave Transmission
    Satellite Transmission
    Wireless Transmission
    An Example of a Communications Channel
Line Configurations
    Point-to-Point Lines
      Switched Line
      Dedicated Line
    Multidrop Lines
Characteristics of Communications Channels
    Types of Signals: Digital and Analog
    Transmission Modes: Asynchronous and
      Synchronous

    Direction of Transmission: Simplex, Half-Duplex,
      and Full-Duplex
    Transmission Rate
Communications Equipment
    Modems
    Multiplexors
    Front-End Processors
Communications Software
Communications Protocols
Communications Networks
    Local Area Networks (LANs)
    Wide Area Networks (WANs)
Network Configurations
    Star Network
    Bus Network
    Ring Network
Connection Networks
An Example of a Communications Network
Summary of Communications

Chapter Review

Chapter 8 provides an overview of communications with an emphasis on the communication of data and information. Terminology, equipment, procedures, and applications that relate to computers and their use as communications devices are also explained. Communications, sometimes called data communications, refers to the transmission of data and information over a communications channel between one computer or terminal and another computer. Telecommunications describes any type of long-distance communications including television signals. Teleprocessing refers to the use of telephone lines to transmit data. Most people refer to the process of transmitting data or information of any type as data communications, or simply communications.

The basic model of a communications system includes communications software and the following equipment: a computer or terminal, communications equipment that can send (and can usually receive) data, the communications channel over which the data is sent, communications equipment that can receive (and can usually send) data, and another computer.

A communications channel, also called a communications line or communications link, is the path that the data follows as it is transmitted from the sending equipment to the receiving equipment in a communications system. Channels are made up of one or more transmission media, including twisted pair wire, coaxial cable, fiber optics, microwave transmission, satellite transmission, and wireless transmission.

Various cables used for communications include the following. Twisted pair wire consists of pairs of copper wires that are twisted together. Twisted pair wire, commonly used for telephone lines, is inexpensive but can be affected by outside electrical interference. Coaxial cable is a high-quality communications line consisting of a copper wire conductor surrounded by a nonconducting insulator that is in turn surrounded by a woven metal outer conductor, and finally a plastic outer coating. Coaxial cable is not susceptible to electrical interference and can transmit data at higher data rates over longer distances than twisted pair telephone wire. Baseband coaxial cable can carry one signal at a time at a very high speed over a short distance. Broadband coaxial cable can carry multiple signals at one time over longer distances. Broadband coaxial cable can carry data, audio, and video transmission over the same line. Fiber-optic cable uses smooth, hair-thin strands of glass to conduct light with high efficiency. Although it is more expensive and difficult to install than metal wiring, fiber-optic cable can transmit thousands of times the data than comparable size metal wiring.

Microwaves provide high-speed data communication of voice and data but are limited to line-of-sight transmission. Microwave stations are characterized by antennas positioned on tops of buildings, towers, or mountains.

Communications satellites receive signals from earth stations, amplify the signals, and retransmit the signals back to other earth stations. The transmission to the satellite is called an uplink and the transmission from the satellite to a receiving earth station is called a downlink. Satellites are usually placed 22,300 miles in space in order to remain over a fixed earth location. This is called a geosynchronous orbit.

Wireless transmission uses one of three techniques to transmit data: light beams, radio waves, or carrier-connect radio which uses the existing electrical wiring of a building. Wireless systems offer design flexibility and portability, but provide slower transmission speed than wired connections.

CHAPTER REVIEW (continued)

Cellular telephones use radio waves to communicate with a local antenna assigned to a specific geographic area called a cell. A central computer monitors the communication activity in each cell and can switch a transmission from one cell to another if necessary. Individual hexagon-shaped cells range from one to ten miles in width and use between 50 and 75 radio channels.

Two major line configurations (types of connections) commonly used in communications are: point-to-point lines and multidrop, or multipoint, lines. A point-to-point line is a direct line between a sending and a receiving device. A switched point-to-point line uses a regular telephone line. The process of establishing the communication connection is referred to as the handshake. Although the quality of the line cannot be controlled, a switched point-to-point line can be used to make a communication connection between any two locations where there is phone service and communications equipment. A dedicated point-to-point line is a line connection that is always established. If the dedicated line is provided by an outside organization, it is sometimes called a leased line or a private line. Dedicated lines are usually charged for on a flat-fee basis depending on the distance between the two connected points and the speed at which data will be transmitted.

A multidrop line, also called a multipoint line, is commonly used to connect multiple devices, such as terminals or personal computers, on a single line to a main computer, sometimes called a host computer. A multidrop line can be used by only one user at a time and therefore the number of terminals to be placed on the line depends on the anticipated amount of communication traffic. A leased line is almost always used for multidrop line configurations.

A modem is a piece of communications equipment used to convert between digital signals used by computers and analog signals carried over voice phone lines. Some telephone companies now offer digital data service, communications channels designed to carry digital instead of voice signals. With digital data service, users connect to the communications line through a device called a data service unit.

In asynchronous transmission mode, individual characters (made up of bits) are transmitted at irregular intervals. The asynchronous transmission mode is used for lower speed data transmission and is used with most communications equipment designed for personal computers. In the synchronous transmission mode, large blocks of data are transmitted at regular intervals. Synchronous transmission requires more sophisticated equipment, but gives much higher speed and accuracy than asynchronous transmission.

The direction of data transmission is classified as either simplex, half-duplex, or full-duplex. In simplex transmission, data flows in one direction only. In half-duplex transmission, data can flow in both directions but in only one direction at a time. In full-duplex transmission, data can be sent in both directions at the same time.

The transmission rate of a communications channel is determined by its bandwidth and its speed. The bandwidth is the range of frequencies that a channel can carry. The wider the bandwidth, the more frequencies, and the more data that can be transmitted. The speed at which data is transmitted is usually expressed as bits per second or as a baud rate. Bits per second (bps) is the number of bits that can be transmitted in one second. Baud rate is the number of times the signal changes. With each signal change, one or more bits can be transmitted.

The word modem comes from a combination of the words modulate, which means to change into a sound or analog signal, and demodulate, which means to convert an analog signal into a digital signal. A modem is needed at both the sending and receiving ends of a communications channel. An external modem is a separate, or stand-alone device attached to the computer or terminal by a cable and the telephone outlet by a standard telephone cable. An internal modem is a circuit board that is installed inside a computer or terminal. An acoustic modem or acoustic coupler is a modem designed to be used with a telephone handset.

A multiplexor, or MUX, combines more than one input signal into a single stream of data that can be transmitted over a communications channel. A multiplexor at the receiving end separates the combined signal into its original parts. A multiplexor increases the efficiency of communications and saves the cost of individual communications channels.

A front-end processor is a computer that is dedicated to handling the communications requirements of a larger computer. These tasks include polling (checking connected terminals or computers to see if they have data to send), error checking and correction, and access security.

Communications software is sometimes needed to perform such tasks as dialing, file transfer, terminal emulation, and data encryption. Terminal emulation software allows a personal computer to imitate or appear to be a specific type of terminal. Data encryption is the conversion of data at the sending end into an unrecognizable string of characters or bits and the reconversion of the data at the receiving end.

A protocol is a set of rules and procedures for exchanging information between computers. Protocols define how the communications link is established, how information is transmitted, and how errors are detected and corrected.

CHAPTER REVIEW (continued)

A communications network is a collection of terminals, computers, and other equipment that uses communications channels to share data, information, hardware, and software. Networks can be classified as either local area networks or wide area networks. A local area network (LAN) is a communications network that is privately owned and that covers a limited geographic area such as an office, a building, or a group of buildings. Two common applications of local area networks are hardware resource sharing and information resource sharing. Hardware resource sharing allows each network user to access and use devices that would be too expensive or otherwise unjustified to provide for each user. Information resource sharing allows network users to access data stored on any other computer in the network. The server, or network control unit, is a computer dedicated to handling the communications needs of the other computers in the network.

Information resource sharing is usually provided by using either the file-server or client-server method. Using the file-server method, the server sends an entire file at a time. With the client-server method, as much processing as possible is done on the server system before data is transmitted.

A site license is sometimes necessary to allow multiple users to use a commercial software package.

A wide area network (WAN) is geographic in scope (as opposed to local) and uses telephone lines, microwaves, satellites, or a combination of communications channels. Public wide area network companies include so-called common carriers such as the telephone companies. Value-added carriers lease channels from common carriers to provide specialized communications services referred to as value-added networks. Packet-switching combines individual packets of information from various users and transmits them together over a high-speed channel. Most common carriers now offer Integrated Services Digital Network (ISDN), an international standard for the digital transmission of both voice and data using different channels and communications companies.

The configuration, or physical layout, of the equipment in a communications network is called topology. Devices connected to a network are referred to as nodes. The three most common topologies are star, bus, and ring networks. A star network contains a central computer and one or more terminals or computers. On a bus network, all devices in the network are connected to and share a single cable. In a ring network, all computers are connected in a continuous loop. Data flows around the ring in one direction only.

Networks can be connected using gateways and bridges. A gateway is a combination of hardware and software that allows users on one network to access the resources on a different type of network. A bridge is a combination of hardware and software that is used to connect similar networks.

CHAPTER EIGHT

Key Terms

Acoustic coupler, *see* **Acoustic modem**

Acoustic modem: A communications device used with a telephone handset; also called acoustic coupler.

Analog signal: A signal used on communications lines that consists of a continuous electrical wave.

Asynchronous transmission mode: A data communication method which transmits one character at a time at irregular intervals using start and stop bits.

Bandwidth: The range of frequencies that a communications channel can carry.

Baseband: Coaxial cable that can carry one signal at a time at very high rates of speed.

Baud rate: The number of times per second that a data communications signal being transmitted changes; with each change, one or more bits can be transmitted.

Bits per second (bps): A measure of the speed of data transmission; the number of bits transmitted in one second.

Bridge: A combination of hardware and software that is used to connect *similar* networks.

Broadband: Coaxial cable that can carry multiple signals at one time.

Bus network: A communications network in which all the devices are connected to and share a single cable.

Cellular telephone: A wireless telephone available to the general public that uses radio waves to communicate with a local antenna assigned to a specific geographic area called a cell.

Client-server: In information resource sharing on a network, as much processing as possible is done on the server system before data is transmitted to the requesting computer.

Coaxial cable: A high-quality communications line that is used in offices and laid underground and under the ocean. Coaxial cable consists of a copper wire conductor surrounded by a nonconducting insulator that is in turn surrounded by a woven metal mesh outer conductor, and finally a plastic outer coating.

Common carriers: Public wide area network companies such as the telephone companies.

Communications: The transmission of data and information over a communications channel such as a standard telephone line, between one computer or terminal and another computer. *See also* **Telecommunications**

Communications channel: The link, or path, that the data follows as it is transmitted from the sending equipment to the receiving equipment in a communications system.

Communications line, *see* **Communications channel**

Communications link, *see* **Communications channel**

Communications satellites: Man-made space devices that receive, amplify, and retransmit signals from earth.

Communications software: Programs that perform data communications tasks such as dialing, file transfer, terminal emulation, and data encryption.

Data communications, *see* **Communications**

Data encryption: Communications software that protects confidential data during transmission. The data is converted at the sending end into an unrecognizable string of characters or bits and reconverted at the receiving end.

Data service unit (DSU): In digital data service, a device that connects users to the communications line.

Dedicated line: A communications line connection between devices that is always established.

KEY TERMS (continued)

Dialing software: Communications software that stores, selects, and dials telephone numbers.

Digital data service: A service offered by telephone companies with communications channels specifically designed to carry digital instead of voice signals.

Digital signals: A type of signal for computer processing in which individual electrical pulses represent bits that are grouped together to form characters.

Downlink: The transmission from a satellite to a receiving earth station.

Earth stations: Communications facilities that contain large, dish-shaped antennas used to transmit data to and receive data from communications satellites.

External modem: A separate, or stand-alone, device attached to the computer or terminal by a cable and to the telephone outlet by a standard telephone cord.

Fiber optics: A technology based on the capability of smooth, hair-thin strands of glass that conduct light waves to rapidly and efficiently transmit data.

File-server: In information resource sharing on a network, allows an entire file to be sent at a time, on request. The requesting computer then performs the processing.

File transfer software: Communications software that allows the user to move one or more files from one system to another. The software generally has to be loaded on both the sending and receiving computers.

Front-end processor: A computer that is dedicated to handling the communications requirements of a larger computer.

Full-duplex transmission: A data transmission method in which data can be sent in both directions at the same time.

Gateway: A combination of hardware and software that allows users on one network to access the resources on a *different* type of network.

Geosynchronous orbit: An orbit about 22,300 miles above the earth in which communications satellites are placed. The satellite rotates with the earth, so that the same dish antennas on earth that are used to send and receive signals can remain fixed on the satellite at all times.

Half-duplex transmission: A data transmission method in which data can flow in both directions, but in only one direction at a time.

Handshake: The process of establishing the communications connection on a switched line.

Hardware resource sharing: A procedure used in local area networks, allowing all network users to access a single piece of equipment rather than each user having to be connected to his or her own device.

Host computer: In a data communications system, a main computer that is connected to several devices (such as terminals or personal computers).

Information resource sharing: A procedure that allows local area network users to access data stored on any other computer in the network.

Integrated Services Digital Network (ISDN): An international standard for the digital transmission of both voice and data using different channels and communications companies.

Internal modem: A circuit board containing a modem that is installed inside a computer or terminal.

Leased line: A dedicated communications line provided by an outside organization; also called private line.

Line configurations: The types of line connections used in communications systems. The major line configurations are point-to-point lines and multidrop, or multipoint, lines.

Local area network (LAN): A communications network that is privately owned and covers a limited geographic area such as an office, a building, or a group of buildings.

Microwaves: Radio waves that can be used to provide high-speed transmission of both voice and data.

Modem (*mo***dulate-***dem***odulate):** A communications device that converts data between the digital signals of a terminal or computer and the analog signals that are transmitted over a communications channel.

Multidrop line: A communications line configuration using a single line to connect multiple devices, such as terminals or personal computers, to a main computer; also called multipoint line.

Multiplexor (MUX): An electronic device that converts multiple input signals into a single stream of data that can be efficiently transmitted over a communications channel.

Multipoint line, *see* **Multidrop line**

Network: In data communications, a collection of terminals, computers, and other equipment that use communications channels to share data, information, hardware, and software.

Network control unit, *see* **Server**

Nodes: Devices connected to a network, such as terminals, printers, or other computers.

Open Systems Interconnection (OSI) model: A set of communications protocols defined by the International Standards Organization based in Geneva, Switzerland.

KEY TERMS (continued)

Packet-switching: In communications networks, individual packets of information from various users are combined and transmitted over a high-speed channel.

Parity bit: One extra bit for each byte that is used for error checking.

Point-to-point line: A line configuration used in communications which is a direct line between a sending and a receiving device. It can be either a switched line or a dedicated line.

Polling: Polling is used by a front-end processor to check the connected terminals or computers to see if they have data to send.

Private line, *see* **Leased line**

Protocol: In data communications, a set of rules and procedures for exchanging information between computers.

Ring network: A communications network that has a series of computers connected to each other in a ring.

Server: In local area networks, a computer that is dedicated to handling the communications needs of the other computers in the network; also called network control unit.

Simplex transmission: A data transmission method in which data flows in only one direction.

Site license: A special agreement, obtained from the software vendor, that allows a commercial software package to be used by many users within the same organization.

Star network: A communications network that contains a central computer and one or more terminals or computers connected to it, forming a star.

Switched line: A point-to-point line using a regular telephone line to establish a communications connection.

Synchronous transmission: A data communication method which transmits blocks of data at regular intervals using timing signals to synchronize the sending and receiving equipment.

Telecommunications: Any type of long-distance communications including television signals.

Teleprocessing: Teleprocessing is the use of telephone lines to transmit data.

Terminal emulation software: Communications software that allows a personal computer to imitate or appear to be a specific type of terminal, so that the personal computer can connect to another usually larger computer.

Topology: Topology is the configuration, or physical layout, of the equipment in a communications network.

Transmission media: Communications channels are made up of one or more transmission media, including twisted pair wire, coaxial cable, fiber optics, microwave transmission, satellite transmission, and wireless transmission.

Twisted pair wire: Color-coded pairs of copper wires twisted together and commonly used for telephone lines.

Uplink: Uplink is the transmission to a satellite.

Value-added carriers: Companies that lease channels from common carriers to provide specialized communications services.

Value-added networks: Networks provided by companies that lease channels from common carriers to provide specialized communications services.

Wide area network (WAN): A communications network that covers a large geographic area and uses telephone lines, microwaves, satellites, or a combination of communications channels.

Wireless transmission: Connects devices that are in the same general area such as an office or business park, using one of three transmission techniques: light beams, radio waves, or carrier-connect radio.

CHAPTER EIGHT—PROJECT ONE

ClassNotes

WHAT IS COMMUNICATIONS?

1. Communications is the _____ of data and information over a communications channel.

2. _____ is any type of long-distance communications including television signals.

3. Teleprocessing uses _____ to transmit data.

A COMMUNICATIONS SYSTEM MODEL

1.–3. Label the various components in this illustration. Choose your answers from the following list.

   computer or terminal   communications equipment   communications network
   communications channel

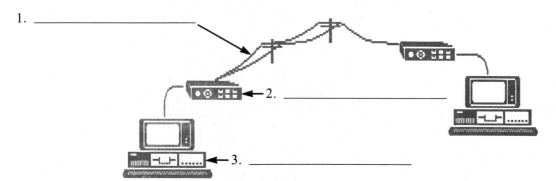

1. _____

2. _____

3. _____

COMMUNICATIONS CHANNELS

1.–3. The illustrations below represent three forms of transmission media. Label each illustration, choosing your answers from the following list.

   fiber optics   twisted pair wire   telephone cable   coaxial cable

1. _____   2. _____   3. _____

CLASSNOTES (continued)

4. This illustration is another example of transmission media. The type of transmission media this represents is

_____.

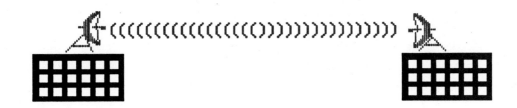

5.-7. This illustration represents an example of data transmission using satellites. Label the illustration.

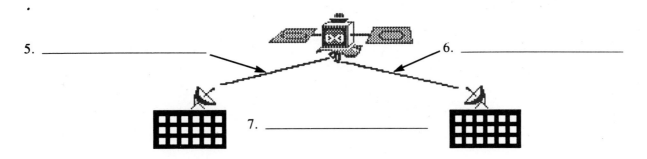

5. _____

6. _____

7. _____

LINE CONFIGURATIONS

1.-2. Label these illustrations of line configurations. Choose your answers from the following list.

satellite network   point-to-point   ring   multidrop

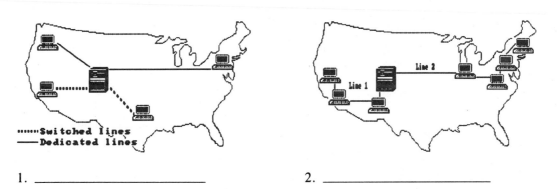

1. _____   2. _____

CHARACTERISTICS OF COMMUNICATIONS CHANNELS

Complete these statements about communication channels, choosing your answers from the following list.

full-duplex   simplex   synchronous   half-duplex   bits per second   multileaved

asynchronous   bits per second   analog   digital

1. The two types of signals used in communications channels are _____ and

_____.

2. In _____ transmission, special characters are transmitted in order to coordinate the transmission.

CLASSNOTES (continued)

3. In _____ transmission, the data that is transmitted is marked in the transmission stream by start and stop bits.

4. In _____ transmission, data transmission proceeds in one direction only.

5. In _____ transmission, data transmission proceeds in two directions but not at the same time.

6. In _____ transmission, data transmission proceeds in two directions at the same time.

7. The speed of data transmission along communications channels is measured in _____.

COMMUNICATIONS EQUIPMENT

1. The piece of equipment shown here is an external _____.

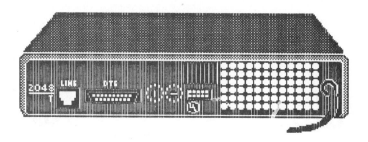

2. This modem located within the personal computer is called a(n) _____ modem.

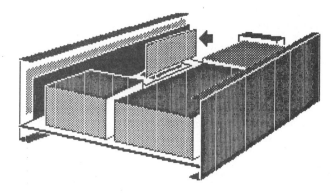

3. The equipment shown here is a(n) _____.

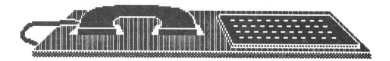

CLASSNOTES (continued)

4. The device illustrated below is routing data to various computing resources and is called a(n) _____.

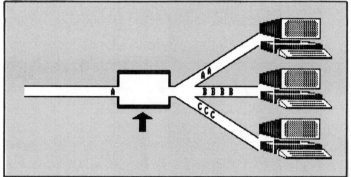

5. _____ is the process of checking connected terminals to see if they have data to send.

COMMUNICATIONS SOFTWARE

1. Name four major functions of communications software, choosing your answers from the following list.
   data encryption   communication validation   file transfer   dialing   terminal emulation

   _____   _____

   _____   _____

COMMUNICATIONS PROTOCOLS

1. A protocol is a set of rules and procedures for exchanging _____ between computers.

COMMUNICATIONS NETWORKS

1. List two major advantages of local area networks (LANs).

   _____

   _____

2. In a LAN, a _____ server would request an individual customer's file.

3. WAN is an acronymn for _____.

NETWORK CONFIGURATIONS

1.–3. Label the following network configurations, choosing your answers from the following list.

star network   crisscross network   hierarchical network   ring network   bus network

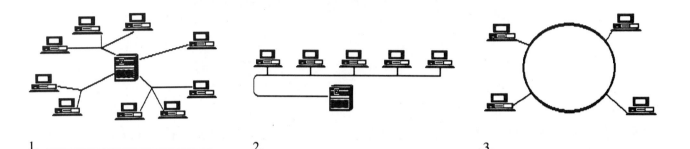

1. _____   2. _____   3. _____

CONNECTING NETWORKS

1. A _____ is a combination of hardware and software that allows users on one network to access the resources on a different type of network.

AN EXAMPLE OF A COMMUNICATIONS NETWORK

1. The marketing department and administration department are connected with a(n) _____.

2. A(n) _____ allows different types of network systems to be connected.

3. All communications with the mainframe computer are controlled by a(n) _____.

CHAPTER EIGHT—PROJECT TWO

elf-Test
WORKBOOK AND PC VERSIONS

Match the following:

_____ 1. Bridge

_____ 2. Ring Network

_____ 3. Topology

_____ 4. Wide Area Network

_____ 5. Broadband Coaxial Cable

_____ 6. Acoustic Coupler

_____ 7. Transmission Rate

_____ 8. Full-duplex Transmission

1. A series of computers connected to each other in a ring
2. Network covering a large georgraphical area
3. Sends and receives simultaneously
4. Device used with telephone handset
5. Carries multiple signals at a time
6. A combination of hardware and software used to connect similar networks
7. Configuration of the equipment in a communications network
8. Depends on bandwidth and speed
9. A direct line between a sending and receiving device

You can complete the remainder of Project 2 in two ways—either by marking or filling in your answers in this workbook, or by using the PC version of Project 2. The PC version (available from your instructor) automatically corrects your answers for you. It also calculates the percent of your answers that are correct.

Answer the following questions.

1. T   F   Communications is the transmission of information over telephones.

2. _____ uses telephone lines to transmit data.

   a. Telecommunications

   b. Teleprocessing

3. Transmission of data from one computer to another computer over communications channels is called

_____.

   a. networking   c. downloading

   b. data communications   d. data transfer

4. For a personal computer to access other computers through data communications, it must have

_____.

   a. a modem   c. a phone line

   b. communications software   d. all of the above

SELF-TEST (continued)

5. The arrow in the following illustration is pointing to which component of the data communications system?

    a. multidrop line   c. communications channel

    b. communications equipment   d. earth station

6. The arrow in the following illustration is pointing to which component of the data communications system?

    a. personal computer or terminal   c. communications channel

    b. communications equipment   d. mainframe computer

7. The arrow in the following illustration is pointing to which component of the data communications system?

    a. personal computer or terminal   c. communications channel

    b. communications equipment   d. mainframe computer

8. T   F   Communications channels include various transmission media, such as twisted pair wire, coaxial cable, fiber optics, microwaves, and communications satellites.

9. Baseband coaxial cable carries _____.

    a. one signal at a time   c. multiple signals

    b. radio signals   d. radio waves

10. Broadband coaxial cable carries _____.

    a. one signal at a time   c. multiple signals

    b. radio signals   d. radio waves

11. The illustration at the top of the next page shows which type of communications channel?

    a. fiber optics   c. satellite

    b. microwave

PLAZA BUSINESS INSTITUTE

MEMORANDUM

PROCEDURES FOR USING INFORMATION PROCESSING/COMPUTER CLASSROOM

1. NO FOOD OR BEVERAGES OF ANY KIND ARE PERMITTED IN ANY CLASSROOM.

2. IT IS THE STUDENT'S RESPONSIBILITY TO CHECK DISK WHEN ISSUED; THEREAFTER, THE COLLEGE IS NOT RESPONSIBLE FOR A LOST OR DAMAGED DISK. NEW DISKS MAY BE PURCHASED FOR CASH FROM THE FINANCIAL AID OFFICE.

3. NO PENS ARE TO BE USED IN ROOM 8; ONLY PENCILS ARE PERMITTED. STUDENTS SHOULD NOT BE TYPING WITH PENCILS OR PENS IN THEIR HANDS.

4. WHEN LEAVING THE COMPUTER, MAKE SURE TO CLEAN THE AREA OF ALL PAPERS AND CLOSE DISK DRIVE DOOR TO PREVENT DUST FROM GETTING INTO THE SYSTEM.

5. TURN OFF THE COMPUTER AND THE PRINTER YOU USED.

6. IF A COMPUTER IS NOT WORKING, REPORT IT TO THE TECHNICAL ASSISTANT OR FACULTY MEMBER ON DUTY AT THE TIME.

7. DO NOT REST ANYTHING ON THE TOP OF THE COMPUTER. DOING THIS WILL PREVENT THE COMPUTER FROM BREATHING AND COULD RESULT IN SERIOUS DAMAGE TO THE CPU.

8. DO NOT LEAN ON MACHINE OR REST BOOKS ON THE KEYBOARD.

9. TO BORROW ANY PROGRAMS, YOU MUST PRESENT YOUR I.D. CARD TO THE TECHNICAL ASSISTANT OR FACULTY MEMBER. IF YOU DO NOT HAVE AN I.D. CARD, YOU MUST FILLOUT AN INDEX CARD WITH YOUR NAME, DATE, AND THE PROGRAM YOU BORROWED.

10. WHEN USING ROOM 8 DURING INDEPENDENT STUDY PERIODS, YOU MUST SIGN IN WITH THE TECHNICAL ASSISTANT. IF YOU DO NOT SIGN IN, YOU MAY BE ASKED TO LEAVE THE ROOM. WHEN LEAVING THE ROOM, YOU MUST SIGN OUT.

11. IT IS THE POLICY OF THE COLLEGE TO RESTRICT THE USE OF ROOM 8 DURING SCHEDULED CLASS TIME.

12. BE CONSIDERATE; KEEP VOICES LOW IN THE COMPUTER ROOM; YOUR FELLOW STUDENTS NEED QUIET TO CONCENTRATE.

13. THE TECHNICAL ASSISTANTS' ROLES ARE TO DISTRIBUTE PROGRAMS AND TO ASSIST STUDENTS IN TURNING ON MACHINES AS WELL AS MAINTAINING ORDER. THEY ARE NOT INSTRUCTORS. IF YOU HAVE A SPECIFIC PROBLEM WITH COURSE WORK, MAKE AN APPOINTMENT TO SEE YOUR INSTRUCTOR WHO WILL PROVIDE YOU WITH ASSISTANCE.

14. PROGRAMS SUPPLIED TO STUDENTS MAY NOT LEAVE THE PREMISES; DUPLICATION OF PROGRAMS IS PROHIBITED.

SELF-TEST (continued)

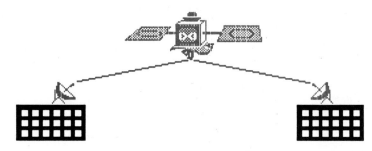

12. _____ are classified as either point-to-point or multidrop.

    a. Receiving locations   c. Line configurations

    b. Host locations   d. Networks

13. T   F   A point-to-point line is a direct line between sending and receiving devices.

14. Multidrop lines commonly use a single line to connect multiple devices such as terminals and

    _____.

    a. modems   c. fiber optics

    b. telephone wires   d. a host computer

15. _____ signals are used by computer equipment.

    a. Digital   c. Morse code

    b. Analog   d. Microwave

16. _____ signals are used by telephone equipment.

    a. Digital   c. Morse code

    b. Analog   d. Microwave

17. The following illustration represents _____ transmission.

    a. synchronous   b. asynchronous

18. The following illustration represents _____ transmission.

    a. synchronous   b. asynchronous

SELF-TEST (continued)

19. T F   In half-duplex transmission, data can be transmitted in both directions along the communications line, but in only one direction at a time.

20. A _____ converts digital signals to analog signals.
    - a. multiplexor
    - b. modem
    - c. telephone wire
    - d. terminal

21. An internal modem is actually a _____.
    - a. box inside the computer
    - b. chip inside the computer
    - c. circuit board inside the computer
    - d. demodulator

22. The following illustration is an example of what type of communications equipment?
    - a. a telephone keyboard
    - b. an acoustic coupler
    - c. telephone
    - d. calculator

23. The following diagram illustrates _____.
    - a. networking
    - b. data transmission
    - c. multiplexing
    - d. communications channels

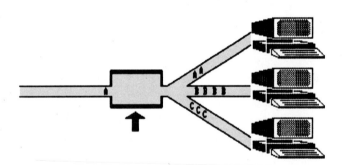

24. _____ allows the user to move one or more files from one system to another.
    - a. Dialing software
    - b. File transfer software
    - c. Terminal emulation software
    - d. Data encryption

25. _____ allows the user to store, review, select, and dial telephone numbers that can be called.
    - a. Dialing software
    - b. File transfer software
    - c. Terminal emulation software
    - d. Data encryption

26. T F   Protocols are rules and procedures for exchanging information between computers.

27. One of the benefits of a local area network is _____.
    - a. hardware resource sharing
    - b. information resource sharing
    - c. both a and b

28. The server unit sends an entire file at a time using the _____.
    - a. file-server method
    - b. client-server method
    - c. neither a nor b

SELF-TEST (continued)

29. A wide area network uses _____ as a means of communications channels.
    a. telephone lines   c. satellites
    b. microwaves   d. all of the above

30. The configuration or physical layout of the equipment in a communications network is called

    _____.
    a. bus design   c. star diagram
    b. a node   d. topology

31. A _____ is a collection of terminals, computers, and other equipment that use communications channels to share data.
    a. system   c. network
    b. topology   d. hardware resource sharing

32. The following illustration represents a _____ network.

33. For a personal computer to access other computers through data communications, it must have

    _____.
    a. a modem   c. a phone line
    b. communications software   d. all of the above

34. T F   A bridge is a combination of hardware and software that allows users on one network to access the resources on a different network.

35. The marketing department operates a _____ network of

    _____ personal computers.
    a. bus, 3   c. bus, 4
    b. star, 3   d. star, 4

36. A _____ connects different types of networks so that multiple departments will have access to necessary information.
    a. bridge   c. both a and b
    b. gateway

37. Every component in the mainframe network must channel through the _____.
    a. bridge   c. front end processor
    b. mainframe computer   d. modem

CHAPTER EIGHT—PROJECT THREE

Identifying the Basic Components of a Communications System

Instructions: The diagram below illustrates the basic components of a communications system. Identify each component in the space provided.

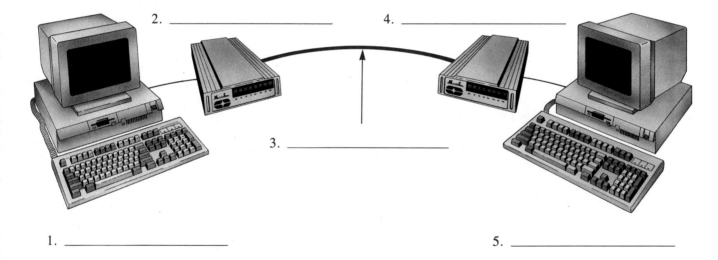

2. _____   4. _____

3. _____

1. _____   5. _____

CHAPTER EIGHT–PROJECT FOUR

Long-Distance Communications

Instructions: The diagram below illustrates the use of various communications channels to allow a personal computer to communicate with a host computer located across the country. Analyze the diagram and briefly explain each of the steps as identified by the numbers 1 through 7.

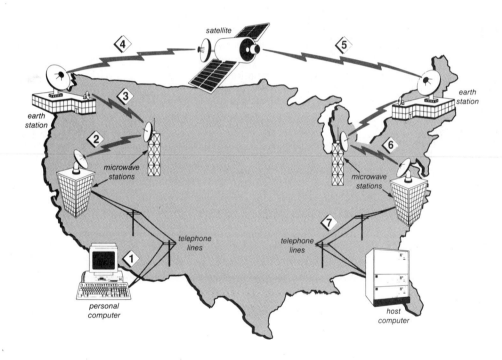

Step 1: _____

Step 2: _____

Step 3: _____

Step 4: _____

Step 5: _____

Step 6: _____

Step 7: _____

CHAPTER EIGHT—PROJECT FIVE

Developing Communication Skills

Instructions: Prepare an oral or written report on one or more of the following subjects.

1. Prepare a report on the use of fiber-optic cable for communications.
2. Find an organization that uses microwave transmission (look for a microwave antenna on top of a building). Prepare a report on how it uses the microwave communications equipment.
3. Prepare a report on satellite communications services that are currently available to businesses.
4. Contact a wireless communications equipment manufacturer or distributor and ask if there are any users in your area. Interview a local user and prepare a report on how the equipment is used.
5. Contact your local phone company and obtain information about establishing a dedicated communications line from your school to a city at least 1,000 miles away. Ask about cost, installation time, and line speed. Report on your findings.
6. Read several articles about communications software. Discuss your findings and your recommendation for the best package for a home computer user.
7. Interview someone who uses a network of personal computers. Prepare a report on how the network is used to share information and equipment. Include comments about how reliable the network is and how much time is spent in managing the network.
8. Investigate the availability of cellular phone service in your area. Prepare a report on the cost of equipment and service and the capability to transmit data over a cellular phone connection.
9. Visit your local computer store or read several articles to obtain information about modems. Discuss with your class the different modems available.

CHAPTER NINE

Operating Systems and Systems Software

◆ OBJECTIVES

- ◆ Describe the three major categories of systems software
- ◆ Define the term operating system
- ◆ Describe the various types of operating systems and explain the differences in their capabilities
- ◆ Describe the functions of an operating system, including allocating system resources, monitoring system activities, and disk and file management
- ◆ Explain the difference between proprietary and portable operating systems
- ◆ Name and briefly describe the major operating systems that are being used today
- ◆ Discuss utilities and language translators

◆ CHAPTER OUTLINE

CHAPTER NINE

Chapter eview

 Chapter 9 discusses operating system features of both large and small computer systems. Systems software consists of all the programs including the operating system that are related to controlling the operations of the computer equipment. Systems software can be classified into three major categories; operating systems, utilities, and language translators.

For a computer to operate, the most frequently used portions of the operating system must be stored in the main memory of the computer. This resident portion of the operating system can be called several different names including supervisor, monitor, executive, master program, control program, or kernel. The less frequently used instructions are stored on disk and can be read into memory when necessary. The process of loading an operating system into main memory is called booting the system. When the computer is turned on, a series of instructions stored in read only memory (ROM) called the boot routine issue commands to load the operating system into main memory. A copy of the operating system is then copied from either a diskette or a hard disk into memory. Control of the computer is then transferred to the operating system. The operating system prompt indicates that the operating system has been loaded and is ready to accept commands. Once the operating system is loaded, it usually remains in memory until the computer is turned off.

Types of operating systems include single program, multiprogramming, multiprocessing, and virtual machine. They are classified by two criteria: (1) whether they allow more than one user to use the computer at the same time and (2) whether they allow more than one program to run at the same time. Single computer operating systems, which are common on personal computers, allow only a single user to run a single program at one time. Multiprogramming operating systems, also called multitasking operating systems, allow more than one program to be run at the same time on one computer. A multiuser-multiprogramming operating system allows more than one user to run more than one program. Computers that have more than one CPU are called multiprocessors. A multiprocessing operating system coordinates the operations of computers with more than one CPU. By using redundant CPU, memory, and other components, fault-tolerant computers can continue to operate even if one of the components fails. Fault-tolerant systems are used in applications where it is important to keep the computer operating at all times. A virtual machine (VM) operating system allows a single computer to run two or more different operating systems. The VM operating system allocates system resources such as memory and processing time to each operating system.

The operating system performs three types of functions: allocating system resources, monitoring system activities, and disk and file management. System resources include the CPU, main memory, and the input and output devices such as disk and tape drives and printers.

A common way of allocating CPU processing is time slicing where a fixed amount of time, usually measured in milliseconds (thousandths of a second) is allocated to each user. When a user's time slice has expired, the operating system directs the CPU to work on another user's program instructions, and the most recent user moves to the end of the line to await the next time slice. Another way of assigning processing priorities is to designate each job as either foreground or background. Foreground jobs receive a higher processing priority and therefore more

CHAPTER REVIEW (continued)

CPU time. Background jobs receive a lower processing priority and less CPU time. The operating system allocates areas of memory for use in storing programs, data, calculations, and work space. Some of these areas are fixed in size and are called partitions. Other areas of memory called buffers are used to store data that has been read from an input device or is waiting to be sent to an output device.

Virtual memory management increases the effective (or virtual) limits of memory by expanding the amount of main memory to include disk space. With virtual memory management, only the portion of the program that is currently being used is required to be in main memory. Virtual memory management is accomplished by transferring the least recently used portion of memory back to disk. In paging, a fixed number of bytes (called a page or frame) is transferred to or from the disk. In segmentation, programs are divided into logical portions called segments for transfer to or from the disk. The memory management process of transferring data to and from memory and the disk is called swapping.

System performance is usually measured by users in terms of response time which is the amount of time from the moment a user enters data until the computer responds. A more precise measurement of performance is CPU utilization; the amount of time that the CPU is working and not idle, waiting for data to process. A system with a heavy work load and insufficient memory can get into a situation called thrashing, where the system is spending more time moving pages to and from the disk than processing data.

To provide for system security, most multiuser operating systems provide for a logon code, a user ID, and a password that must all be entered correctly before a user is allowed to use an application program. A logon code usually identifies the application that will be used. A user ID identifies the user. A password is usually confidential and known only to the user and the system administrator.

The trend today is away from proprietary operating systems that are limited to a specific computer manufacturer or model toward portable operating systems that will run on many manufacturers' computers. Portable operating systems allow the user to change computer systems yet retain their existing program and data files. UNIX is one of the most popular portable operating systems. UNIX has an extensive library of over 400 instruction modules that can be linked together to perform almost any programming task.

MS-DOS and PC-DOS are two versions of the leading operating system for IBM and IBM-compatible personal computers. Both versions of this operating system are often referred to simply as DOS. The Apple Macintosh multiprogramming operating system provides a graphic interface that uses icons and windows. The Macintosh operating system has set the standard for operating system ease of use and has been the model for most of the new graphic user interfaces developed for non-Macintosh systems. The OS/2 operating system is designed to run on IBM's PS/2 line of personal computers. OS/2 can run larger and more complex programs and has the capability to do multiprogramming (up to 12 programs can run at the same time). Other popular operating systems include: ProDos for Apple II computers; PICK, a portable operating system that runs on microcomputers, minicomputers, and mainframes; DOS/VS, MVS, and VM, all IBM mainframe operating systems; and MACH, considered a streamlined version of UNIX.

An operating environment, sometimes called a windowing environment, is a graphic interface between the user and the operating system. Common features and advantages of operating environments include the use of a mouse, pull-down menus, the capability to have several applications open at the same time, and the capability to easily move data from one application to another. Like an operating environment, a shell program acts as an interface between the user and the operating system, but usually offers a limited number of utility functions and does not offer applications windowing or graphics. Utilities are programs that provide commonly needed tasks such as file backups, sorting, and editing. An editor is a utility program that allows users to make direct changes to programs and data. Utility programs are usually supplied as part of the system software that is delivered with the computer system.

Language translators are used to convert the programming instructions written by programmers into the machine instructions that a computer can understand. Language translators are written for specific programming languages and computer systems.

Key Terms

Background (jobs): Jobs assigned a lower processing priority and less CPU time. Compare with foreground jobs.

Booting: The process of loading an operating system into main memory.

Buffers: Areas of main memory used to store data that has been read or is waiting to be sent to an output device.

Control program: The resident portion of the operating system; also called supervisor, monitor, master program, executive, or kernel.

CPU utilization: The amount of time that the CPU is working and not idle, waiting for data to process.

Device drivers: Programs used by the operating system to control input and output devices.

Editor: A utility program that allows users to make direct changes to programs and data.

Executive, *see* **Control program**

Fault-tolerant computers: Computers built with redundant components to allow processing to continue if any single component fails.

Foreground (jobs): Jobs assigned a higher processing priority and more CPU time. Compare with background jobs.

Frame, *see* **Page**

Kernel: The resident portion of the operating system.

Language translators: Special-purpose systems software programs that are used to convert the programming instructions written by programmers into the machine instructions that a computer can understand.

Logon code: In multiuser operating systems, a logon code, consisting of a word or series of characters, must be entered correctly before a user is allowed to use an application program.

Macintosh (operating system): A multiprogramming operating system developed by Apple Computers, which provides a graphic interface that uses icons (figures) and windows.

Master program, *see* **Control program**

Monitor, *see* **Control program**

MS-DOS (Microsoft Disk Operating System): A single-user operating system originally developed by Microsoft Corporation for IBM personal computers. The IBM version is called PC-DOS. MS-DOS quickly became an industry standard for personal computer operating systems.

Multiprocessing (operating system): A multiprocessing operating system that coordinates the operations of computers with more than one CPU.

Multiprocessors: Computers that have more than one CPU.

Multiprogramming (operating system): A multiprogramming operating system that allows more than one program to be run at the same time; also called multitasking operating system.

Multitasking (operating system), *see* **Multiprogramming (operating system)**

Multiuser-multiprogramming (operating system): A multiprogramming operating system that supports more than one user running more than one program.

Operating environment: A graphic interface between the user and the operating system; also called windowing environment.

Operating system (OS): One or more programs that manage the operations of a computer and function as an interface between the user, the application programs, and the computer equipment.

KEY TERMS (continued)

Operating system prompt: A prompt that indicates to the user that the operating system has been loaded and is ready to accept a command.

OS/2: The operating system released by IBM for its family of PS/2 personal computers, developed by Microsoft Corporation.

Page: In virtual memory management, the fixed number of bytes that are transferred from disk to memory each time new data or program instructions are required.

Paging: In virtual memory management, a fixed number of bytes (a *page*) is transferred from disk to memory each time new data or program instructions are required.

Password: A value, such as a word or number, which identifies the user. In multiuser operating systems, the password must be entered correctly before a user is allowed to use an application program. The password is usually confidential.

PC-DOS: The IBM single-user operating system developed by Microsoft Corporation for personal computers.

Portable operating systems: Operating systems that will run on many manufacturers' computers.

Print spool: The reports stored on disk that are waiting to be printed.

Proprietary operating systems: Operating systems that are privately owned and limited to a specific computer model.

Response time: The amount of time from the moment a user enters data until the computer responds.

Segmentation: In virtual memory management, programs are divided into logical portions called segments, which are brought into main memory from disk only when needed.

Segments: In virtual memory management, programs that are divided into logical portions.

Shell (programs): Programs that act as an interface between the user and the operating system and offer a limited number of utility functions such as file maintenance, but not applications windowing, or graphics.

Single program operating systems: Systems that allow only a single user to run a single program at one time.

Spooling: Spooling is used when a report is first written (saved) to the disk and then it is printed at a later time. Spooling is used to increase printer efficiency.

Supervisor, *see* **Control program**

Swapping: When using paging or segmentation, the operating system sometimes needs to *swap* data in memory with new data on disk.

Systems software: All the programs including the operating system that are related to controlling the operations of the computer equipment, classified into three major categories: operating systems, utilities, and language translators.

Time slice: A common way for a multiprogramming operating system to allocate CPU processing time.

Thrashing: A condition where the operating system is spending more time swapping pages to and from the disk than processing data.

UNIX (operating system): A popular operating system from AT&T that was originally developed to manage a variety of scientific and specialized computer applications. With the deregulation of the telephone companies in the 1980s, a multiuser version of UNIX has become available to run on most major computers.

User ID: In multiuser operating systems, a user ID identifies the user, and must be entered correctly before a user is allowed to use an application program.

Utilities: Programs that provide commonly needed tasks such as file backups, sorting, and editing.

Virtual machine (VM) operating system: An operating system that allows a single computer to run two or more different operating systems.

Virtual memory management: A technique that increases the effective (or *virtual*) limits of memory by expanding the amount of main memory to include disk space.

Windowing environment, *see* **Operating environment**

CHAPTER NINE—PROJECT ONE

ClassNotes

WHAT IS SYSTEMS SOFTWARE?

1. Name the two categories of software.

   System   Application

2. _System_ software controls computer equipment operation.

3. Give some examples of system software, choosing your answers from the following list.

   performs what-if scenarios   retrieves information from a database   storing and retrieving files
   starting up the computer   loading, executing, and storing application programs
   produces publication-quality materials   utility functions

   Storing application programs   _Starting up the Computer_
   Utility functions   _Loading_
   retrieving files   _Executing_

4. _application_ software utilizes the computer resources to produce information from data.

5. Give some examples of application software, choosing your answers from the following list.

   spreadsheet   database   operating system   graphics   word processing   disk formatting

   Spreadsheet   _DataBase_
   graphics   _word processing_

WHAT IS AN OPERATING SYSTEM?

1. The operating system is the interface between the end user, the application software, and the computer

   Equiptment or hardware

2. The OS supervisor is essential and resides in main memory. Name some other terms for the OS supervisor, choosing your answers from the following list.

   monitor   kernel   general   executive   master program   control program   loader

   Monitor   _Master program_
   Executive   _Control Program_
   Kernel   _Supervisor_

9.6

CLASSNOTES (continued)

3. The _Non Resident_ portion of the operating system remains stored on a disk and is available to be loaded into main memory whenever it is needed.

LOADING AN OPERATING SYSTEM

Complete these steps for booting the system.

1. Insert the _OS (Operating System) or turned Compacter while OS is on hard disk_ disk.
2. Turn on the _Computer_.
3. The _OS (operating System)_ execution begins.

4.–6. The following activities are handled by the operating system after it has been loaded. Complete the statements, choosing your answers from the following list.

   commands   application   OS   data   execution   allocation

4. Loads _Application_ programs to main memory
5. Manages the _Execution_ of application programs
6. Processes _Commands_ from the user

TYPES OF OPERATING SYSTEMS

Complete the classification criteria for types of operating systems.

1. Number of _Simultaneous_ users
2. Number of _Programs_ running

3.–6. Label the operating systems in the illustrations. Choose your answers from the following list.

   multiprogramming/multitasking   single program   multiprocessing   virtual machine

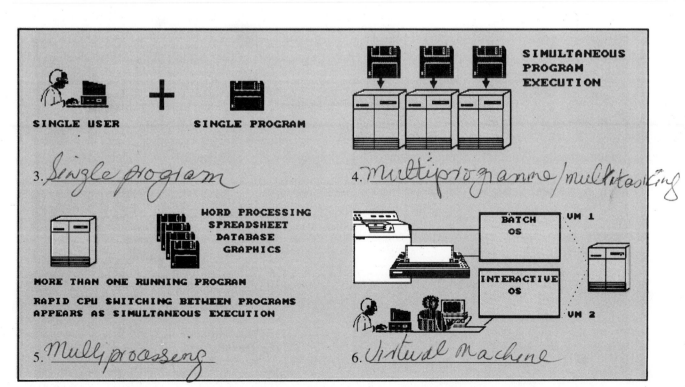

SINGLE USER + SINGLE PROGRAM

SIMULTANEOUS PROGRAM EXECUTION

3. _Single program_

4. _multiprogramme/multitasking_

WORD PROCESSING
SPREADSHEET
DATABASE
GRAPHICS

MORE THAN ONE RUNNING PROGRAM

RAPID CPU SWITCHING BETWEEN PROGRAMS APPEARS AS SIMULTANEOUS EXECUTION

BATCH OS   VM 1

INTERACTIVE OS   VM 2

5. _Multiprocessing_

6. _virtual machine_

CLASSNOTES (continued)

7.–12. Complete the following table.

	SINGLE PROGRAM	MULTI-PROGRAMMING	MULTI-PROCESSING	VIRTUAL MACHINE
NUMBER OF PROGRAMS RUNNING	ONE	7.	9.	11.
NUMBER OF USERS	ONE	8.	10.	12.

FUNCTIONS OF OPERATING SYSTEMS

1.–3. In this diagram, fill in three functions of operating systems. Choose your answers from the following list.

maintaining databases   utilities   publishing materials   monitoring activities

allocating system resources   allocating resources   CPU management

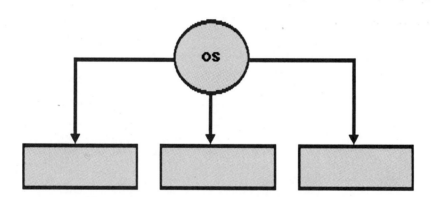

4. With the concept of _____, the operating system allocates the CPU to various programs, sharing the CPU resource over time.

5.–6. In these illustrations of time slicing, label one as time slicing without priority and one as time slicing with priority.

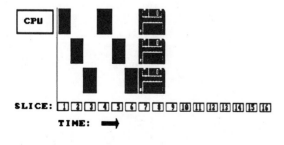

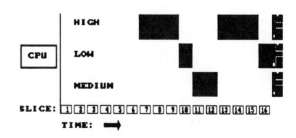

5. _____

6. _____

CLASSNOTES (continued)

7.-11. Complete the following statements about memory management, choosing your answers from the following list.

segmentation   paging   inactive   resident   swapping   replacing   active   partitioning

7. The operating system manages memory by _____ the memory into distinct units, each capable of holding programs and/or data.

8. In virtual memory situations, only the _____ portion of a program resides in memory. The rest of the program resides on disk.

9. When using a(n) _____ approach to virtual memory management, the program is divided into logical portions and loaded to memory as the portions are required.

10. When using a(n) _____ approach to virtual memory management, the program is divided into fixed portions (pages or frames) and loaded to memory as the frames are required.

11. In virtual memory management, _____ occurs when memory is full and an additional page is required for execution but that page is not in main memory.

12.-13. Complete the following statements about input and output management, choosing your answers from the following list.

single   multiplexing   multiple   spooling

12. Operating systems for mainframe computers typically manage the sharing of disk drives among

_____ users.

13. _____ is a term used to describe the collection of several print tasks on a disk drive with the subsequent printing occurring under control of an operating system program.

14. Name two system performance items that the operating system might monitor. Choose your answers from the following list.

CPU utilization   password protection   system access   response time

_____   _____

15. All of the system activities identified in this illustration relate to system _____.

16. The functions of file management, sorting, and editing all fall into the general category of _____ when associated with the operating system.

CLASSNOTES (continued)

POPULAR OPERATING SYSTEMS

The characteristics below apply to popular operating systems. Assign the appropriate heading to each characteristic, choosing your answers from the following list.

MS-DOS   portable operating system   PC-DOS   proprietary operating system   UNIX   OS/2

1. _____

    privately owned
    one vendor

2. _____

    licensed by numerous universities
    portable operating system
    library of instructions
    offered by most manufacturers

3. _____

    for IBM PS/2 personal computers
    used with 80286 and 80386 microprocessor chips
    requires 5MB hard disk and 2MB main memory
    runs complex programs
    multiprogramming
    one version has graphics windowing environment

4. _____

    multiple vendors
    retain existing software and data files

5. _____

    Microsoft Disk Operating System
    industry standard for personal computers
    single-user operating system
    IBM version is PC-DOS

OPERATING ENVIRONMENTS

1. The operating environment is a _____ between the user and the operating system.

UTILITIES

1. _____ are programs that provide commonly needed tasks such as file backups, sorting, and editing.

2. A(n) _____ is a utility program that allows users to make direct changes to programs and data.

LANGUAGE TRANSLATORS

1. Language translators are used to convert the programming instructions written by programmers into the _____ that a computer can understand.

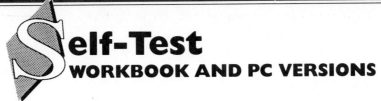

CHAPTER NINE—PROJECT TWO

Self-Test
WORKBOOK AND PC VERSIONS

Match the following:

_____ 1. UNIX, OS/2

_____ 2. Single Program

_____ 3. Device Driver

_____ 4. Operating Environment

_____ 5. Virtual Memory Management

_____ 6. Time Slicing

_____ 7. Booking

_____ 8. Spooling

1. Writes a report to a disk before it is printed
2. Graphics interface between the user and the operating system
3. Logon code, user ID, and password
4. Popular operating systems
5. Allocates CPU processing time
6. Program that controls different input and output equipment
7. Process of loading operating system into the main memory of a computer
8. Swaps segments or pages
9. Allows single user to run a single program at one time

You can complete the remainder of Project 2 in two ways—either by marking or filling in your answers in this workbook, or by using the PC version of Project 2. The PC version (available from your instructor) automatically corrects your answers for you. It also calculates the percent of your answers that are correct.

Answer the following questions.

1. T F A program that tells the computer how to calculate the correct amount to print on a paycheck is an example of system software.

2. The program responsible for formatting disks is classified as _____ software.
   a. systems   b. applications

3. T F In managing computer resources, the operating system may interface with application software or directly with the end user.

4. T F For a computer to operate, the kernel must be stored in main memory.

5. The routine used to boot the operating system is stored in/on a _____.
   a. primary memory   c. ROM   e. the application program
   b. hard disk   d. floppy disk

6. T F The operating system prompt indicates to the user that the OS is ready to accept a command.

SELF-TEST (continued)

7. A multiprogramming operating system is classified as supporting _____ user(s) and
_____ running program(s).

   a. one, one   c. multiple, one

   b. one, multiple   d. multiple, multiple

8. Which type of operating system best supports fault-tolerant computing?

   a. single program   c. multiprocessing   e. virtual machine

   b. multiprogramming   d. multitasking

9. T F The functions of an operating system include allocating system resources, monitoring system activities, and utilities.

10. T F The system resources allocated by the OS are limited to the CPU, main memory, and output devices.

11. _____ slicing is a common way for an operating system to allocate the CPU resource.

   a. Program   c. Input   e. Time

   b. Memory   d. Output

12. _____ is the memory allocation technique that the OS uses to transfer fixed size portions of a program between disk and primary memory.

   a. Paging   b. Segmentation

13. T F The CPU is responsible for managing the input and output processes of the computer.

14. T F Passwords and logon IDs are used by the operating system for monitoring system security.

15. T F Popular operating systems used today include UNIX, MS-DOS, OS/2, and PASCAL.

16. T F An operating environment is a text interface between the user and the operating system.

17. Programs that help manage and sort MS-DOS files are called _____.

   a. virtual memory management   c. control programs

   b. utilities   d. passwords

18. Language translators are used to convert the programming _____ written by programmers into the machine instructions that a computer can understand.

   a. instructions   b. languages

CHAPTER NINE—PROJECT THREE

Loading an Operating System

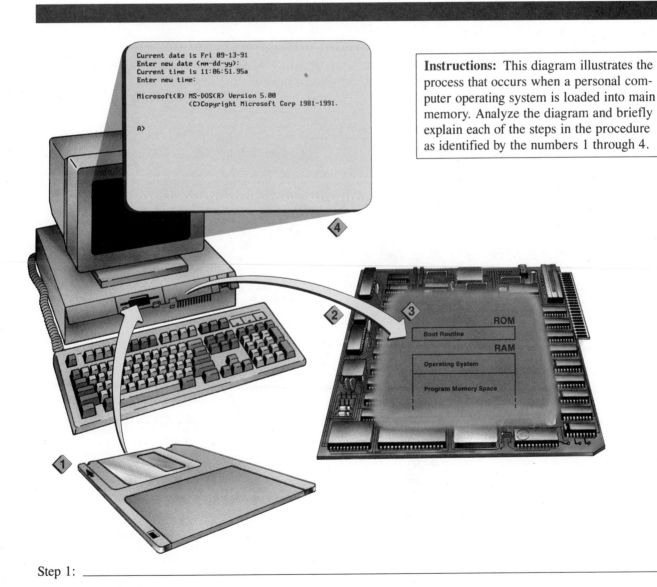

```
Current date is Fri 09-13-91
Enter new date (mm-dd-yy):
Current time is 11:06:51.95a
Enter new time:

Microsoft(R) MS-DOS(R) Version 5.00
          (C)Copyright Microsoft Corp 1981-1991.


A>
```

Instructions: This diagram illustrates the process that occurs when a personal computer operating system is loaded into main memory. Analyze the diagram and briefly explain each of the steps in the procedure as identified by the numbers 1 through 4.

ROM
Boot Routine
RAM
Operating System
Program Memory Space

Step 1: _____

Step 2: _____

Step 3: _____

Step 4: _____

CHAPTER NINE—PROJECT FOUR

Identifying How System Software Acts as an Interface

Instructions: In the space provided, label the diagram below to show how the system software (including the operating system) acts as an interface between the user, the applications software, and the computer equipment.

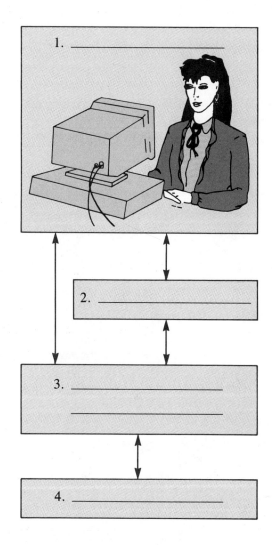

1. _____

2. _____

3. _____

_____

4. _____

CHAPTER NINE—PROJECT FIVE

Developing Communication Skills

Instructions: Prepare an oral or written report on one or more of the following subjects.

1. Prepare a report that explains in detail what happens when a microcomputer is first turned on and the operating system is loaded.
2. Visit a minicomputer installation and interview the person responsible for operating the computer. Prepare a report on the differences between the minicomputer operating system and a personal computer operating system.
3. Interview a user of a fault-tolerant computer. Ask him or her why he or she acquired a fault-tolerant system and if the fault-tolerant capabilities of the system have ever been used.
4. Interview a representative of a minicomputer or mainframe computer manufacturer. Prepare a report on how the system performs virtual memory management.
5. Discuss a print spooling software package available for use on microcomputers.
6. Interview a person responsible for computer system security at a medium or large organization. Ask him or her what computer and noncomputer methods he or she uses to prevent unauthorized access or use of the system.
7. Research the differences between the Microsoft Windows operating environment and the Macintosh operating system.
8. Review several articles on utility software packages. Prepare a report describing the capabilities of these packages and how they make using the computer easier and more efficient.
9. Contact a representative of a mainframe computer manufacturer and ask him or her to discuss proprietary operating system(s) and support of portable operating systems such as Unix used at the company.

Management Information Systems

◆ OBJECTIVES

- ◆ Define the term management information systems
- ◆ Describe why information is important to an organization
- ◆ Discuss the different levels in an organization and how the information requirements differ for each level
- ◆ Explain the qualities that all information should have
- ◆ Define the term information system and identify the six elements of an information system
- ◆ Describe the different types of information systems and the trend toward integration
- ◆ Explain how personal computers are used in management information systems

◆ CHAPTER OUTLINE

CHAPTER TEN

Chapter Review

Chapter 10 discusses management information systems (MIS) which is defined to mean any computer-based system that provides timely and accurate information for managing an organization. Information is an important asset that must be protected. Like tangible assets, information assets have both a present and future value and have costs associated with their acquisition, maintenance, and storage.

Factors that have contributed to the increased need for timely and accurate information include expanded markets, increased competition, shorter product life cycles, and government regulation. The primary users of information are managers. Managers of an organization are the men and women responsible for directing the use of resources such as people, money, materials, and information so the organization can operate efficiently and prosper. Managers perform the four management tasks of planning, organizing, directing, and controlling. Planning involves establishing goals and objectives. Organizing includes identifying and bringing together the resources necessary to achieve the plans of an organization. Directing involves instructing and authorizing others to perform the necessary work. Controlling involves measuring performance and, if necessary, taking corrective action. These four management tasks are usually performed in a sequence that becomes a recurring cycle. All managers perform these four management tasks but their area of focus, such as finance or production, and the information they need to perform the tasks is influenced by their level in the organization.

Management is usually classified into three levels: senior management, middle management, and operational management. These three levels are above a fourth level of the organization consisting of the production, clerical, and nonmanagement staff. Senior management, also called executive, or top, management, is concerned with the long-range direction of the organization. Senior managers are primarily responsible for strategic decisions that deal with the overall goals and objectives of an organization. Senior management is also responsible for monitoring how current operations are meeting the objectives of previously made strategic decisions and for supervising middle management personnel. Middle management is responsible for implementing the strategic decisions of senior management. Middle managers make tactical decisions that implement specific programs and plans necessary to accomplish the stated objectives. Middle managers are more concerned with the internal operations of the organization and, therefore, rely on information generated by the organization. Middle management supervises operations management. Operational management supervises the production, clerical, and nonmanagement staff of an organization. Operational managers make operational decisions that usually involve an immediate action. The decision time frame of operational managers tasks is usually very short, such as a day, a week, or a month. Nonmanagement employees also have a frequent need for information. There is a trend toward giving lower level, nonmanagement employees the information they need to make decisions made formerly by managers. In the real world there is often a crossover from one organizational level to another. Organizations have realized that formal or informal distinctions between managers and employees hinder communication and can restrict the flow of useful ideas and information. Recent technology, including the personal computer, has significantly contributed to the flow of timely information to all levels within an organization.

CHAPTER REVIEW (continued)

The qualities that information should have are: accurate, verifiable, timely, organized, meaningful, useful, and cost effective. Although accurate data does not guarantee accurate information, it is impossible to produce accurate information from erroneous data. GIGO is computer jargon for Garbage In, Garbage Out. Verifiable means that if necessary, the user can confirm the information. Timely means that the information is still current and has not lost value because of the passage of time. Organized means that information is in an order that suits the users needs. Meaningful information indicates that the information is relevant to the person who receives it. To be useful, information should result in an action being taken or specifically being not taken, depending on the situation. Cost effective means that the cost to produce the information must be less than the value of the information.

An information system is a collection of elements that provides accurate, timely, and useful information. Information systems that are implemented on a computer are generally classified into four categories: (1) operational systems; (2) management information systems; (3) decision support systems; and (4) expert systems. Operational systems process data generated by the day-to-day transactions of an organization. Operational systems are often a part of management information systems. Management information systems focus on the summary information and exceptions that managers use to perform their jobs. Executive information systems (EIS) are management information systems that have been designed for the information needs of senior management and have features that make them easier for executives to use. EIS rely heavily on graphic presentation of both the processing options and data. Because executives focus on strategic issues, EIS often have access to external databases that can provide current information on interest rates, commodity prices, and other leading economic indicators. EIS have often failed because they were not modified to meet the specific needs of the individual executives who use them.

A decision support system (DSS) is a system designed to help someone reach a decision by summarizing or comparing data from either or both internal and external sources. Decision support systems often include query languages, statistical analysis capabilities, spreadsheets, and graphics to help the user evaluate the decision data. Some DSS can create models that allow the user to ask what-if questions by changing one or more of the variables and seeing what the projected results would be. Compared to EIS, DSS are more analytical and are designed to work on unstructured problems that do not have a predefined number of variables.

Expert systems combine the knowledge on a given subject of one or more human experts into a computerized system that simulates the human experts' reasoning and decision making processes. Expert systems are made up of the combined subject knowledge of the human experts, called the knowledge base and the inference rules that determine how the knowledge is used to reach decisions. Although they may appear to think, the current expert systems actually operate within narrow preprogrammed limits and cannot make decisions based on common sense or on information outside of their knowledge base. Although expert systems can be used at any level in an organization, to date they have been primarily used by nonmanagement employees for job-related decisions. Expert systems are part of a branch of computer science called artificial intelligence, the application of human intelligence to computer systems.

It is difficult to classify an information system into only one of the four categories. Often, an information system will have features of more than one of the four types. The trend is to combine all of an organization's information needs into a single, integrated information system.

The personal computer is playing an increasingly significant role in modern management information systems by giving both management and nonmanagement employees access to the information they need to perform their jobs. For many MIS applications, personal computers are more cost effective than larger systems. Many professionals believe that the ideal MIS decision involves a network of personal computers attached to a central computer that stores the common information that many users access. A centralized data and decentralized computing arrangement allows users and organizations the most flexibility over controlling their information resources.

Key Terms

Artificial intelligence (AI): A branch of computer science applying human intelligence to computer systems.

Decision support system (DSS): A system designed to help someone reach a decision by summarizing or comparing data from either or both internal and external sources.

Executive information systems (EIS): Management information systems that have been designed for the information needs of senior management.

Expert system: A system that combines the knowledge on a given subject of one or more human experts into a computerized system that simulates the human experts' reasoning and decision-making processes.

GIGO: An acronym that stands for Garbage In, Garbage Out.

Inference rules: In expert systems, rules that determine how the knowledge is used to reach decisions.

Information system: A collection of elements that provides accurate, timely, and useful information. These elements include: equipment, software, accurate data, trained information systems personnel, knowledgeable users, and documented procedures. Information systems are classified into four categories: (1) operational systems, (2) management information systems, (3) decision support systems, and (4) expert systems.

Knowledge base: In expert systems, the combined subject knowledge of the human experts.

Management information systems (MIS): Any computer-based system that provides timely and accurate information for managing an organization.

Managers: The men and women responsible for directing the use of resources such as people, money materials, and information so the organization can operate efficiently and prosper. Managers are responsible for the tasks of planning, organizing, directing, and controlling.

Middle management: The managers in an organization who make tactical decisions and are responsible for implementing the strategic decisions of senior management.

Models: In decision support systems, models allow users to ask *what-if* questions by changing one or more of the variables and seeing what the projected results would be.

Operational decisions: Decisions made by operational manag017ement that involve an immediate action such as accepting or rejecting an inventory delivery or approving a purchase order.

Operational management: The management level that makes operational decisions and provides direct supervision over the production, clerical, and nonmanagement staff of an organization.

Operational systems: Information systems that process data generated by the day-to-day transactions of an organization.

Senior management: The top managers in an organization who make strategic decisions and are concerned with the long-range direction of the organization; also called executive, or top, management.

Strategic decisions: Decisions made by senior management that deal with the overall goals and objectives of an organization.

Tactical decisions: The decisions made by middle management, implementing specific programs and plans necessary to accomplish the strategic objectives of an organization.

CHAPTER TEN—PROJECT ONE

ClassNotes

WHY IS INFORMATION IMPORTANT TO AN ORGANIZATION?

1. List the four factors that have contributed to the increased need for timely and accurate information.

_____   _____

_____   _____

2.–5. Match the following:

_____ 2. Businesses must sell their products in as many markets as possible.

_____ 3. Competing companies are financially stronger and better organized.

_____ 4. Companies have less time to perfect a product.

_____ 5. An example of this is human resource management.

a. Shorter product life cycle
b. Expanded markets
c. Government regulation
d. Increased competition

HOW DO MANAGERS USE INFORMATION?

1. _____ of an organization are the men and women responsible for directing the use of resources such as people, money, materials, and information, so the organization can operate efficiently and prosper.

2. Label the following diagram with the four tasks of a manager.

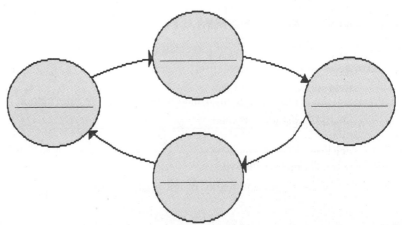

CLASSNOTES (continued)

3. Planning involves establishing _____ and _____.

4. Organizing includes identifying and bringing together the _____ necessary to achieve the plans of an organization.

5. Directing involves _____ and _____ others to perform the necessary work.

6. Controlling involves measuring _____ and, if necessary, taking _____.

MANAGEMENT LEVELS IN AN ORGANIZATION

1. Label the three levels of management with an operational level in the following diagram.

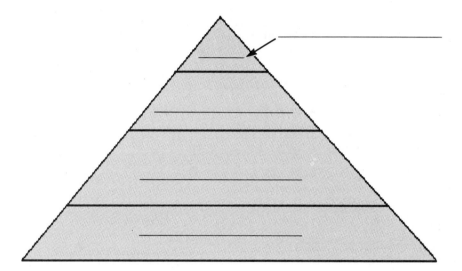

2. Senior management responsibilities include making _____ and monitoring

   _____.

3. Middle management responsibilities include making _____ and examining

   _____.

4. Operational management responsibilities include making _____ and

   supervising _____ and _____ of the product or service.

QUALITIES OF INFORMATION

1.–4. Complete the statements about the qualities of information. Choose your answers from the following list.

accurate   timely   meaningful   cost-effective   verifiable   organized   useful

1. _____ information means that the information is relevant to the person who receives it.

2. The information must be _____ to suit users' requirements.

3. If information is _____, the cost to produce the information must be less than the value of the information.

4. The first and most important quality of information is that it is _____.

CLASSNOTES (continued)

WHAT IS AN INFORMATION SYSTEM?

1. A collection of elements that provide accurate, timely, and useful information is an _____.

2. Name the elements of an information system.

   _____   _____

   _____   _____

   _____   _____

3. _____ process day-to-day transactions.

4. _____ provide information to management.

5. _____ are MIS that have been designed for the information needs of senior management.

6. A(n) _____ is designed to help someone reach a decision by summarizing or comparing data from either or both internal and external sources.

7. _____ combine the knowledge on a given subject of one or more human experts into a computerized system.

INTEGRATED INFORMATION SYSTEMS

1. The trend is clear: combine all of an organization's information needs into a single _____ system.

THE ROLE OF PERSONAL COMPUTERS IN MANAGEMENT INFORMATION SYSTEMS

1. For many information MIS applications, personal computers are more _____ and more _____ than larger computers.

CHAPTER TEN—PROJECT TWO

Self-Test
WORKBOOK AND PC VERSIONS

Match the following:

_____ 1. GIGO

_____ 2. Middle Management

_____ 3. Information Systems

_____ 4. Operational Systems

_____ 5. Expert Systems

_____ 6. Operational Decisions

_____ 7. Information

_____ 8. Increased Competition

1. Collection of elements that provide accurate, timely, and useful information
2. Key ingredients in both short- and long-range decision making
3. Type of computer information system
4. Garbage In, Garbage Out
5. Includes approving a purchase order
6. Contributes to increased need for information
7. Accurate, verifiable, timely, useful, and cost-effective
8. Make tactical decisions
9. Process data generated by day-to-day transactions of an organization

You can complete the remainder of Project 2 in two ways—either by marking or filling in your answers in this workbook, or by using the PC version of Project 2. The PC version (available from your instructor) automatically corrects your answers for you. It also calculates the percent of your answers that are correct.

Answer the following questions.

1. T   F   Information is the key ingredient for both short- and long-range decision making.

2. Having the ability to sell in _____ today is essential for the success of many businesses.

    a. expanded markets   b. foreign markets   c. both a and b

3. T   F   It isn't important for organizations to have current information on how competitors are selling their products.

4. _____ includes identifying and bringing together the resources necessary to achieve the plans of an organization.

    a. Planning   c. Directing

    b. Organizing   d. Controlling

5. _____ involves measuring performance and, if necessary, taking corrective action.

    a. Planning   c. Directing

    b. Organizing   d. Controlling

SELF-TEST (continued)

6. _____ management is responsible for examining variances in performance.
   a. Senior   b. Middle   c. Operational

7. Senior management will make _____ decisions for the company.
   a. strategic   b. tactical   c. operational

8. T   F   Since information is easily available at the operational level, decisions are more complex.

9. Garbage In, Garbage Out best describes which term?
   a. organized   c. meaningful   e. useful
   b. timely   d. accurate

10. The information must be relevant to the person who receives it, best describes which term?
    a. organized   c. meaningful   e. useful
    b. timely   d. accurate

11. _____ arc information systems that are designed for the information needs of senior management.
    a. operating systems c. MIS   e. Expert systems
    b. DSS   d. EIS

12. A system that uses a model and what-if questions is a(n) _____.
    a. operating system   c. MIS   e. Expert system
    b. DSS   d. EIS

13. The _____ uses a knowledge base and inference rules.
    a. operating system   c. MIS   e. Expert system
    b. DSS   d. EIS

14. T   F   Companies today must combine all of an organization's information needs into a single integrated information system.

15. T   F   By using personal computers, management information systems are less flexible and more expensive.

CHAPTER TEN—PROJECT THREE

Identifying Management Tasks and Terms

Instructions: In the space provided, identify the terms that are associated with the four management tasks.

MANAGEMENT TASKS	TERMS
PLAN	1. _____
	2. _____
	3. _____
ORGANIZE	4. _____
	5. _____
	6. _____
	7. _____
DIRECT	8. _____
	9. _____
	10. _____
CONTROL	11. _____
	12. _____

CHAPTER TEN—PROJECT FOUR

Identifying Management Decisions

Instructions: In the space provided, place the number of the organization level (1 through 4) that best matches the type of decision and decision time frame.

ORGANIZATION LEVELS

1. Senior
2. Middle
3. Operational
4. Nonmanagement

Type of Decision

_____ 1. On-the-job

_____ 2. Strategic

_____ 3. Operational

_____ 4. Tactical

Decision Time Frame

_____ 5. Short (day, week, month)

_____ 6. Immediate (what to do next)

_____ 7. Long-range (one or more years)

_____ 8. Medium (up to one year)

CHAPTER TEN—PROJECT FIVE

Developing Communication Skills

Instructions: Prepare an oral or written report on one or more of the following subjects.

1. Obtain the organization chart from a medium or large organization in your local area. Review the chart with a member of the personnel or human resources department and identify the different levels of management.
2. Interview the information systems manager of a medium or large organization and review the computerized systems. Identify the types of operational, management, decision support, and expert systems information provided.
3. Contact a developer or distributor of an Executive Information System (EIS). Prepare a report on the system it offers.
4. Contact local companies that lend money such as banks, savings and loans, mortgage companies, or personal finance companies. Report on the company that uses the most computerized system to determine whether or not to make a loan.
5. Design an expert system to solve a problem of your choice. Specify what information would need to be included in the knowledge base and how inference rules would use that knowledge to reach decisions.
6. Contact a medium or large organization in your area and interview at least one person from each level of the organization. Try to interview people from the same functional area such as finance, manufacturing, or marketing. Discuss the different types of information required for decision making at each level.
7. Interview a manager who works for a company in a competitive industry. Prepare a report on the types of information the company maintains on its competition and how the information is used.
8. Interview a personnel or human resources manager who has been in such a position for at least ten years. Ask him or her to comment on the changes that have taken place in the amount and kind of information that has to be maintained and reported to the government.
9. Interview a manager and prepare a report on the specific things he or she does while performing the four management tasks; planning, organizing, directing, and controlling.

CHAPTER ELEVEN

The Information System Life Cycle

◆ OBJECTIVES

- ◆ Explain the phases of the information system life cycle
- ◆ Explain the importance of project management and documentation
- ◆ Define commercial application software and describe the difference between horizontal and vertical applications
- ◆ Discuss each of the steps of acquiring commercial application software
- ◆ Discuss the reasons for developing custom software
- ◆ Describe how various analysis and design tools, such as data flow diagrams, are used
- ◆ Explain how program development is part of the information system life cycle
- ◆ Explain several methods that can be used for a conversion to a new system
- ◆ Discuss the installation and maintenance of an information system

◆ CHAPTER OUTLINE

CHAPTER ELEVEN

Chapter eview

Chapter 11 explains the phases and paths of the information system life cycle (ISLC); an organized approach to acquiring or developing an information system. The phases of the information system life cycle are: analysis, acquisition or design, customizing or development, implementation, and maintenance. The acquisition path includes the acquisition and customizing phases. The development path includes the design and development phases. If an organization does not find a suitable system during the acquisition phase, it will move to the design phase of the development path. All systems have analysis, implementation, and maintenance phases.

Project management involves planning, scheduling, reporting, and controlling the individual activities that make up the ISLC. Project management activities are usually recorded in a project plan on a week-by-week basis that includes an estimate of the time to complete the activity and the start and finish dates. Project management is a place for realistic, not wishful, thinking and should be practiced throughout the development process.

Documentation refers to written materials that are produced as part of the ISLC. Documentation should be identified and agreed on prior to beginning a project and should be an ongoing part of the development process. Well-written, thorough documentation can extend the useful life of a system.

Every person who will be affected by a new system should have the opportunity to participate in its development. ISLC participants fall into two categories: users and information systems personnel. The systems analyst works closely with both the users and the programmers to define the system. A systems analyst's job is challenging, requiring good communications, analytical, and diplomatic skills.

During the analysis phase, a system is separated into its parts to determine how the system works. The analysis phase includes the identification of a proposed solution to the problems identified in the current system. The analysis phase is usually initiated by a written request for assistance from a user department. The first step in the analysis phase is the preliminary investigation.

The purpose of the preliminary investigation is to determine if a request justifies further detailed investigation and analysis. The most important aspect of the preliminary investigation is problem definition, the identification of the true nature of the problem. Often the stated problem and the real problem are not the same. The preliminary investigation usually includes interviews and concludes with a report to management that recommends the next action.

Detailed system analysis involves both a thorough study of the current system and at least one proposed solution to the problems found. An important reason for studying the current system is to build a relationship with the user. Fact-gathering techniques used during detailed system analysis include interviews, questionnaires, reviewing current system documentation, and observing current procedures. Information gathered during this phase includes the output of the current system, the input to the current system, and the procedures used to produce the output.

Structured analysis is the use of analysis and design tools such as data flow diagrams, data dictionaries, process specifications, structured English, decision tables, and decision trees to document the specifications of an information system. Data flow diagrams use symbols such as arrows and circles to graphically represent the flow of data through a system. The data dictionary describes the elements that make up the data flow. Process specifications describe what happens to data and are often written in an organized style using structured English. A decision table or a decision tree identifies the actions that should be taken under different conditions.

CHAPTER REVIEW (continued)

At the end of the analysis phase, the user, systems analyst, and management must make a decision on how to proceed. Sometimes, the systems analyst is asked to prepare a feasibility study and a cost/benefit analysis. The feasibility study discusses whether the proposed solution is practical and capable of being accomplished. The cost/benefit analysis identifies the estimated costs of the proposed solution and the benefits that are expected. The end of the analysis phase is usually when organizations decide either to acquire a commercial software package from an outside source or to develop the software.

The acquisition phase includes four steps: (1) summarizing the application requirements; (2) identifying potential software vendors; (3) evaluating software alternatives; and (4) making the purchase.

Commercial applications software is software that has already been developed and is available for purchase. Horizontal application software can be used by many different types of organizations. Vertical application software is developed for a unique way of doing business, usually within a specific industry. A request for proposal, or RFP, is a written list of an organization's software requirements that is given to prospective vendors to help them determine if they have a possible software solution.

Software houses are businesses that specialize in developing software for sale. System houses not only sell software but also sell the equipment. Other possible sources of software suppliers are computer stores, computer manufacturers, trade publications, computer magazines, and consultants.

Evaluating software alternatives includes: (1) matching each alternative against your original requirements list; (2) talking to existing users of the software; and (3) trying the software yourself. To evaluate whether or not a software package can handle a certain work load, a benchmark test can be used to measure the time it takes to process a set number of transactions. When software is acquired, the user usually purchases a software license and not the software itself. The license gives the user the right to use the software under certain terms and conditions. Copying or making the licensed software available for use by others is usually prohibited. A common reason for developing instead of acquiring commercial software is that an organization's requirements are so unique that it is unable to find a package that will meet its needs. Application software developed by the user or at the user's request is called custom software. It is often difficult to make custom software work with purchased software. A good guideline for evaluating your need for custom or commercial software is to look for a package with an 80% or better fit with your requirements.

Modifying a commercial application package is usually referred to as customizing, or tailoring. Some vendors do not recommend or support modifications to their packages.

During the logical design step of the design phase, a design is developed without regard to a specific computer or programming language and no attempt is made to identify which procedures should be automated and which procedures should be manual. These decisions are made later during the physical design step.

Top-down design, also called structured design, breaks down the major functions of the system into smaller and smaller activities called modules that can be programmed. Bottom-up design focuses on system output and moves up to the processes needed to produce the output. Most systems analysts use a combination of top-down and bottom-up designs.

Design activities include designs for the output, input, database, processes, system controls, and testing. During output design, the systems analyst and the user document specific screen and report layouts for output to display or report information. During input design, the systems analyst and the user identify what information needs to be entered into the system to produce the desired output, and where and how the data will be entered. During database design the systems analyst uses the data dictionary information and merges it into new or existing system files. During process design, the systems analyst specifies exactly what actions will be taken on the input data to create output information. The relationship of different actions or processes are sometimes documented through the use of a system flowchart. Design logic errors can be discovered during a step-by-step review of the process design called a structured walk-through.

Four types of system controls are used to ensure that only valid data is accepted and processed. These control types are: (1) source document controls; (2) input controls; (3) processing controls; and (4) accounting controls. Test specifications should be designed by an impartial third party and should be designed to test each system control that is part of the system by using both valid and invalid data.

At the end of the design phase, a management design review takes place and a decision is made on how to proceed. Canceling or restarting a project is less costly than implementing an inadequate solution. Prototyping is an accelerated method of system design and development based on building and refining a working model. The prototype continues to be refined until it is acceptable to the user. Computer-aided software engineering (CASE) refers to the use of automated computer-based tools to design and manage a software system.

CHAPTER REVIEW (continued)

The development phase includes two parts: program development and equipment acquisition. Program development is the process of developing the required software. Equipment acquisition involves determining what, if any, additional equipment will be required for the new system.

The implementation phase is when people begin using the new system and includes the following steps: training and education, conversion, and post-conversion evaluation. Training consists of showing people exactly how they will use the new system. Education consists of learning new principles or theories that help people to understand and use the system.

Conversion refers to the process of changing from the old system to the new system. With direct conversion, the user stops using the old system one day and begins using the new system the next. Parallel conversion consists of continuing to process data on the old system while some or all of the data is also processed on the new system. Phased conversion is used with larger systems that can be broken down into individual modules that can be implemented separately at different times. Pilot conversion means that the new system will be used first by only a portion of the organization.

A post-implementation evaluation is made to determine if system performance and costs are as anticipated.

Maintenance is the process of supporting the system after it is implemented and consists of three activities: performance monitoring, change management, and error correction. Performance monitoring is the process of comparing response times, file sizes, and other system performance measures against the estimates that were prepared during the preceding ISLC phases. Change management is the process of controlling requests for changes to the new system. Error correction deals with problems that are caused by programming and design errors that are discovered after the system is implemented.

Accounting controls: System controls to provide assurance that the dollar amounts recorded in the accounting records are correct.

Acquisition: The phase of the information systems life cycle that follows the analysis phase and consists of four steps: summarizing the application requirements; identifying potential software vendors; evaluating software alternatives; and making the purchase.

Analysis: The phase in the information system life cycle where the system is separated into its parts in order to determine how the system works. This phase consists of the preliminary investigation, detailed system analysis, and making the decision to proceed.

Benchmark test: A test performed on software that measures the time it takes to process a set number of transactions.

Bottom-up design: A design approach that focuses on the data, particularly the output of the system.

CASE workbench: An integrated package of several CASE tools. These tools might include (1) analysis and design tools, (2) prototyping tools, (3) code generators, (4) information repository, and (5) management tools.

Commercial applications software: Software that has already been developed and is available for purchase.

Computer-aided software engineering (CASE): CASE is the use of automated, computer-based tools to design and manage a software system.

Conversion: During the implementation phase of the system development process, conversion refers to the process of changing from the old system to the new system.

Cost/benefit analysis: During the analysis phase of the information system life cycle, identifies the estimated costs of the proposed solution and the benefits (including potential cost savings) that are expected.

Custom software: Applications software that is developed by the user or at the user's request.

Customizing: The modification of a commercial application software package.

Database design: In information system design, the data dictionary information developed during the analysis phase is merged into new or existing system files.

Data dictionary: The data dictionary defines each data field, or element, to be used in the database.

Data flow diagram (DFD): The graphic representation of the flow of data through a system.

Decision tables: A way of documenting the system during the analysis phase; identifies the actions that should be taken under different conditions.

Decision trees: Like a decision table, illustrates the action to be taken based on given conditions, but presents it graphically.

Design: The second phase in the development path of the information system life cycle, where the logical design that was created in the analysis phase is transformed into a physical design.

Design review: The design review is performed by management at the end of the design phase to evaluate the work completed thus far to determine whether to proceed.

Detailed system analysis: Analysis that involves both a thorough study of the current system and at least one proposed solution to any problems found.

Development: Phase three in the information system life cycle, performed after the design phase. The development phase consists of program development and equipment acquisition.

KEY TERMS (continued)

Dialogue: The sequence of inputs and computer responses that a user will encounter when he or she enters data on an interactive system.

Direct conversion: With direct conversion, the user stops using the old system one day and begins using the new system the next.

Documentation: Documentation is written materials that are produced as part of the information system life cycle.

Feasibility study: During the analysis phase of the information system life cycle, the feasibility study discusses whether the proposed solution is practical and capable of being accomplished.

Horizontal application software: Software packages that can be used by many different types of organizations, such as accounting packages.

Implementation: The phase of the system development process when people actually begin using the new system. This phase includes training and education, conversion, and the post-implementation evaluation.

Information system life cycle (ISLC): An organized approach to obtaining an information system, grouped into distinct phases: (1) analysis, (2) acquisition or design, (3) customizing or development, (4) implementation, and (5) maintenance.

Input controls: System controls established to assure the complete and accurate conversion of data from the source documents or other sources to a machine-processable form.

Input design: The identification of which data needs to be entered into the system to produce the desired output, and where and how the data will be entered.

Logical design: In the analysis phase of the information system life cycle, a design that offers a solution to an existing problem without regard to a specific computer or programming language.

Maintenance: Maintenance is the final phase in the information system life cycle. It is the process of supporting the system after it is implemented, consisting of three activities: performance monitoring, change management, and error correction.

Output design: The design of specific screen and report layouts that will be used for output to display or report information from the new system.

Parallel conversion: The conversion method that continues to process data on the old system while some or all of the data is also processed on the new system.

Performance monitoring: During the maintenance phase of the information system life cycle, the ongoing process of comparing response times, file sizes, and other system performance measures against the values that were estimated when the system was designed.

Phased conversion: The conversion method used with larger systems that can be broken down into individual modules that can be implemented separately at different times.

Physical design: In the information system life cycle, the logical design that was created during the analysis phase is transformed into physical design, identifying the procedures to be automated, choosing the programming language, and specifying the equipment needed for the system.

Pilot conversion: With pilot conversion, the new system will be used first by only a portion of the organization, often at a separate location.

Post-implementation evaluation: The evaluation conducted after a system is implemented to determine if the system is performing as designed, if operating costs are as anticipated, and if any modifications are necessary to make the system operate more effectively.

Preliminary investigation: The determination if a request for development or modification of an information system justifies further detailed investigation.

Problem definition: An aspect of the preliminary investigation where the true nature of the problem is identified.

Process design: In information systems design, the systems analyst specifies exactly what actions will be taken on the input data to create the output information.

Processing control: Procedures that are established to determine the accuracy of information after it has been input to the system.

Process specifications: Specifications that describe and document what happens to a data flow when it reaches a process circle.

Program development: The process of developing the software, or programs, required for a system. Program development includes the following steps: (1) review of the program specifications, (2) program design, (3) program coding, (4) program testing, and (5) finalizing the documentation.

Project management: Involves planning, scheduling, reporting, and controlling the individual activities that make up the information system life cycle.

KEY TERMS (continued)

Project plan: A week-by-week record of individual activities that make up the information system life cycle, and includes an estimate of the time to complete the activity and the start and finish dates.

Prototyping: In information system development, building a working model of the new system.

Request for proposal (RFP): A written list of an organization's software requirements that is given to prospective software vendors.

Software houses: Businesses that specialize in developing software for sale.

Software license: A license from the software manufacturer to the buyer that describes the right to use the software under certain terms and conditions.

Source document control: A system control that includes serial numbering of input documents such as invoices and paychecks, document registers in which each input document is recorded and time-stamped as it is received, and batch totaling and balancing to predetermined totals to assure the accuracy of processing.

Structured analysis: The use of analysis and design tools such as data flow diagrams, data dictionaries, process specifications, structured English, decision tables, and decision trees to document the specifications of an information system.

Structured design, *see* **Top-down design**

Structured English: One way of writing process specifications; a style of writing and presentation that highlights the alternatives and actions that are part of the process.

Structured walk-through: A step-by-step review performed on the process design to identify any design logic errors, and to continue the communication between the systems analyst and the user; also used during program development.

System controls: During the design phase, system controls are established to (1) ensure that only valid data is accepted and processed, and (2) to prevent computer-related fraud.

System flowchart: A graphical depiction of the major processes, reports, data files, and types of input devices that provide data to the system.

System houses: Software companies that not only sell software but also sell the equipment.

Tailoring (software), *see* **Customizing**

Top-down design: A design approach that focuses on the major functions of an information system and keeps breaking those functions down into smaller and smaller activities, sometimes called modules, that can eventually be programmed; also called structured design.

Vertical application software: Software developed for a unique way of doing business, usually within a specific industry.

CHAPTER ELEVEN—PROJECT ONE

ClassNotes

WHAT IS THE INFORMATION SYSTEM LIFE CYCLE?

1. An information system system life cycle is an organized approach to obtaining an _____.

2. Name the five phases of the information system life cycle.

   _____   _____

   _____   _____

   _____

3. Identify the four tasks involved in project management.

   _____   _____

   _____   _____

4. _____ is written materials that are produced as part of the information system development life cycle.

ANALYSIS PHASE

1. Define the term analysis as it applies to the information system development life cycle.

   _____

2. What is the most important aspect of the preliminary investigation?

   _____

3. A detailed _____ involves a thorough study of the current system but does not produce solutions to any problems that are identified.

4. Name four key fact-gathering techniques used during detailed system analysis.

   _____   _____

   _____   _____

5. Describe the three types of information gathered during detailed system analysis.

   _____   _____   _____

CLASSNOTES (continued)

6. Structured analysis is the use of analysis and _____ such as data flow diagrams, data dictionaries, structured English, and decision tables and trees.

7. A _____ discusses whether a proposed solution is practical and capable of being accomplished.

8. A _____ identifies the estimated costs of a proposed solution and the benefits, including potential cost savings, that are expected.

ACQUISITION PHASE

1. The acquistion phase involves _____ the application requirements, _____ potential software vendors, and _____ the purchase.

2. _____ software is software that has been previously written and is available for purchase.

3. Nonindustry-specific software has _____ applications, and industry-specific software has _____ applications.

4. A_____ is a list of software requirements given to prospective vendors for identifying a possible software solution.

5. _____ are businesses that specialize in developing software for sale.

6. _____ provide software and equipment for an entire system.

7. A(n) _____ measures the time it takes to process a set number of transactions.

8. A(n) _____ is the right to use software under certain terms and conditions.

COMMERCIAL APPLICATIONS VERSUS CUSTOM SOFTWARE

1. An _____ is applicable to many different types of organizations; _____ is unique to a specific organization or business.

CUSTOMIZING PHASE

1. The first step in the customizing phase is _____ potential modifications.

2. The last step in the customizing phase is choosing which _____ will be made.

DESIGN PHASE

1. _____ design is concerned with the programming language that will be used in the development of a system.

2. A(n) _____ design identifies the procedures to be automated and the programming language, and specifies the equipment needed for the system.

3. _____ focuses on the major functions of the system and breaking them down into smaller activities.

4. _____ focuses on the data or output of the system and *moves up* to the processes that are needed to produce the desired output.

CLASSNOTES (continued)

5. The illustration below involves the transformation of data from a screen format to a hard-copy format.

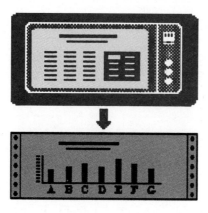

    That process is called _____.

6. Input design, as illustrated below, is concerned with a sequence of inputs and computer responses known as

    a(n) _____.

7. During _____, a systems analyst uses data dictionary information developed during the analysis phase and merges it into new or existing system files.

8. During process design, the systems analyst specifies exactly what actions will be taken on the _____ to create _____ information.

9. The symbols shown below are used in diagramming a _____.

CLASSNOTES (continued)

10. System _____ ensure that only valid data is accepted and processed.

11. Name the four basic types of system controls that must be considered by a systems analyst.

    _____   _____

    _____   _____

12. T F   Test specifications should be developed by an impartial third party, with no assistance from users and systems analysts.

test specifications

13. At the end of the design phase, management evaluates the work completed thus far by conducting a

    _____.

14. Building a working model of a new system is known as _____.

15. Computer-aided software engineering (CASE) uses automated _____ tools to design and manage a software system.

DEVELOPMENT PHASE

1. The two steps of system development are _____ and _____.

IMPLEMENTATION PHASE

1. Name three steps in the implementation process.

    _____   _____   _____

MAINTENANCE PHASE

1. Define system maintenance.

    _____

2. Identify the three key elements of system maintenance.

    _____   _____   _____

CHAPTER ELEVEN—PROJECT TWO

Self-Test
WORKBOOK AND PC VERSIONS

Match the following:

_____ 1. Conversion

_____ 2. Benchmark Test

_____ 3. Preliminary Investigation

_____ 4. Structured Walk-through

_____ 5. CASE

_____ 6. Design Review

_____ 7. Prototyping

_____ 8. Software License

1. Building a working model of the new system
2. Determines if a request warrants further investigation
3. Changing from old to new system
4. Evaluates the work completed thus far
5. Step-by-step review
6. Use of automated computer-based tools to design and manage a software system
7. Measures the time it takes to process a set number of transactions
8. Request for proposal
9. Right to use the software under certain terms and conditions

You can complete the remainder of Project 2 in two ways—either by marking or filling in your answers in this workbook, or by using the PC version of Project 2. The PC version (available from your instructor) automatically corrects your answers for you. It also calculates the percent of your answers that are correct.

Answer the following questions.

1. T F   The information system life cycle is an organized approach to developing an information system.

2. _____ involves planning, scheduling, reporting, and controlling the individual activities that make up the information system development life cycle.
   a. Documentation   c. Project management
   b. Analysis   d. Maintenance

3. _____ refers to written materials that are produced throughout the information system development life cycle.
   a. Documentation   c. Gantt chart
   b. Analysis   d. Flowcharting

4. The _____ phase consists of the separation of a system into its parts to determine how the system works.
   a. analysis   c. development   e. maintenance
   b. design   d. implementation

SELF-TEST (continued)

5. _____ involves both a thorough study of the current system and at least one proposed solution to any problems found.

   a. Preliminary investigation   b. Detailed system analysis   c. Logical design

6. T F A feasibility study and a cost/benefit analysis are performed in the development phase to show whether the proposed system is practical and to show the expected cost and benefits.

7. Software that has already been written and is available for purchase is called _____.

   a. vendor software   c. commercial application software

   b. custom software   d. public domain software

8. An accounting software package is an example of _____ application software.

   a. vertical   c. business

   b. horizontal   d. general

9. _____ application software is developed for a unique way of doing business, usually within a specific industry.

   a. Vertical   b. Horizontal   c. General

10. T F Identifying potential software vendors for a personal computer can usually be done at a local computer store.

11. A benchmark test involves measuring the time it takes to process a set number of transactions and is used to measure the relative _____ of different software packages on the same equipment.

    a. performance   c. ease-of-use

    b. compatibility   d. capability

12. A _____ is the right to use software under certain terms and conditions.

    a. contract   c. software license

    b. certificate   d. statement of authorization

13. If you needed a program to control the fuel intake rate for the space shuttle, you would most likely decide on which one of the following types of software solutions?

    a. horizontal application   b. vertical application   c. custom software

14. If you were using a program to manage the inventory of a distribution center for a major shoe manufacturer, you would more than likely be using _____.

    a. horizontal application   b. vertical application   c. custom software

15. Modifying a commercial application package is usually referred to as _____.

    a. customizing   c. tailoring

    b. editing   d. both a and c

16. T F An essential part of customizing is specifying the amount of work required to make the modifications and the correspnding costs.

17. A physical design is developed in the _____ phase.

    a. analysis   c. development   e. maintenance

    b. design   d. implementation

18. A physical design identifies _____.

    a. the procedures to be automated

    b. the programming language(s) to be used

    c. the equipment needed for the system

    d. all of the above

SELF-TEST (continued)

19. T F   There are two major structured design methods: top-down and bottom-up.

20. A way of documenting the process design is with a(n) _____.
    a. input and output design   c. system flowchart
    b. database design   d. process design

21. A working model of the new system is called a _____.

22. The _____ phase consists of the program development and equipment acquisition.
    a. analysis   c. development   e. maintenance
    b. design   d. implementation

23. T F   Writing program specifications, designing the program, coding the program, testing the program, and finalizing the program documentation are included in the implementation phase.

24. The _____ phase is when people actually begin using the system.
    a. analysis   c. development   e. maintenance
    b. design   d. implementation

25. Implementation includes _____, conversion, and post-implementation evaluation.
    a. performance monitoring   c. training and education
    b. equipment acquisition   d. error correcting

26. T F   Conversion to the new system is a process of change that can be managed using appropriate methods.

27. The _____ is the process of supporting the information system after it is implemented.
    a. analysis phase   c. development phase   e. maintenance phase
    b. design phase   d. implementation phase

28. T F   Maintenance consists of performance monitoring, change management, and error correction.

CHAPTER ELEVEN—PROJECT THREE

Identifying the Phases of the Information System Life Cycle

Instructions: Identify the phases of the information system life cycle in the spaces provided in the diagram below.

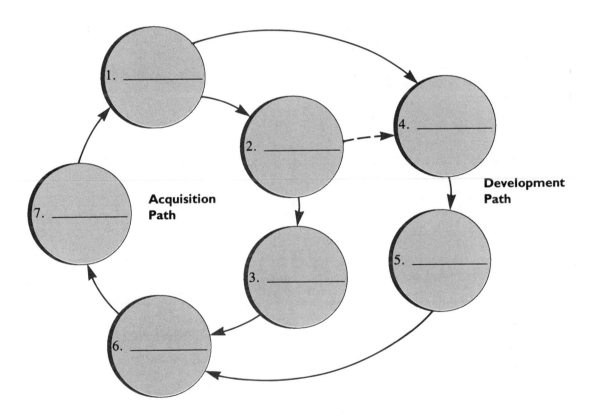

CHAPTER ELEVEN—PROJECT FOUR

Completing a Decision Tree

Instructions: A structured English process specification and a partially completed decision tree for an organization's order processing policy are shown below. Use the information given in the process specification to complete the decision tree.

Process specification:

If the order amount exceeds $5,000,
    If customer has any unpaid invoices over 60 days old,
        Reject order,
        Write message on order reject report.
    Otherwise (account is in good standing),
        Issue order confirmation.
Otherwise (order is $5,000 or less),
    If customer has any unpaid invoices over 60 days old,
        Confirm order,
        Write message on credit follow-up report,
    Otherwise (account is in good standing),
        Confirm order.

Decision tree:

```
                        ┌ Invoices > 60 days          — Reject Order
            ┌ Order > $5,000 ┤
            │           └ No Past Due Invoices        — 3. _____
Order Policy┤
            │           ┌ 1. _____       — 2. _____
            └ Order ≤ $5,000 ┤                  — Credit Follow-Up
                        └ 4. _____       — 5. _____
```

CHAPTER ELEVEN—PROJECT FIVE

Developing Communication Skills

Instructions: Prepare an oral or written report on one or more of the following subjects.

1. Interview someone who has participated in a system development project within the last year. Ask him or her to comment on the things that could have been done differently.
2. Contact a local software developer or distributor and ask him or her to discuss a request for proposal to which he or she responded in the past.
3. Obtain information about the kinds of software available for a hobby in which you are interested. What resources did you use to locate information about the software?
4. Research sales management software packages available for use on personal computers. Use at least three sources for your report.
5. Obtain a copy of a software license for a commercial application software package. Summarize the key features of the license and what the user can and cannot do with the software package.
6. Interview someone who chose to develop custom software instead of acquiring a commercial package. Discuss the factors that led to the decision.
7. Interview a user of an existing business application such as accounts payable or accounts receivable. Prepare a report on the number and type of system controls that are used.
8. Interview someone who uses computer-aided software engineering (CASE) tools to develop software. Ask him or her to comment on the effect of CASE on development productivity.
9. Interview someone who has recently (within the last year) converted from one software application to another. Prepare a report on how the conversion was handled.

CHAPTER TWELVE

Program Development

◆ OBJECTIVES

- ◆ Define the term computer program
- ◆ Describe the five steps in program development: review of program specifications, program design, program coding, program testing, and finalizing program documentation
- ◆ Explain the concepts of structured program design including modules, control structures, and single entry/single exit
- ◆ Explain and illustrate the sequence, selection, and iteration control structures used in structured programming
- ◆ Define the term programming language and discuss the various categories of programming languages
- ◆ Briefly discuss the programming languages that are commonly used today, including BASIC, COBOL, C, FORTRAN, Pascal, and Ada
- ◆ Explain and discuss application generators
- ◆ Explain and discuss object-oriented programming
- ◆ Explain the factors that should be considered when choosing a programming language

◆ CHAPTER OUTLINE

Chapter Review

 Chapter 12 focuses on the steps taken to write a program and the available tools that make the program development process more efficient. The chapter also discusses the different languages used to write programs.

A computer program is a detailed set of instructions that directs a computer to perform the tasks necessary to process data into information. A program can be coded (written) in a variety or programming languages.

Program development is the process of producing one or more programs to perform specific tasks on a computer. The process of program development has evolved into a series of five steps: (1) review of program specifications; (2) program design; (3) coding; (4) testing; and (5) finalizing documentation. Program specifications can consist of data flow diagrams, system flowcharts, process specifications, a data dictionary, screen formats, report layouts, and actual documents. The programmer uses the specifications to determine what work needs to be done by the program. During program design, a logical solution to the programming task is developed and documented. The logical solution, or logic, for a program is a step-by-step solution to a programming problem. The logic is often developed using a method called structured program design.

Structured program design is a methodology that emphasizes three main program design concepts: modules, control structures, and single entry/single exit. Use of these concepts helps to create programs that are easy to write, read, understand, check for errors, and modify. Each module, sometimes referred to as a subroutine, performs a given task within the program. Modules are combined to form a complete program. Structure charts, also called hierarchy charts, are often used to decompose (break down) and show the relationship of the modules within a program.

All logic problems can be solved by using one or more of three basic control structures: sequence, selection, and iteration. In the sequence structure, one process occurs immediately after another. In the selection structure, also called the if-then-else structure, a test of a condition is used to direct the program to one process or another based on the results of the test. The case structure is a variation of the selection structure and is used when there are more than two alternatives. The iteration, or looping, structure means that one or more processes continue to occur as long as a given condition remains true. Two forms of the iteration structure are the do-while structure and the do-until structure.

The single entry/single exit rule means that there is only one entry point and one exit point for each of the three control structures. An entry point is where a control structure is entered and an exit point is where the control structure is exited.

A program flowchart uses a combination of text and standardized symbols to represent the logical steps of a program. For many years, program flowcharts were used as the primary means of program design. Alternatives to flowcharts are pseudocode and Warnier-Orr diagrams. In pseudocode, the logical steps in the solution of a problem are written as English statements and indentations are used to represent the control structures. Using the Warnier-Orr technique, the programmer produces diagrams that show the processing modules necessary to produce the desired output.

During a structured walk-through, the programmer meets with other programmers and the systems analyst to review the program design and look for logic errors.

CHAPTER REVIEW (continued)

Coding the program refers to the process of writing the program instructions that will process the data and produce the output specified in the program design. If the program design is thorough, logical, and well structured, the coding process is greatly simplified and can sometimes be a one-for-one translation of a design step into a program step.

Before a program is put into use it should be thoroughly tested. Desk checking is the process of reading the program and mentally reviewing its logic. Syntax errors are violations of grammar rules of the language in which the program was written. During logic testing, the sequence of program instructions is tested to make sure it provides the correct result. Logic testing is performed with test data, data that simulates the type of input that the program will process when it is implemented. Debugging refers to the process of locating and correcting program errors, or bugs, found during testing.

Documentation should be an ongoing part of developing a program and should only be finalized after the program is successfully tested and ready for implementation. Documentation developed during the programming process should include a narrative description of the program, program design documents such as flowcharts or pseudocode, program listings, and test results. Proper documentation can substantially reduce program maintenance time.

Program maintenance includes all changes to a program once it is implemented and processing real transactions. Maintenance programming should be subject to the same policies and procedures that are required for new programs. Maintaining high standards for program maintenance can lower overall programming costs and lengthen the useful life of programs.

A programming language is a set of written words and symbols that allow the programmer or user to communicate with the computer. As with spoken languages, programming languages have rules, called syntax, that govern their use. Programming languages can be classified into one of four categories: machine language, assembly language, high-level languages, and fourth-generation languages.

A machine language is the fundamental language of the computer's processor. Programs written in all other categories of languages are eventually converted into machine language before they are executed. Because they are written for specific processors, machine languages are different for computers that have different processors. Machine languages are also called low-level languages.

An assembly language is similar to a machine language, but uses abbreviations called mnemonics or symbolic operation code to represent the machine operation code. Assembly languages also allow symbolic addressing and macroinstructions. Assembly language programs are converted into machine language instructions by a special program called an assembler.

High-level languages closely resemble spoken languages in that they contain nouns, verbs, and mathematical, relational, and logical operators that can be grouped together to form sentences called program statements. High-level languages are usually machine independent, which means they can run on different types of computers. High-level languages are translated into machine language by either a compiler or an interpreter. A compiler converts an entire source program into a machine language object code, also called an object program. An interpreter translates one program statement at a time and then executes the resulting machine language before translating the next program statement.

Fourth-generation languages (4GLs), sometimes called very high-level languages, are easier to use and are described as nonprocedural, meaning that the programmer does not specify the actual procedures to be used to accomplish a task. Instead of telling the computer how to do the task, the programmer tells the computer what is to be done, usually by describing the desired output.

A natural language, sometimes called a fifth-generation language, is a type of query language that allows the user to enter a question as if he or she were speaking to another person.

Programming languages used today include BASIC, COBOL, C, FORTRAN, Pascal, and Ada. BASIC, which stands for Beginner's All-purpose Symbolic Instruction Code, is one of the most popular programming languages in use on microcomputers and minicomputers. COBOL (COmmon Business Oriented Language) is one of the most widely used programming languages for business applications. C is a general-purpose programming language often used with the UNIX operating system. FORTRAN (FORmula TRANslator) was designed to be used by scientists, engineers, and mathematicians and is noted for its capability to easily express and efficiently calculate mathematical equations. Pascal was developed for teaching programming so that programmers would be encouraged to develop programs that follow structured program design. Ada was developed with the support of the U.S. Department of Defense and is required on all U.S. military projects.

CHAPTER REVIEW (continued)

Application generators, also called program generators, are programs that produce source-language programs based on input, output, and processing specifications entered by the user. By using standard processing modules, they greatly reduce the amount of time required to develop a program. A menu generator lets the user specify a menu (list) of processing options that can be selected. A screen generator, sometimes called a screen painter, allows the user to design an input or output screen by entering the names and descriptions of the input and output data directly on the screen.

Object-oriented programming (OOP) is a new approach to developing software that allows programmers to create objects, a combination of data and program instructions. Objects can be used repeatedly by programmers whenever they need them. Specific instructions, called methods, define how the object acts when it is used by a program. Classes of objects contain the methods that are unique to that class. Each class can have one or more subclasses which can inherit the methods of the higher classes. A specific instance of an object contains all methods from its higher level classes plus any methods that are unique to the object. When a program wants an OOP object to do something, it sends the object a message. The message does not have to tell the object what to do because that is defined by the methods that the object contains or has inherited.

Factors to consider when choosing a programming language include: (1) programming standards of the organization; (2) the need to interface with other programs; (3) the suitability of a language to the application to be programmed; (4) the expertise of the programmers; (5) the availability of the language; (6) the need for the application to be portable; and (7) the anticipated maintenance requirements.

Key Terms

Ada: A programming language supported by the U.S. Department of Defense. Its use is required on all U.S. government military projects. Ada was designed to facilitate the writing and maintenance of large programs that would be used over a long period of time.

Application generators: Programs that produce source-language programs, such as BASIC or COBOL, based on input, output, and processing specifications entered by the user; also called program generators.

Assembler: A special program that converts assembly language programs into machine language instructions.

Assembly language: A low-level language that is similar to machine language, but uses abbreviations called mnemonics or symbolic operation code to represent the machine operation code.

BASIC (Beginner's All-purpose Symbolic Instruction Code): A simple, interactive programming language. BASIC is one of the most commonly used programming languages on microcomputers and minicomputers.

Bugs, *see* **Debugging**

C: A programming language originally designed for writing systems software, but it is now considered a general-purpose programming language. C requires professional programming skills to be used effectively.

Case structure: A variation of the selection structure, used when a condition is being tested that can lead to more than two alternatives.

Class: In object-oriented programming, programmers define classes of objects. Each class contains the methods that are unique to that class.

COBOL (COmmon Business Oriented Language): One of the most widely used programming languages for business applications, which uses an English-like format.

Coding: The process of writing the program instructions that will process the data and produce the output specified in the program design.

Compiler: A program that translates high-level source programs into machine language object code.

Computer program: The detailed set of instructions that tells the computer exactly what to do, so it can perform the operations in the information processing cycle; also called program instructions, or software.

Control structures: In structured program design, used to form the logic of a program. The three control structures are: the sequence structure, selection structure, and iteration structure.

Debugging: The process of locating and correcting program errors, or bugs, found during testing.

Desk checking: The process of reading the program and mentally reviewing its logic, before the program is used to process real data.

Do-until structure: The control structure where a condition is tested at the end of a loop. Processing continues until the condition is met.

Do-while structure: The control structure where a condition is tested at the beginning of a loop. If the condition is true, the process is performed. The program then loops back and tests the condition again. This looping continues until the condition being tested is false.

Entry point: The point where the control structure is entered.

Exit point: The point where the control structure is exited.

KEY TERMS (continued)

FORTRAN (FORmula TRANslator): A programming language designed to be used by scientists, engineers, and mathematicians. FORTRAN is noted for its capability to easily express and efficiently calculate mathematical equations.

Fourth-generation languages (4GLs): Programming languages that are easy to use, both for programmers and nonprogrammers, because the user tells the computer *what* is to be done, not *how* to do it; also called very high-level languages.

Hierarchy charts, *see* **Structure charts**

High-level languages: Computer languages that are easier to learn and use than low-level languages and contain nouns, verbs, and mathematical, relational, and logical operators that can be grouped together in what appear to be sentences. These sentences are called program statements.

If-then-else structure, *see* **Selection structure**

Inheritance: In object-oriented programming, the capability to pass methods to lower levels of classes or objects.

Instance: In object-oriented programming, a specific instance of an object contains all methods from its higher level classes plus any methods that are unique to the object.

Interpreter: An interpreter translates a program in a high-level language one program statement at a time into machine language and then executes the resulting machine language before translating the next program statement.

Iteration structure: The control structure where one or more processes continue to occur as long as a given condition remains true; also called a looping structure. Two forms of this structure are the do-while structure and the do-until structure.

Logic: Logic is the step-by-step solution to a programming problem.

Logic testing: The sequence of program instructions is tested for incorrect results using test data.

Looping structure, *see* **Iteration structure**

Low-level language, *see* **Machine language**

Machine language: The fundamental language of the computer's processor; also called low-level language. All programs are converted into machine language before they can be executed.

Macroinstructions: Instructions in assembly language programs that generate more than one machine language instruction.

Menu generator: Software that lets the user specify a menu (list) of processing options that can be selected. The resulting menu is automatically formatted.

Message: In object-oriented programming, the instruction to do something that is sent to an object.

Methods: In object-oriented programming, specific instructions that define how the object acts when it is used by a program.

Mnemonic: A simple, easily remembered abbreviation used in assembly language programming to represent a machine operation code; also called symbolic operation code.

Module: A module performs a given task within a program and can be developed individually and then combined to form a complete program; sometimes called a subroutine.

Natural language: A type of query language that allows the user to enter a question as if he or she were speaking to another person.

Nonprocedural: Nonprocedural is said of fourth-generation languages because the programmer does not specify the actual procedures that the program must use to solve a problem.

Object: An object is a combination of data and program instructions used in object-oriented programming.

Object code, *see* **Object program**

Object-oriented operating systems: Operating systems specifically designed to run object-oriented programming applications.

Object-oriented programming (OOP): A new approach to developing software that allows programmers to create objects, which can be used repeatedly by programmers whenever they need them.

Object-oriented software: Applications that are developed using object-oriented programming techniques.

Object program: The machine instructions produced by a compiler from a program originally written in a high-level language; also called object code.

Pascal: A programming language developed for teaching programming. Pascal contains programming statements that encourage the use of structured program design.

Program design: A logical solution, or logic, for a program is developed and documented.

Program development: The process of developing the software, or programs, required for a system. Program development includes the following steps: (1) review of the program specifications, (2) program design, (3) program coding, (4) program testing, and (5) finalizing the documentation.

KEY TERMS (continued)

Program flowchart: A program design tool in which the logical steps of a program are represented by a combination of symbols and text.

Program generators, *see* **Application generators**

Program maintenance: Maintenance includes all changes to a program once it is implemented and processing real transactions.

Programming language: A set of written words and symbols that allow a programmer or user to communicate with the computer.

Program specifications: Specifications that can include many documents such as data flow diagrams, system flowcharts, process specifications, a data dictionary, screen formats, and report layouts.

Program statements: Program statements are the *sentences* of a high-level programming language.

Pseudocode: The logical steps in the solution of a problem are written as English statements and indentations are used to represent the control structures.

Screen generator: Software that allows the user to design an input or output screen by entering the names and descriptions of the input and output data directly on the screen.

Screen painter, *see* **Screen generator**

Selection structure: The control structure used for conditional program logic; also called if-then-else structure.

Sequence structure: The control structure where one process occurs immediately after another.

Single entry/single exit: From each of the control structures, there is only one entry point and one exit point.

Source program: A program written in high-level language and later converted by a compiler or interpreter to machine language.

Structure charts: Charts used to decompose and represent the modules of a program; also called hierarchy charts.

Structured program design: A methodology that emphasizes three main program design concepts: modules, control structures, and single entry/single exit.

Subroutine, *see* **Module**

Symbolic addressing: Assembly language allows a specific computer memory location to be referenced by a name or symbol.

Symbolic operation code, *see* **Mnemonic**

Syntax errors: Violations of the grammar rules of the language in which the program is written.

Test data: Data that simulates the type of input that the program will process when it is implemented; used during logic testing.

Very high-level languages, *see* **Fourth-generation languages**

Warnier-Orr technique: The programmer analyzes output to be produced from an application and develops processing modules that are needed to produce the output (named after Jean Dominique Warnier and Kenneth Orr).

CHAPTER TWELVE–PROJECT ONE

ClassNotes

WHAT IS A COMPUTER PROGRAM?

1. Name the four items that make up a computer program, choosing your answers from the following list.

instructions   storage   data   output   language   process   input   information

_____   _____

_____   _____

WHAT IS PROGRAM DEVELOPMENT?

1. List in order the five steps of program development.

Step 1: _____   Step 4: _____

Step 2: _____   Step 5: _____

Step 3: _____

STEP 1—REVIEWING THE PROGRAM SPECIFICATIONS

1. Program specifications usually consist of one or more documents. Name the seven documents.

_____   _____

_____   _____

_____   _____

_____

Complete the statements about program specifications, choosing your answers from the following list.

writers   programmer   analyst   users   customer   designer

2. The _____ and _____, through the system design, have specified *what* is to be done.

3. The _____ determines *how* it is to be done.

CLASSNOTES (continued)

STEP 2—DESIGNING THE PROGRAM

1. During program design, a _____ is developed and documented.

2. _____ is a methodology that emphasizes three main program design concepts.

Structured Program Design

3. Identify the three key concepts of structured program design, choosing your answers from the following list.

   modules   single entry/single exit   structured programming   control structures
   multiple subroutines

   _____   _____   _____

4. Modules are often referred to as _____.

5. _____ are often used to decompose and represent the modules of a program.

6. At the conclusion of program decomposition, the entire structure of a program is illustrated by the

   _____ and the relationship of the _____ within the program.

7. All logic problems can be solved by three basic control structures:

   _____   _____   _____

8. One process occurs immediately after another in the _____ structure.

9. _____ gives programmers a way to represent conditional program logic.

10. _____ means that one or more processes continue to occur so long as a given condition remains true.

11. In the _____ structure, a condition is tested to determine when the looping will terminate.

12. With the _____ control structure, the conditional test is at the end instead of the beginning of the loop.

13. _____ means that there is only one entry point and one exit point for each of the three control structures.

Program Design Tools

14. Name three major design tools, choosing your answers from the following list.

   flowcharts   Warnier-Orr   data flow diagrams   Jackson charts   pseudocode   data dictionaries

   _____   _____   _____

CLASSNOTES (continued)

15.–22. Label the following flowchart symbols.

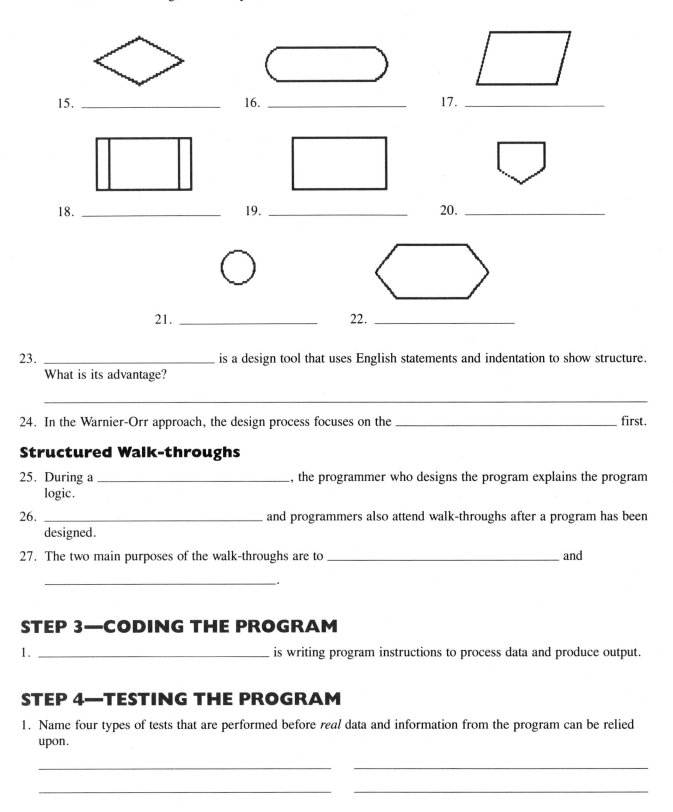

15. _____   16. _____   17. _____

18. _____   19. _____   20. _____

21. _____   22. _____

23. _____ is a design tool that uses English statements and indentation to show structure. What is its advantage?

_____

24. In the Warnier-Orr approach, the design process focuses on the _____ first.

Structured Walk-throughs

25. During a _____, the programmer who designs the program explains the program logic.

26. _____ and programmers also attend walk-throughs after a program has been designed.

27. The two main purposes of the walk-throughs are to _____ and

_____.

STEP 3—CODING THE PROGRAM

1. _____ is writing program instructions to process data and produce output.

STEP 4—TESTING THE PROGRAM

1. Name four types of tests that are performed before *real* data and information from the program can be relied upon.

_____   _____

_____   _____

CLASSNOTES (continued)

2.–5. Match the following definitions to the listed terms.

2. desk checking _____

3. syntax error checking _____

4. logic testing _____

5. debugging _____

a. identifying violations of the program language's grammar rules

b. locating and correcting program errors during testing

c. breaking the code into small bits

d. using test data (expected and unexpected data) to test the program

e. similar to proofreading a letter

STEP 5—FINALIZING PROGRAM DOCUMENTATION

1. Name items that should be included in program documentation, choosing your answers from the following list.

narrative description   pseudocode   program flowcharts   test results   comments within program

debugging steps   program listings   opinions on design   notes on structured walk-through

_____   _____

_____   _____

_____   _____

PROGRAM MAINTENANCE

1. Program maintenance is used to correct _____ and make required changes in users' needs.

WHAT IS A PROGRAMMING LANGUAGE?

1. A programming language is a set of words, symbols, and instructions used to _____ with the computer.

CATEGORIES OF PROGRAMMING LANGUAGES

1. What are the four categories of programming languages?

_____   _____

_____   _____

2. _____ is the fundamental language of the processor.

3. Programs written in other categories of languages are eventually _____ to machine language before they are executed.

4. Assembly language is similar to machine language, but uses abbreviations called _____ or symbolic operation codes.

5. In assembly language, the programmer uses _____ to refer to a memory location rather than its specific numeric locations.

6. _____ generate more than one machine language instruction.

CLASSNOTES (continued)

7. Circle the statements that apply to high-level languages.

   a. They contain program statements.

   b. They are usually machine dependent.

   c. They are usually machine independent.

   d. They are converted to machine language by a compiler or an interpreter.

   e. They contain program generators.

8.–9. Fill in the missing labels.

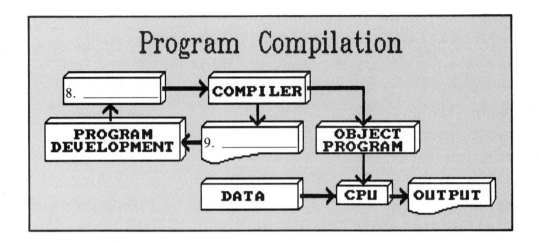

10.–12. Fill in the missing labels.

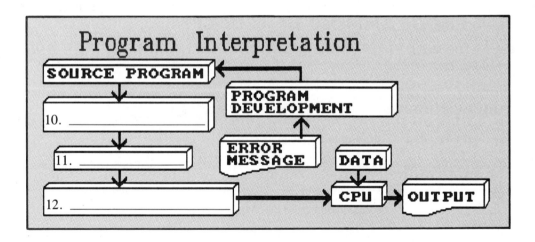

13. Fourth-generation languages (4GLs) are sometimes called _____ and are often

    referred to as _____.

14. These languages tell the computer _____ to do versus _____
    to do it.

15. An example of a 4GL is a _____.

16. A fifth-generation language is a _____ language, or query language, simi-
    lar to the way we speak.

CLASSNOTES (continued)

PROGRAMMING LANGUAGES USED TODAY

1. BASIC stands for _____.

2. BASIC is used primarily on _____ and _____.

3. COBOL stands for _____.

4. COBOL has an Englishlike format and is widely used for _____ applications.

5. C is a language used for writing _____ software on microcomputers and minicomputers that requires professional programming skills.

6. FORTRAN stands for _____.

7. Because FORTRAN handles _____ easily, it is often used by scientists, engineers, and mathematicians.

8. Pascal was named for _____.

9. Pascal encourages the use of _____ program design.

10. Ada was named for the mathematician _____.

11. Ada facilitates very large _____ and has portability across computers.

12. RPG stands for _____.

13. RPG was designed to allow _____ to be generated quickly and easily.

14. Circle the statement that correctly identifies what enables RPG to be used with a minimum of training.
    a. It uses special forms filled out describing the report.
    b. It uses special formulas to format the reports.

15. _____ is a structured programming language used for scientific and mathematical applications.

16. _____ is a powerful language for manipulating data stored in a table (matrix) format.

17. _____ is similar to C.

18. _____ and _____ are used for artificial intelligence.

19. _____ is used as an educational tool to teach problem-solving skills.

20. _____ is similar to Pascal.

21. _____ is used by educators to write computer-aided instruction programs.

22. _____ combines many of the features of FORTRAN and COBOL.

APPLICATION GENERATORS

1. Another name for application generators is _____.

2. Application generators produce _____.

3. A(n) _____ lets the user specify a menu (list) of processing options that can be selected.

4. A(n) _____ allows the user to design an input or output screen by entering the names and descriptions of the input and output data directly on the screen.

OBJECT-ORIENTED PROGRAMMING

1. Object-oriented programming (OOP) is a new approach to developing software that allows programmers to create _____, a combination of data and program instructions.

2. Specific instructions, called _____, define how the object acts when it is used by a program.

3. The OOP capability to pass methods to lower levels is called _____.

4. A specific _____ of an object contains all methods from its higher level classes plus any methods that are unique to the object.

HOW TO CHOOSE A PROGRAMMING LANGUAGE

1. Although each programming language has its own unique characteristics, selecting a language for a programming task can be a difficult decision. Circle the factors to be considered in making a choice.

   a. programming standards
   b. portability
   c. language suitability
   d. maintenance requirements
   e. programmer expertise
   f. user friendliness
   g. language availability
   h. interfacing needs

CHAPTER TWELVE—PROJECT TWO

Self-Test
WORKBOOK AND PC VERSIONS

Match the following:

_____ 1. Logic
_____ 2. Control Structures
_____ 3. Coding
_____ 4. Debugging
_____ 5. Machine Language
_____ 6. C
_____ 7. Forms of Iteration
_____ 8. Module

1. Locating and correcting program errors
2. Writing the program instructions
3. Do-while and do-until structures
4. Sequence, selection, and iteration
5. Subroutine
6. Programming language that requires professional programming skills
7. Fundamental language of computers
8. Step-by-step solution
9. Programming language developed by the U.S. Department of Defense

You can complete the remainder of Project 2 in two ways—either by marking or filling in your answers in this workbook, or by using the PC version of Project 2. The PC version (available from your instructor) automatically corrects your answers for you. It also calculates the percent of your answers that are correct.

Answer the following questions.

1. A computer program is a set of instructions that _____.
   a. processes data into information
   b. are usually written by a programmer
   c. are usually written in one of many languages
   d. all of the above

2. The first step in program development is _____.
   a. review of program specifications   c. program design
   b. program coding   d. initiating program documentation

3. After reviewing program specifications, the next step is _____.
   a. review of program specifications   c. program design
   b. program coding   d. initiating program documentation

4. In structured program design, programs are separated into _____.
   a. subsets   b. modules   c. nodes   d. pages

5. The control structure used to repeat a process is called _____.
   a. sequence   b. iteration   c. selection   d. what-if

SELF-TEST (continued)

6. Looping is accomplished in two forms, DO WHILE and DO _____.
   a. GO TO   c. UNTIL
   b. LOOP   d. AS

7. In _____, the logical steps in the solution of a problem are written as Englishlike statements and indentations are used to represent the control structures.
   a. program flowchart   c. Warnier-Orr
   b. pseudocode

8. In structured program design, control structures should have _____.
   a. a single condition   c. fewer than two GOTOs
   b. no more than 10 statements d. a single entry/exit

9. Once a program is coded, the next step is _____.

10. Program logic testing is accomplished by _____.
    a. using expected data   c. using unexpected data
    b. desk and syntax checking   d. all of the above

11. In program development, documenting a program is _____.
    a. the final step   c. the first step
    b. an ongoing process   d. none of the above

12. T F   Program maintenance is required for user data entry.

13. T F   A programming language is a set of symbols, instructions and words used to communicate with the computer.

14. High-level languages are designed with the _____ in mind.

15. T F   Machine language is the language to which all other languages are converted.

16. T F   Assembly language is a high-level language because it is closely related to the design of the computer.

17. The function of a compiler is to _____ high-level languages.
    a. execute   c. specify programming
    b. translate   d. interpret

18. The definition of a fourth-generation language is that it is nonprocedural, user-friendly, and deals with

    _____.
    a. what versus how   b. how versus what

19. The first programming language to encourage structured program design was _____.
    a. BASIC   c. FORTRAN
    b. COBOL   d. Pascal

20. Two common business-oriented languages are _____.
    a. C and FORTRAN   c. BASIC and Pascal
    b. COBOL and RPG   d. Ada and BASIC

21. Programs designed to shorten program development time include program, menu, and screen

    _____.
    a. producers   c. generators
    b. applications   d. modules

22. T F   Inheritance refers to the capability of passing methods to lower levels of classes or objects.

23. T F   A factor to consider when choosing a language is future maintenance.

CHAPTER TWELVE—PROJECT THREE

Describing Program Development Steps

Instructions: Program development requires the completion of five steps. In the space provided, identify and briefly describe each of the steps in the sequence they are normally performed.

Program Development Steps

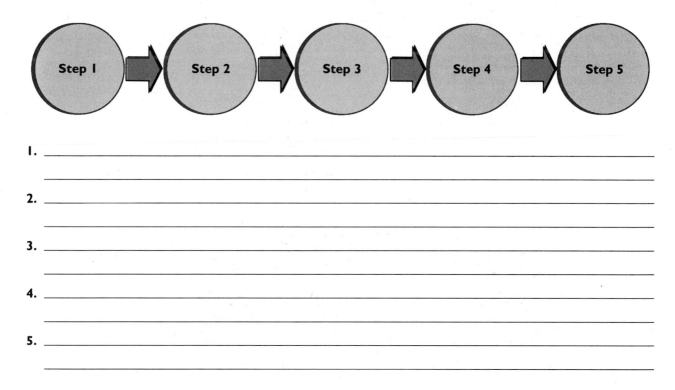

1. _____
   _____

2. _____
   _____

3. _____
   _____

4. _____
   _____

5. _____
   _____

CHAPTER TWELVE—PROJECT FOUR

Identifying Logic Control Structures

Instructions: All programming logic problems can be solved by using a combination of control structures. In the space provided, label each of the control structures shown below.

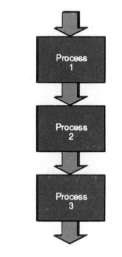

1. _____

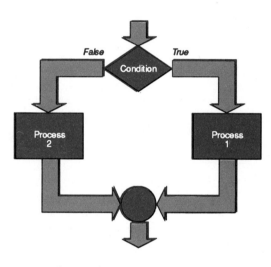

2. _____

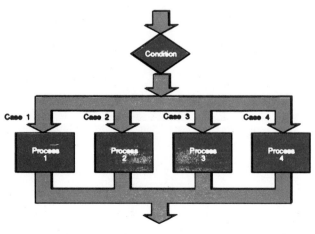

3. _____

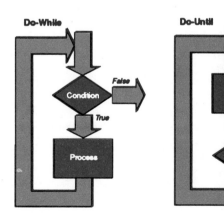

4. _____

CHAPTER TWELVE–PROJECT FIVE

Developing Communication Skills

Instructions: Prepare an oral or written report on one or more of the following subjects.

1. Contact the manager of an information systems department and obtain a copy of a typical program. Review the program with the manager or someone on the information systems staff and prepare a report on the program. Include information on the type of language used, the date the program was originally written, the purpose of the program, the size of the program, and changes that have been made to the program since it was originally written.

2. Interview a placement counselor at a local technical school that offers programming classes. Ask the counselor about the different programming language skills that he or she believes to be important.

3. Interview a person who has been working as a programmer for two years or less. Discuss how the programmer spends a typical day.

4. Prepare a list of the educational institutions in your area that teach programming. Summarize the languages taught and the differences between the institutions.

5. Interview a programming manager at a local computer installation. Prepare a report on the types of program design tools used in developing systems at the installation.

6. Contact someone who has used an application generator to develop a system. Ask him or her to comment on how long he or she thinks the system would have taken to develop using conventional programming techniques.

7. Interview a programmer who has used an object-oriented programming (OOP) language to develop a system. Prepare a report that discusses how the OOP concepts of classes and inheritance were used in developing the system.

8. Contact a local elementary school and interview the person responsible for computer training. Prepare a report on how the elementary school is using LOGO or some other language to teach beginning programming concepts.

9. Prepare a report on the current development of fifth-generation languages.

Career Opportunities in Information Processing

◆ OBJECTIVES

- ◆ Discuss the three areas that provide the majority of computer-related jobs
- ◆ Describe the career positions available in an information systems department
- ◆ Describe information processing career opportunities in sales, service and repair, consulting, and education and training
- ◆ Discuss the compensation and growth trends for information processing careers
- ◆ Discuss the three fields in the information processing industry
- ◆ Discuss career development, including professional organizations, certification, and professional growth and continuing education

◆ CHAPTER OUTLINE

CHAPTER THIRTEEN

Chapter Review

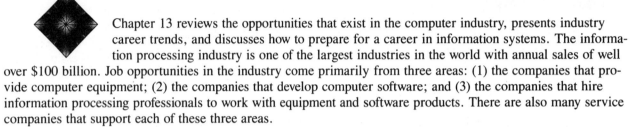

Chapter 13 reviews the opportunities that exist in the computer industry, presents industry career trends, and discusses how to prepare for a career in information systems. The information processing industry is one of the largest industries in the world with annual sales of well over $100 billion. Job opportunities in the industry come primarily from three areas: (1) the companies that provide computer equipment; (2) the companies that develop computer software; and (3) the companies that hire information processing professionals to work with equipment and software products. There are also many service companies that support each of these three areas.

The computer equipment, or hardware, industry includes all manufacturers and distributors of computers and computer-related equipment. The five largest minicomputer and mainframe manufacturers in the United States are IBM, Digital Equipment Corporation (DEC), UNISYS, Hewlett-Packard, and NCR. Major microcomputer manufacturers include IBM, Apple, Compaq, and Tandy. The computer equipment industry is also known for the many new start-up companies that appear each year by taking advantage of rapid changes in equipment technology to create new products and new job opportunities.

The computer software industry includes all the developers and distributors of applications and system software. Numerous opportunities in the software industry were provided by the personal computer boom in the early 1980s. Leading software companies include MSA, ASK, Microsoft, Lotus, and Borland.

In addition to management, the jobs in an information systems department can be classified into five categories: (1) operations; (2) data administration; (3) systems analysis an design; (4) programming; and (5) information center. Operations personnel are responsible for carrying out tasks such as operating the computer equipment that is located in the computer center. The primary responsibility of data administration is to maintain and control the organization's database. In systems analysis and design, the various information systems needed by an organization are created and maintained. Programming develops the programs needed for the information systems, and the information center provides teaching and consulting services within an organization to help users meet their departmental and individual information processing needs.

Sales representatives must have a general understanding of computers and a specific knowledge of the product they are selling. Strong interpersonal, or people, skills are important, including listening ability and strong oral and written communications skills. Being a service and repair technician is a challenging job for individuals who like to troubleshoot and solve problems and who have a strong background in electronics. Consultants are people who draw upon their experience to give advice to others. Consultants must have not only strong technical skills in their area of expertise, but also must have the people skills to effectively communicate their suggestions to their clients.

Compensation for computer industry jobs is a function of experience and demand for a particular skill. Demand is influenced by geographic location, with metropolitan areas usually having higher pay than rural areas. According to a survey, the communications, utility, and aerospace industries pay the highest salaries. These industries have many challenging applications and pay the highest rate to obtain the best qualified employees. According to the U.S. Bureau of Labor Statistics, the fastest growing computer career positions through 1995 will be systems analyst, applications programmer, machine operator, and computer repair technician.

CHAPTER REVIEW (continued)

There are three broad fields in the information processing industry: (1) computer information systems (CIS); (2) computer science; and (3) computer engineering. Computer information systems refers to the use of computers to provide the information needed to operate businesses and other organizations. The field of computer science includes the technical aspects of computers such as hardware operation and systems software. Computer engineering deals with the design and manufacturing of electronic components and computer hardware.

Examples of jobs in the computer information systems area include information processing manager, database administrator, systems analyst, business applications programmer, and computer operator. Examples of jobs in the computer science area include computer scientist, language design specialist, and systems software specialist. Examples of jobs in the computer engineering area include computer design engineer and service and repair technician.

Certification and degree programs in computer-related fields can be obtained from trade schools, technical schools, community colleges, colleges, and universities. As in most other industries, the more advanced degree an individual has in a chosen field, the better that individual's chances are for success. Ways for persons employed in the information processing industry to develop their skills and increase their recognition among their peers include professional organizations, certification, and professional growth and continuing education activities.

Computer-related professional organizations exist for people who have common interests and a desire to share their knowledge. The Association for Computing Machinery (ACM) is composed of persons interested in computer science and computer science education. The Association of Information Systems Professionals (AISP) is aimed at word processing and office automation professionals. The Association of Systems Management (ASM) is composed of individuals interested in improving the systems analysis and design field. The Data Processing Management Association (DPMA) is an association of programmers, systems analysts, and information processing managers. The Institute of Electrical and Electronic Engineers (IEEE) and IEEE Computer Society (IEEE/CS) are organizations primarily composed of computer scientists and engineers. In addition to professional organizations, user groups exist for people with common computer equipment or software.

The Institute for the Certification of Computer Professionals (ICCP) offers four certification designations: (1) Certified Computer Programmer (CCP); (2) Certified Data Processor (CDP); (3) Certified Systems Professional (CSP); and (4) Associate Computer Professional (ACP). The CCP, CDP, and CSP designations are earned by passing three examinations. The ACP designation is obtained by passing a general computer knowledge test and any one of seven programming language tests. The CCP, CDP, and CSP examinations require a minimum of five years of information industry experience. The ASP exam is designed for entry level personnel and requires no previous experience.

Professional growth and continuing education include activities such as workshops, seminars, conferences, conventions, and trade shows. These events provide both general and specific information on equipment, software, services, and issues affecting the industry. COMDEX is the largest computer industry trade show in the United States and brings together nearly 2,000 vendors and over 125,000 attendees. Regularly reading computer trade publications is a good way of keeping informed about what is going on in the industry. Some publications are like newspapers and cover a wide range of issues and others focus on a particular topic area.

Key Terms

Association for Computing Machinery (ACM): A professional organization composed of persons interested in computer science and computer science education.

Association of Information Systems Professionals (AISP): A professional organization originally aimed at word processing professionals, but it now includes a much broader membership, including office automation professionals.

Association of Systems Management (ASM): A professional organization composed of individuals interested in improving the systems analysis and design field.

COMDEX: COMDEX is the largest computer trade show in the United States.

Computer engineering: The design and manufacturing of electronic computer components and computer hardware.

Computer information systems (CIS): CIS is the use of computers to provide the information needed to operate businesses and other organizations.

Computer science: The science that includes the technical aspects of computers such as hardware operation and systems software.

Consultants: People who draw upon their experience to give advice to others. They must have not only strong technical skills in their area of expertise, but also have the people skills to effectively communicate with clients.

Data Processing Management Association (DPMA): A professional association of programmers, systems analysts, and information processing managers.

IEEE Computer Society (IEEE/CS), *see* **Institute of Electrical and Electronic Engineers (IEEE) and IEEE Computer Society (IEEE/CS)**

Institute for the Certification of Computer Professionals (ICCP): The institute offers four certification programs as a way of encouraging and recognizing the efforts of its members to attain a level of knowledge about their profession.

Institute of Electrical and Electronic Engineers (IEEE) and IEEE Computer Society (IEEE/CS): Professional organizations that are primarily composed of computer scientists and engineers.

Sales representatives: Persons who must have a general understanding of computers and a specific knowledge of the product they are selling; often the most highly compensated employees in a computer company.

Service and repair technician: A challenging job for individuals who like to troubleshoot and solve problems, and who have a strong background in electronics.

User group: A group of people with common computer equipment or software interests who meet regularly to share information.

CHAPTER THIRTEEN—PROJECT ONE

ClassNotes

THE INFORMATION PROCESSING INDUSTRY

1. Name the three areas where job opportunities in the information processing industry are found.

   _____   _____

   _____

WHAT ARE THE CAREER OPPORTUNITIES IN INFORMATION PROCESSING?

1. Name the five categories of jobs in an information systems department, choosing your answers from the following list.

   operations   data administration   information center   software library   administration

   programming   hardware administration   systems analysis and design

   _____   _____

   _____   _____

   _____

2. _____ personnel are responsible for carrying out tasks such as operating the computer equipment located in the data center, providing telecommunications, control and scheduling services, data entry, and maintaining the tape and/or disk library.

3. Name the two major roles of the data administration section of the information processing department.

   _____   _____

4. What two roles do systems analysis and design personnel fulfill?

   _____   _____

5. Programming personnel include application programmers and _____ programmers.

6. The role of information center personnel is to provide _____ and

   _____ .

7. _____ representatives in the information processing industry must have strong inter-personal, or people, skills, a general knowledge of computers, and a specific understanding of the product they are selling.

CLASSNOTES (continued)

8. Someone who draws upon his or her computer experience to give advice to others is known as a

   _____.

9. T F   The high demand by private industry for teachers with computer education and training experience has helped create a high demand at colleges and universities for qualified instructors with the same skills.

COMPENSATION AND GROWTH TRENDS FOR INFORMATION PROCESSING CAREERS

1. Name the industry in which information processing professionals are likely to receive the highest pay.

   _____

2. Fill in the following salary table indicating what programming personnel with two year's experience could expect to earn.

   Commercial   _____

   Engineering/Scientific   _____

   Microcomputer   _____

   Minicomputer   _____

   Software Engineer   _____

   Systems Software   _____

PREPARING FOR A CAREER IN INFORMATION PROCESSING

1. Name the three major fields in the information processing industry.

   _____   _____   _____

2. Name two career opportunities in computer engineering.

   _____   _____

3. Identify the six career opportunities available in computer information systems.

   _____   _____

   _____   _____

   _____   _____

4. Name three career opportunities in computer science.

   _____   _____   _____

5. Educational institutions and _____ are two sources of information and training in computers.

CAREER DEVELOPMENT IN THE INFORMATION PROCESSING INDUSTRY

1. One way to further your professional growth and continue your education in computers is to join one or more

   _____ organizations, such as the Association of Computing Machinery (ACM) or the Data Processing Management Association (DPMA).

2. _____ programs are a way to encourage and recognize the efforts of professionals who improve their level of knowledge about their professions.

CHAPTER THIRTEEN—PROJECT TWO

Self-Test
WORKBOOK AND PC VERSIONS

Match the following:

_____ 1. Sales Representatives

_____ 2. Consultants

_____ 3. Computer Science

_____ 4. COMDEX

_____ 5. Professional Organizations

_____ 6. CIS

_____ 7. Computer Engineering

_____ 8. CDP

1. Often the most highly compensated employees in a computer company
2. Certificate of data processing
3. Computer information systems
4. Design and manufacturing of electronic computer equipment
5. Draw upon their experience to give advice to others
6. Large computer product trade show
7. Technical aspects of computers
8. Institute of electrical and electronic engineers
9. Have common interests and a desire to share their knowledge

You can complete the remainder of Project 2 in two ways—either by marking or filling in your answers in this workbook, or by using the PC version of Project 2. The PC version (available from your instructor) automatically corrects your answers for you. It also calculates the percent of your answers that are correct.

Answer the following questions.

1. As society becomes more information oriented, _____ are becoming an integral part of most jobs.

2. Computers, tape drives, terminals, and printers are manufactured by companies in the _____ industry.

   a. information   c. computer software

   b. data processing   d. computer equipment

3. _____ is a leading manufacturer of minicomputers and mainframes.

   a. Borland   c. Intel

   b. IBM   d. AT&T

4. Leaders in the computer software industry include _____.

   a. Lotus   c. Borland

   b. Microsoft   d. all of the above

SELF-TEST (continued)

5. In an information systems department, program development would be done by a _____.
   a. database administrator   c. systems analyst
   b. programmer   d. computer operator

6. T F   The primary responsibility of data administration is the maintenance and control of an organization's database.

7. An information center provides _____ services within an organization to help users meet their departmental and individual processing needs.
   a. computer   c. library and information
   b. teaching and consulting   d. software and hardware

8. _____ are often the most highly compensated employees in a computer company.
   a. Programmers   c. Sales representatives
   b. Systems analysts   d. Consultants

9. T F   Service and repair technicians troubleshoot, solve problems, and have a strong background in electronics.

10. _____ draw upon their experience and expertise to give advice to others for tasks such as system selection, system design, and communications network design and installation.
    a. Consultants   c. Managers
    b. Trainers   d. System design specialists

11. Compensation is a function of experience and _____.

12. Research shows that the fastest growing computer career positions between 1982 and 1995 will be _____.
    a. systems analysts   c. applications programmers   e. all of the above
    b. machine operators   d. computer repair technicians

13. Computer Information Systems (CIS) refers to the use of computers in areas relating to _____.
    a. communications   c. business
    b. information processing   d. financial management

14. _____ includes the technical aspects of computers, such as hardware operation and systems software.
    a. Computer science   b. Computer engineering   c. Computer information systems

15. _____ deals with the design and manufacturing of electronic computer components and hardware.
    a. Computer science
    b. Computer engineering
    c. Computer information systems

16. T F   Computer development involves developing skills and increasing recognition among peers.

17. _____ have been formed by people who have common interests and a desire to share their knowledge.
    a. Computer cooperatives   c. Sharewares
    b. Professional organizations   d. COMDEX

18. T F   The Certificate of Data Processing (CDP) is the best known certification program in the information processing industry.

19. T F   Computer professionals can stay current by participating in professional growth and continuing education activities such as conferences, workshops, conventions, and trade shows.

CHAPTER THIRTEEN—PROJECT THREE

Identifying the Main Areas in an Information Systems Department

Instructions: In the space provided, identify the five main areas in an information systems department as represented by the numbers 1 through 5 in the following organization chart.

Area 1: _____

Area 2: _____

Area 3: _____

Area 4: _____

Area 5: _____

CHAPTER THIRTEEN—PROJECT FOUR

Identifying Fields of Study in Information Processing

Instructions: In the space provided, identify each of the three broad fields of study in the information processing industry.

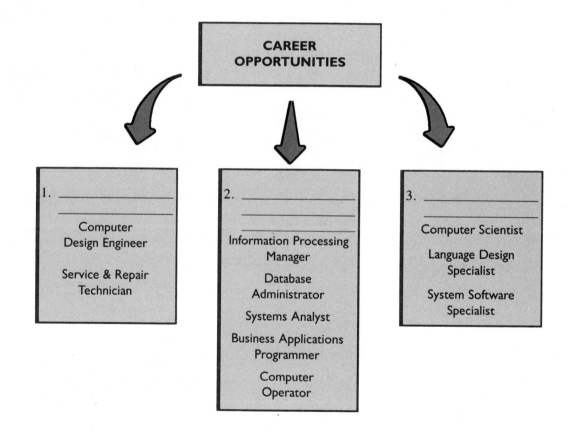

CAREER OPPORTUNITIES

1. _____
   _____
   Computer Design Engineer

   Service & Repair Technician

2. _____
   _____
   _____
   Information Processing Manager

   Database Administrator

   Systems Analyst

   Business Applications Programmer

   Computer Operator

3. _____
   _____
   Computer Scientist

   Language Design Specialist

   System Software Specialist

CHAPTER THIRTEEN—PROJECT FIVE

Developing Communication Skills

Instructions: Prepare an oral or written report on one or more of the following subjects.

1. Prepare a report on the growth over the last three years of one segment of the computer industry such as personal computers, software, or communications equipment.
2. Discuss one of the leading computer software companies such as Microsoft, Borland, or ASK.
3. Contact a recruiting firm that specializes in computer professionals. Prepare a report on how local starting salaries for programmers and systems analysts compare with national averages.
4. Interview three sales representatives at local computer stores. Prepare a report on the background of each sales representative.
5. Survey the educational institutions in your area and report on the types of training available in the fields of computer engineering, computer information systems, and computer science.
6. Contact one of the professional organizations listed in the chapter. Report on the organization and its activities in your area.
7. Contact the Institute for the Certification of Computer Professionals (ICCP) and obtain information on the requirements to obtain the Certified Data Processor designation.
8. Attend a computer user group meeting in your area. Prepare a report on the user group and what was discussed at the meeting.
9. Visit a local bookstore and make a list of all the magazines that deal with computers. Choose two magazines and summarize the major articles in each.

Trends and Issues in the Information Age

◆ OBJECTIVES

- ◆ Discuss the electronic devices and applications that are part of the automated office
- ◆ Describe the technologies that are developing for the automated factory, including CAD, CAE, CAM, and CIM
- ◆ Discuss the trend toward the computer-integrated enterprise
- ◆ Discuss the use of personal computers in the home
- ◆ Describe the methods used in computer-aided instruction (CAI)
- ◆ Explain guidelines for purchasing personal computers
- ◆ Discuss social issues related to computers, such as computer crime and privacy

◆ CHAPTER OUTLINE

CHAPTER FOURTEEN

Chapter Review

 Chapter 14 discusses current and future trends in information processing, including the changes taking place in information systems in the workplace. The chapter also covers the use of personal computers in the home and some of the social issues related to computers such as security and computer crime, privacy, and ethics.

In business, where most computer systems are used, business information systems will continue to undergo profound changes as new technology, software, and methods are applied to the huge installed base of traditional business system users.

Equipment trends include the increased use of networked personal computers, mainframes, and minicomputers used as data storehouses, increased disk storage capacity, high-resolution color graphics screens, increased use of page printers, reduced instruction set computing (RISC), parallel processing, increased use of portable computers, and handwriting recognitions systems. Software trends include fourth-generation and natural languages, object orientation, computer-aided software engineering (CASE), decision support and artificial intelligence systems, widespread implementation of graphic user interfaces, and integrated applications.

Data trends include automatic input of data at the source and compound documents that combine text, numbers, and nontext data such as voice, image, and full-motion video.

Trends affecting users include most people being computer literate, increased user responsibility for design, operation, and maintenance of information processing systems, and increased reliance on computers to manage the proliferation of information. Trends affecting information systems personnel include increased interface with users, a shift from a machine and software orientation to a user application orientation, a shift in emphasis from how to capture and process data to how to more effectively use the data available and create information, reduced staff levels being asked to do more work, some processing operations being outsourced to independent contractors, and a continuous need for retraining and education.

The automated, or electronic, office is a term used to describe the use of electronic devices to make office work more productive. The trend is to integrate office applications such as word processing, electronic mail, voice mail, desktop publishing, facsimile, image processing, and teleconferencing into a network of devices and services that can share information. Electronic mail is the capability to use computers to transmit messages to and receive messages from other computer users. Voice mail can be considered verbal electronic mail and is similar to leaving a message on an answering machine. With voice mail, however, the caller's message digitizes (converts into binary ones and zeros) so that it can be stored on a disk like other computer data. The digitized message can later be reconverted to an audio form. Some software applications can now incorporate voice messages as part of stored documents.

A facsimile, or FAX, machine can transmit a reproduced image of a document containing text, graphics, hand-writing, or a photograph over standard phone lines. A FAX machine at the receiving end converts the digitized data back into its original image. Image processing is the capability to store and retrieve a reproduced image of a document and is often used when an original document must be seen to verify data. Teleconferencing, also referred to as video conferencing, is the use of computers and television cameras to transmit video images and the sound of the conference participants to other participants with similar equipment at a remote location.

CHAPTER REVIEW (continued)

The automated factory uses automated, and often computer-controlled, equipment to increase productivity. Technologies used include computer-aided design, computer-aided engineering, computer-aided manufacturing, and computer-integrated manufacturing. Computer-aided design (CAD) uses special graphics software to aid in product design. CAD software eliminates the manual drafting process and allows the user to view a product from different angles. Computer-aided engineering (CAE) is the use of computers to test product designs by simulating the effects of wind, temperature, weight, and stress on product shapes and materials. Computer-aided manufacturing (CAM) is the use of computers to control production equipment. Computer-integrated manufacturing (CIM) is the total integration of the manufacturing process using computers. Under ideal CIM conditions, a product will move through the entire production process under computer control.

The long-range trend is the computer-integrated enterprise—an organization in which all information storage and processing is performed by a network of computers and intelligent devices. In such an enterprise, all office, factory, warehouse, and communications systems would be linked using a common interface allowing authorized users in any functional area of the organization to access and use data stored anywhere in the organization.

Home computer use usually falls into five general areas: (1) personal services, (2) control of home systems, (3) telecommuting, (4) education, and (5) entertainment. Personal service software includes financial and data management packages to assist the user in managing his or her personal affairs. On-line services such as Prodigy offer teleshopping, electronic banking, travel reservations, stock prices, weather, and headline news. Bulletin board systems, called BBSs, allow users to communicate with one another and share information.

Computers can be used to control home systems such as security, environment, lighting, and landscape sprinkler systems. In the future, many homes will be wired for home control systems during construction and will be considered intelligent homes or smart houses. Telecommuting refers to the capability of individuals to work at home and communicate with their offices by using personal computers and communications lines. It is estimated that by the end of the 1990s, ten percent of the work force will be telecommuters.

Computer-aided instruction (CAI) is the use of personal computers for education. Three types of CAI software are drill and practice, tutorials, and simulations. Drill and practice software uses a flash-card approach to teaching by allowing users to practice skills in subjects such as math and language. With tutorial software, the computer software uses text, graphics, and sometimes sound to teach a user concepts about subjects such as chemistry, music theory, or computer literacy. Simulation software is designed to teach a user by creating a model of a real-life situation.

The six steps that you should follow in purchasing a personal computer are: (1) become computer literate; (2) define and prioritize the type of tasks you want to perform on your computer; (3) select the software packages that best meet your needs; (4) select equipment that will run the software you have selected; (5) select the suppliers for the software and equipment; and (6) purchase the software and equipment.

Computer security refers to the safeguards established to prevent and detect unauthorized use and deliberate or accidental damage to computer systems and data. Computer crime is the use of a computer to commit an illegal act. Software theft, often called software piracy, is a violation of copyright law and is a crime. Software companies take illegal copying seriously and in some cases offenders who have been caught have been vigorously prosecuted.

Unauthorized access can be defined as computer trespassing, in other words, being logged on a system without permission. Unauthorized use is the use of a computer system or computer data for unapproved and possibly illegal activities. The key to preventing both unauthorized access and unauthorized use is computer security that controls and monitors an appropriate level of authorization for each user. Malicious or deliberate damage to the data in a computer system is often difficult to detect. One of the most potentially dangerous types of malicious damage is done by a virus, a computer program designed to copy itself into other software and spread through multiple computer systems. Special programs called vaccines have been developed to locate and remove viruses.

The concern about information privacy has led to federal and state laws regarding the storage and disclosure of personal data. Common points in these laws include: (1) information collected and stored about individuals should be limited to what is necessary to carry out the function of the business or government agency collecting the data; (2) once collected, provisions should be made to restrict access to the data to those employees within the organization who need access to it to perform their job duties; (3) personal information should be released outside the organization collecting the data only when the person has agreed to its disclosure; and (4) when information is collected about an individual, the individual should know that data is being collected and have the opportunity to determine the accuracy of the data.

Key Terms

Automated factory: Factories that use automated, and often computer-controlled, equipment.

Automated office: The use of electronic devices such as computers, facsimile machines, and computerized telephone systems to make office work more productive; also known as an electronic office.

Bulletin board systems (BBSs): System that allow users to communicate electronically with one another and share information using personal computers.

Computer-aided design (CAD): A design method that uses a computer and special graphics software to aid in product design.

Computer-aided engineering (CAE): The use of computers to test product designs.

Computer-aided instruction (CAI): The use of personal computers for education.

Computer-aided manufacturing (CAM): The use of computers to control production equipment.

Computer crime: The use of a computer to commit an illegal act.

Computer-integrated enterprise: An organization in which all information storage and processing is performed by a network of computers and intelligent devices.

Computer-integrated manufacturing (CIM): The total integration of the manufacturing process using computers.

Computer security: The safeguards established to prevent and detect unauthorized use and deliberate or accidental damage to computer systems and data.

Drill and practice software: Software that uses a flash-card approach to teaching by allowing users to practice skills in subjects such as math and language.

Electronic mail: The capability to use computers to transmit messages to and receive messages from other computer users.

Electronic office, *see* **Automated office**

Facsimile, or **FAX:** Machines used to transmit a reproduced image of a document over standard phone lines.

Public domain software: Free software that is not copyrighted and can therefore be distributed among users.

Shareware: Software that users can try out on their own systems before paying a fee.

Simulation software: Software designed to teach a user by creating a model of a real-life situation.

Software piracy: Software piracy is the illegal copying of software; also called software theft.

Telecommuting: Telecommuting gives individuals the capability to work at home and communicate with their offices by using personal computers and communications lines.

KEY TERMS (continued)

Teleconferencing: Teleconferencing usually means video conferencing, the use of computers and television cameras to transmit video images and the sound of the conference participants to other participants with similar equipment at a remote location.

Tutorial software: Software that uses text, graphics, and sometimes sound to teach users concepts about a subject and follows the instruction with questions to help the user ensure that he or she understands the concepts.

Unauthorized access: Computer trespassing, in other words, being logged on a system without permission.

Unauthorized use: The use of a computer system or computer data for unapproved and possibly illegal activities.

Vaccines: Vaccines are programs that locate and remove viruses.

Video conferencing, *see* **Teleconferencing**

Virus: A computer program designed to copy itself into other software and spread through multiple computer systems.

Voice mail: Voice mail is verbal electronic mail made possible by the latest computerized telephone systems.

CHAPTER FOURTEEN—PROJECT ONE

ClassNotes

INFORMATION SYSTEMS IN BUSINESS

1. Important overall trends include more online, interactive systems and less _____ .

2.–8. New devices and services provide increased productivity in the automated office, sometimes known as the electronic office. Match the devices and services shown that are likely to be found in modern automated offices. Choose your answers from the following list.

teleconferencing   word processing   electronic mail   facsimile   image processing

voice mail   desktop publishing   teletype   dictaphone   manual typewriter   copy machine

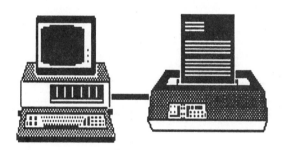

2. _____

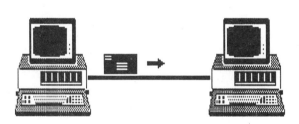

3. _____

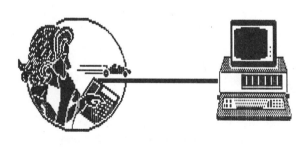

4. _____

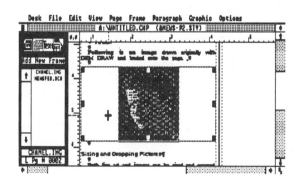

5. _____

CLASSNOTES (continued)

2.–8. (continued)

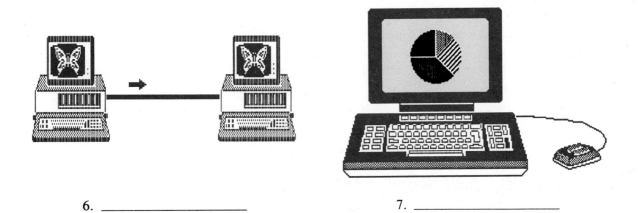

6. _____   7. _____

8. _____

9. CAD is the acronym for _____ .

10. _____ is the use of computers to test product designs.

11. Computer-aided manufacturing (CAM) is the use of computers to control production equipment in an automated _____ .

12.–15. The concept of computer-integrated manufacturing (CIM) is to integrate all phases of the manufacturing process. Fill in the blocks on the diagram, choosing your answers from the following list.

production planning   package designing   product design   computer automation

product distribution   manufacturing

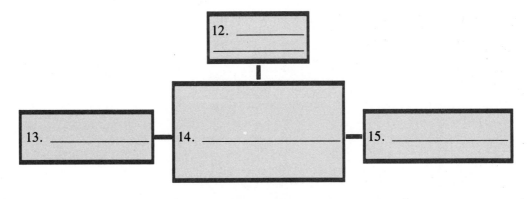

12. _____

13. _____ 14. _____ 15. _____

COMPUTER – INTEGRATED MANUFACTURING

CLASSNOTES (continued)

BRINGING THE INFORMATION AGE HOME

1. The concept of bringing the information age home refers to the use of _____ computers in the home.

2. Name five common uses for personal computers located in the home. Choose the major uses from the following list.

   personal services   telecommuting   entertainment   education   control of home systems
   monitoring cooking devices

   _____   _____

   _____   _____

   _____

3. _____ teaches through drills and practices as well as through simulation.

4. Identify six steps for buying a personal computer, choosing your answers from the following list.

   Select the suppliers for software and equipment.

   Learn the memory-chip manufacturing process.

   Become computer literate.

   Define and prioritize the tasks you want to perform on your computer.

   Select software packages that best meet your needs.

   Select equipment that will run software you have selected.

   Purchase software and equipment.

   Step 1: _____

   Step 2: _____

   Step 3: _____

   Step 4: _____

   Step 5: _____

   Step 6: _____

SOCIAL ISSUES

1. Name the four major social issues that computer users must face.

   _____   _____

   _____   _____

CHAPTER FOURTEEN—PROJECT TWO

Self-Test
WORKBOOK AND PC VERSIONS

Match the following:

_____ 1. Computer-aided Engineering

_____ 2. Bulletin Board System

_____ 3. Simulation Software

_____ 4. Word Processing

_____ 5. Software Privacy

_____ 6. Computer-aided Manufacturing

_____ 7. Vaccines

_____ 8. Voice Mail

1. Designed to teach a user by creating a model of a real-life situation
2. Use of computers to control production equipment
3. Illegal copying of software
4. Programs that locate and remove viruses
5. Verbal electronic mail
6. Allows users to communicate with one another and share information
7. Most widely used office automation technology
8. A long-range trend
9. Use of computers to test product design

You can complete the remainder of Project 2 in two ways—either by marking or filling in your answers in this workbook, or by using the PC version of Project 2. The PC version (available from your instructor) automatically corrects your answers for you. It also calculates the percent of your answers that are correct.

Answer the following questions.

1. Automated offices use electronic devices such as computers, facsimile machines, and computerized telephone systems to improve _____ .
   a. revenues
   b. relationships
   c. productivity
   d. data security

2. Electronically creating, storing, revising, and printing documents is called _____ .
   a. database management
   b. word processing
   c. facsimile
   d. desktop publishing

3. _____ is the ability to transmit messages to and receive messages from other computers.
   a. Electronic mail
   b. Word processing
   c. Facsimilie
   d. Desktop publishing

4. T F   The automated factory uses computer-controlled equipment to increase productivity.

5. _____ uses a computer and special graphics software to aid in product design.
   a. CAE
   b. CAD
   c. CAM

SELF-TEST (continued)

6. _____ is the use of computers to control production equipment.
   a. CAE   b. CAD   c. CAM

7. _____ is the use of computers to test product designs.
   a. CAE   b. CAD   c. CAM

8. T   F   CIM is the total integration of the manufacturing process using computers.

9. T   F   Personal computers in the home are used for business tasks as well as for personal services.

10. T   F   Computers are used in some homes to control the timing for lighting and landscape sprinkler systems.

11. Individuals who work at home and communicate with their offices by using personal computers and communication lines are _____ .
    a. telecommuting   c. not using a modem
    b. cheating   d. highly compensated professionals

12. CAI software is used for _____ in the home.
    a. entertainment   b. education   c. budgeting

13. T   F   Being computer literate is not a great advantage when considering purchasing a computer for the home.

14. T   F   You should be certain that your hardware and software choices are compatible before purchasing them.

15. The term computer _____ refers to the safeguards established to prevent and detect unauthorized use and deliberate or accidental damage to computer systems and data.
    a. passwords   c. security
    b. regulation   d. accident prevention

16. T   F   A very dangerous type of malicious damage is done by a virus, a program designed to copy itself into other software and spread through multiple systems.

CHAPTER FOURTEEN—PROJECT THREE

Identifying Automated Office Applications

Instructions: In the space provided, match the automated office application names on the left with the application descriptions on the right.

1. Word processing
2. Electronic mail
3. Voice mail
4. Desktop publishing
5. Facsimile (FAX)
6. Image processing
7. Teleconferencing

_____ Machines used to transmit a reproduced image of a document over standard phone lines.

_____ The use of computers and television cameras to transmit video images and the sound of conference participants with similar equipment at a remote location.

_____ Allows the user to control the process of creating high-quality newsletters, brochures, and other documents that previously would had to have been developed by professional artists.

_____ This most widely used office automation technology is used to create, edit, and print documents electronically.

_____ The capability of storing and retrieving a reproduced image of a document.

_____ Verbal electronic mail. Caller's messages are digitized and stored on a disk for later retrieval.

_____ The capability to use computers to transmit messages to and receive messages from other computer users.

Name _____   **Date** _____

Computer Viruses

Instructions: In the space provided, answer the questions about computer viruses.

1. How is a computer virus created?

_____

_____

2. How do viruses spread?

_____

_____

_____

3. Why are viruses not detected immediately?

_____

_____

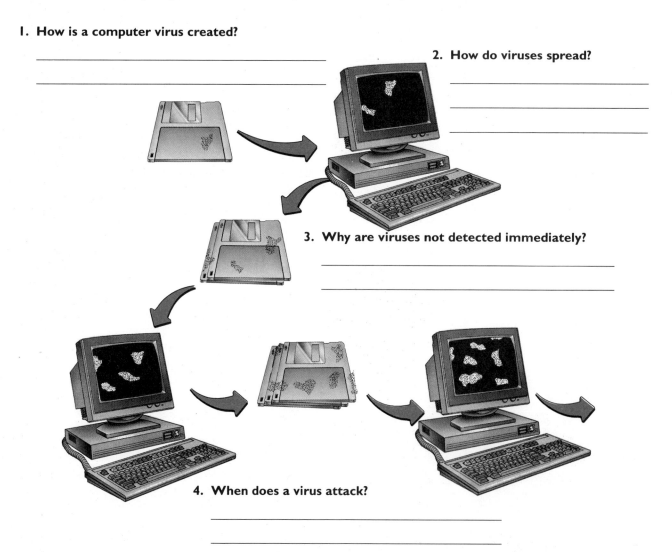

4. When does a virus attack?

_____

_____

CHAPTER FOURTEEN–PROJECT FIVE

Developing Communication Skills

Instructions: Prepare an oral or written report on one or more of the following subjects.

1. Describe how computers will affect the lives of people in the year 2025.
2. Prepare a report on the services currently offered by the leading online information companies such as Prodigy or CompuServe.
3. Investigate the availability of bulletin board systems (BBSs) in your area.
4. Interview a person who spends at least part of his or her job telecommuting. Ask him or her to comment on both the advantages and disadvantages of telecommuting.
5. Contact a local company that uses computer-aided manufacturing (CAM) equipment. Prepare a report on how the equipment is used and how the equipment has affected productivity, staff levels, and overall product quality.
6. Contact a contractor who has installed computer-controlled home systems for such uses as security, environment, and lighting. Obtain information on how such systems work and how much they cost.
7. Contact several medium-sized businesses in your area and ask each for a copy of its company policy on the illegal use of personal computer software. Report on the steps that the companies take to make sure the policy is followed.
8. Prepare a report on computer crimes that have been reported in the past year.
9. Discuss the increasing amount of personal information that is now being accumulated on computers. Consider both the advantages and possible disadvantages of the availability of this information.

PART II
Computer Lab Software Projects

COMPUTER LAB SOFTWARE PROJECTS

Home Banking

PROJECT OBJECTIVES

◆ Dial and connect to a remote computer

◆ Use a menu on which selections are identified by numbers

◆ Inquire and retrieve information from a database

◆ Enter a payment to be made by the bank

PROJECT DESCRIPTION

◆ This project consists of nine assignments requiring the use of a computer and associated software. The user enters a phone number to connect to the bank's computer system and an account number and password to gain access to the home banking system. The projects allow the user to make inquiries regarding account balances and transactions, transfer funds between accounts, and schedule a bill for automatic payment. The screen below illustrates the Main Menu from which the user can choose processing options.

ASSIGNMENT 1: PROGRAM EXECUTION

Load the program for this project into main memory and execute the program.

Step 1: The method for loading and executing the program for this project will vary between different computers. Obtain the necessary instructions from your instructor or the computer center.

Step 2: Load and execute the program for this project.

Step 3: A message about the use of this computer lab software project will appear on the screen. Read the message and press the Spacebar.

Step 4: Sometimes you will be able to enter any one of several responses to a program prompt. Other times, only one response will be correct. If you make an incorrect entry, an error message will appear on the screen. To clear the error message, press the Spacebar. You can then reenter the data. A table at

```
        H O M E   B A N K I N G
                MAIN MENU
----------------------------------------
    1. Account Balances Inquiry
    2. Checking Account Activity Summary
    3. Deposits and Credits Transaction Inquiry
    4. Checks and Charges Transaction Inquiry
    5. Transfer Funds
    6. Bill Payment Inquiry
    7. Enter or Change Bill Payments
    8. Log Off
            ENTER SELECTION: ⌊
```

LAB3

Home Banking (Assignment 1 – continued)

the end of this project contains the error messages, the cause of the errors, and the corrective action you can take. Review the table now before beginning this project. Anytime an error message is displayed you can exit the software project by typing the letter Q (for quit).

ASSIGNMENT 2: CONNECTING TO THE BANK COMPUTER

Connect to the bank computer system.

Step 1: When the prompt "ENTER BANK ACCESS TELEPHONE NUMBER:" appears on the screen, enter the telephone number 555-5050 and press the Enter key.

Step 2: When the prompt "ENTER ACCOUNT NUMBER:" appears on the screen, enter the account number 143-062070 and press the Enter key.

Step 3: When the prompt "ENTER PASSWORD:" appears on the screen, enter the password MYCODE and press the Enter key. (Enter the password using only capital letters. For security reasons, most passwords do not appear on the screen as they are entered.) If the password is correctly entered, the system will display the Main Menu shown below.

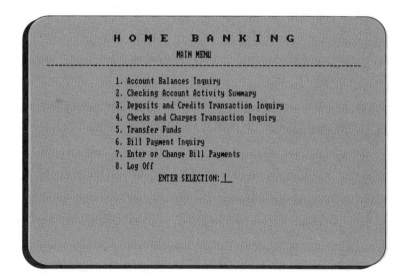

```
H O M E   B A N K I N G
              MAIN MENU
----------------------------------------------
    1. Account Balances Inquiry
    2. Checking Account Activity Summary
    3. Deposits and Credits Transaction Inquiry
    4. Checks and Charges Transaction Inquiry
    5. Transfer Funds
    6. Bill Payment Inquiry
    7. Enter or Change Bill Payments
    8. Log Off
              ENTER SELECTION: |
```

ASSIGNMENT 3: ACCOUNT BALANCES INQUIRY

Display the account balance in your checking and savings accounts and the amount you currently owe on your bank credit card.

Step 1: From the Main Menu, type the number 1 after the prompt "ENTER SELECTION:" and press the Enter key.

Question 1: What is the balance in the checking account? _____

Question 2: What is the balance in the savings account? _____

Question 3: What is the amount owed on the bank credit card? _____

Step 2: Return to the Main Menu by pressing Enter.

ASSIGNMENT 4: CHECKING ACCOUNT ACTIVITY INQUIRY

Display and answer questions about the activity in the checking account since the last bank statement.

Step 1: From the Main Menu, type the number 2 after the prompt "ENTER SELECTION:" and press Enter.

Question 1: What was the checking account balance on the previous statement? _____

Question 2: What is the deposits total? _____

Home Banking (Assignment 4 – continued)

> **Question 3:** How many checks have cleared since the last statement? _____
>
> **Question 4:** According to the banks records, what is the current checking account
>
> balance? _____

Step 2: Return to the Main Menu by pressing Enter.
Selection 3 on the Main Menu, Deposits and Credits Transaction Inquiry, is not used in this project.

ASSIGNMENT 5: CHECKS AND CHARGES TRANSACTION INQUIRY

Display and answer questions about posted checks and other bank charges.

Step 1: From the Main Menu, type the number 4 after the prompt "ENTER SELECTION:" and press Enter.

> **Question 1:** What is the amount of the check that was posted on 05-12? _____
>
> **Question 2:** What is the date of the last check posted? _____
>
> **Question 3:** What is the description of the $11.00 charge on 05-15? _____

Step 2: Return to the Main Menu by pressing Enter.

ASSIGNMENT 6: TRANSFER FUNDS

Use the home banking system to transfer **$1,000** from your savings account to your checking account.

Step 1: From the Main Menu, type the number 5 after the prompt "ENTER SELECTION:" and press Enter.

Step 2: Select the Savings to Checking Transfer type. Enter the appropriate Transfer Type Code.

Step 3: Type the amount to be transferred from your savings account to your checking account. Transfer $1,000.00.

> **Question 1:** Should the system allow any amount to be transferred? What limits do banks place on
>
> amounts to be transferred from one account to another? _____
>
> _____
>
> _____
>
> _____
>
> _____

Step 4: Review the transaction. If the amounts entered are correct, type Y to make the transfer. If you want to enter the data again, type N.

> **Question 1:** Why is it important to allow the user a way of reviewing a transaction before it is
>
> recorded? _____

Step 5: Check to make sure the transfer is recorded. From the Main Menu, type the number 1 and press Enter.

> **Question 1:** What is the checking account balance? _____
>
> **Question 2:** What is the savings account balance? _____

Step 6: Return to the Main Menu by pressing Enter.

Home Banking (continued)

ASSIGNMENT 7: BILL PAYMENT INQUIRY

Home banking systems allow the user to instruct the bank to make payments to companies and organizations that have agreed to accept such payments from the bank. This assignment will allow you to review the bill payments that have already been established. The next assignment will allow you to enter a bill payment.

Step 1: From the Main Menu, type the number 6 after the prompt "ENTER SELECTION:" and press Enter.

Question 1: What is the amount of bill payment #502? _____

Question 2: Who is scheduled to be paid on 05-30? _____

Question 3: What is the total amount of bill payments? _____

Step 2: Return to the Main Menu by pressing Enter.

ASSIGNMENT 8: ENTER A BILL PAYMENT

Use the home banking system to enter a bill.

Step 1: From the Main Menu, type the number 7 after the prompt "ENTER SELECTION:" and press Enter.
Step 2: Type N to indicate that you want to enter a new bill payment.
Step 3: Enter a payment. Schedule the payment for 05-22 to payee number 1008 for $150.25. After you enter the payee number, the system will display the payee name.

Question 1: What is the total of the bill payments after you enter the payment to Acme Musical

Supply? _____

Step 4: Return to the Main Menu by pressing Enter.

ASSIGNMENT 9: END THE PROJECT

When you are finished with all the assignments, exit the program.

Step 1: From the Main Menu, type the number 8 after the prompt "ENTER SELECTION:" and press Enter.
Step 2: The simulated Home Banking system you have used in this project is similar to systems offered by many banks.

Question 1: What safeguards do you think such a system should have to protect the privacy and

accuracy of a bank customers' information? _____

Home Banking (continued)

ERROR MESSAGES

◆ The following table contains the error messages that you might encounter when you make incorrect entries. The cause and the corrective action is given for each error.

ERROR MESSAGE	CAUSE	CORRECTIVE ACTION
INVALID TELEPHONE NUMBER. PLEASE REDIAL.	An incorrect telephone number was entered. For this project, the only valid telephone number is 555-5050.	Enter the correct phone number as 555-5050.
INVALID ACCOUNT NUMBER. PLEASE REENTER.	An incorrect account number was entered. For this project, the only valid account number is 143-062070.	Enter the correct account number as 143-062070.
INVALID PASSWORD. PLEASE REENTER.	An incorrect password was entered. For this project, the only valid password is MYCODE.	Enter the password as MYCODE.
INVALID TRANSFER TYPE CODE. PLEASE REENTER.	An invalid transfer type code was entered. For this project, the only valid transfer type code is 2; a Savings to Checking transfer.	Type transfer type code 2.
INVALID TRANSFER AMOUNT. PLEASE REENTER.	An invalid transfer amount was entered. For this project, the only valid transfer amount is $1,000.	Type a transfer amount of $1,000.
ONLY NEW PAYMENTS MAY BE ENTERED.	An entry other than N was made on the Enter Or Change Bill Payments screen. For this project, changing existing payments is not provided.	Type N to enter a new payment or press Enter to return to the Main Menu.
INVALID PAYMENT DATA. PLEASE REENTER.	Payment data other than that specified in the workbook was entered.	Enter the payment data as given in the workbook.

COMPUTER LAB SOFTWARE PROJECTS

On-Line Information Services

PROJECT OBJECTIVES

◆ Dial and connect to a remote location computer
◆ Follow a logon procedure using an identification code and password to gain access to the on-line system
◆ Learn to use a simulated on-line information services system

PROJECT DESCRIPTION

◆ This project consists of seven assignments requiring the use of a computer and associated software. The user enters a phone number to connect to the information services computer and an account number and password to gain access to the on-line services. The student asssignments allow the user to access information on national news, weather, stocks, and sports. The screen below illustrates the Main Menu from which the user can choose processing options.

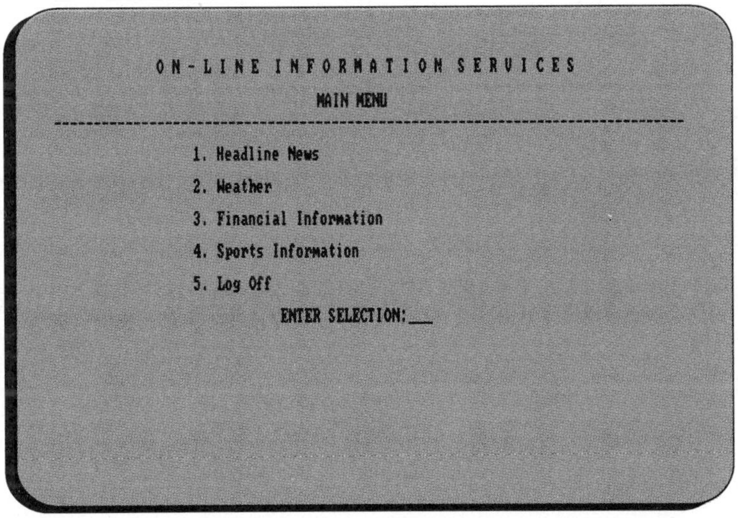

```
          ON-LINE INFORMATION SERVICES
                   MAIN MENU
----------------------------------------------------
        1. Headline News

        2. Weather

        3. Financial Information

        4. Sports Information

        5. Log Off

              ENTER SELECTION:___
```

On-Line Information Services (continued)

ASSIGNMENT 1: PROGRAM EXECUTION

Load the program for this project into main memory and execute the program.

Step 1: The method for loading and executing the program for this project will vary between different computers. Obtain the necessary instructions from your instructor or the computer center.

Step 2: Load and execute the program for this project.

Step 3: A message about the use of this computer lab software project will appear on the screen. Read the message and press the Spacebar.

Step 4: Sometimes you will be able to enter any one of several responses to a program prompt. Other times, only one response will be correct. If you make an incorrect entry, an error message will appear on the screen. To clear the error message press the Spacebar. You can then reenter the data. A table at the end of this project contains the error messages, the cause of the errors, and the corrective action to be taken. Review the table now before beginning this project. Anytime an error message is displayed, you can exit the software project by typing the letter Q (for quit).

ASSIGNMENT 2: CONNECTING TO THE INFORMATION SERVICES COMPUTER

Connect to the information services computer system.

Step 1: When the prompt "ENTER TELEPHONE NUMBER:" appears on the screen, enter the telephone number 555-5050 and press the Enter key.

Step 2: When the prompt "ENTER ACCOUNT NUMBER:" appears on the screen, enter the account number 2109-908 and press the Enter key.

Step 3: When the prompt "ENTER PASSWORD:" appears on the screen, enter the password MYCODE and press the Enter key. (Enter the password using only capital letters. For security reasons, most passwords do not appear on the screen as they are entered.) If the password is correctly entered, the system will display the Main Menu.

ASSIGNMENT 3: HEADLINE NEWS

Review the top stories of the day.

Step 1: From the Main Menu, type the number 1 after the prompt "ENTER SELECTION:" and press the Enter key.

Step 2: From the Headline News menu, type the number 2 to review the story on the United Nations world health conference.

Question 1: In what city and country is the health conference being held? _____

Question 2: How many countries will be represented at the conference? _____

Step 3: After answering the questions, press Enter to return to the Headline News menu.

Step 4: Review the other Headline News stories and answer the following questions.

Question 3: How much does the president think the proposed education programs will cost the government? _____

Question 4: How many acres of land were burned in the western states forest fires?

_____

Question 5: What is the estimated value of trade covered by the agreements being discussed by European leaders? _____

Step 5: After answering the questions, return to the Main Menu by pressing the Enter key twice.

On-Line Information Services (continued)

ASSIGNMENT 4: WEATHER

Display the U.S. weather map and answer questions about the forecasted weather for several U.S. cities.

Step 1: From the Main Menu, type the number 2 after the prompt "ENTER SELECTION:" and press Enter.

Step 2: From the Weather Information menu, choose selection 1, the United States Weather Map.

Question 1: What type of weather conditions are forecast for the east coast? _____

Step 3: Press Enter to return to the Weather Information menu.

Step 4: From the Weather Information menu, choose selection 2, the Major U.S. Cities Forecast.

Question 1: What U.S. city has the highest forecasted temperature? _____

Question 2: What type of weather conditions are forecast for New Orleans? _____

Step 5: After answering the questions, return to the Main Menu by pressing the Enter key twice.

ASSIGNMENT 5: FINANCIAL INFORMATION

Display information and answer questions about the ten most active stocks on the New York and American Stock Exchanges.

Step 1: From the Main Menu, type the number 3 after the prompt "ENTER SELECTION:" and press Enter.

Step 2: At the prompt for Exchange, type the letter N and press Enter.

Question 1: What was the volume of the most active New York Stock Exchange stock?

_____

Question 2: What New York Stock Exchange company had the largest change?

_____

Step 3: Press Enter to return to the Financial Information menu.

Step 4: At the prompt for Exchange, type the letter A and press Enter.

Question 1: What American Stock Exchange company has the highest last price?

_____

Question 2: What was the last price of Tekstar? _____

Step 5: Return to the Main Menu by pressing Enter twice.

ASSIGNMENT 6: SPORTS INFORMATION

Display information and answer questions about the baseball and football standings.

Step 1: From the Main Menu, type the number 4 after the prompt "ENTER SELECTION:" and press Enter.

Step 2: From the Sports Information menu, choose selection 1, Baseball Standings.

Question 1: What baseball team is leading the American League East? _____

Question 2: What team has won the most games? _____

Step 3: Press Enter to return to the Sports Information menu.

On-Line Information Services (Assignment 6 – continued)

> **Step 4:** From the Sports Information menu, choose selection 2, Football Standings.
>
>> **Question 1:** What team is leading the American Conference East? _____
>>
>> **Question 2:** How many teams are undefeated?
>>
>> _____
>
> **Step 5:** Return to the Main Menu by pressing Enter twice.

ASSIGNMENT 7: END THE PROJECT

When you are finished with all the assignments, exit the program.

> **Step 1:** From the Main Menu, type the number 5 after the prompt "ENTER SELECTION:" and press the Enter key.

ERROR MESSAGES

◆ The following table contains the error messages that you might encounter when you make incorrect entries. The cause and the corrective action is given for each error.

ERROR MESSAGE	CAUSE	CORRECTIVE ACTION
INVALID TELEPHONE NUMBER. PLEASE REENTER.	An incorrect telephone number was entered. For this project, the only valid telephone number is 555-5050.	Enter the telephone number as 555-5050.
INVALID ACCOUNT NUMBER. PLEASE REENTER.	An incorrect account number was entered. For this project, the only valid account number is 2109-908.	Enter the account number as 2109-908.
INVALID PASSWORD. PLEASE REENTER.	An incorrect password was entered. For this project, the only valid password is MYCODE.	Enter the password as MYCODE. Enter only capital letters.
ACCESS DENIED . . . End of Transmission	Three attempts to enter the password were made without success.	Begin project again. Enter the correct password as MYCODE. Enter the password in capital letters only.
INVALID MENU SELECTION.	An entry other than the numbers listed on the menu was entered.	Enter a selection from the numbers listed on the menu.
INVALID STOCK EXCHANGE CODE. N OR A ONLY.	A Stock Exchange Code other than N or A was entered. For this project, the only valid codes are N for the New York Stock Exchange and A for the American Stock Exchange.	Type either N or A.

COMPUTER LAB SOFTWARE PROJECTS

Airline Reservations

PROJECT OBJECTIVE

◆ Learn to use a simulated on-line airline reservation system

PROJECT DESCRIPTION

◆ This project consists of eight assignments requiring the use of a computer and associated software. Each assignment requires the user, acting as a travel agent, to use an on-line airline reservation system. As a travel agent, your job responsibilities include checking available airline flights, checking airline fares, making ticket reservations, reserving seat assignments, and making inquiries on previously entered reservations. The screen below illustrates the Main Menu from which you can choose processing options.

```
A I R L I N E    R E S E R V A T I O N S
                  MAIN MENU
----------------------------------------------------
        1. Available Flights
        2. Fares
        3. Flight Reservations
        4. Seat Assignments
        5. Open Reservations Inquiry
        6. Log Off
              ENTER SELECTION: 1
```

ASSIGNMENT 1: PROGRAM EXECUTION

Load the program for this project into main memory and execute the program.

Step 1: The method for loading and executing the program for this project will vary between different computers. Obtain the necessary instructions from your instructor or the computer center.

Step 2: Load and execute the program for this project.

Airline Reservations (Assignment 1 – continued)

Step 3: A message about the use of this computer lab software project will appear on the screen. Read the message and press the Spacebar.

Step 4: Sometimes you will be able to enter any one of several responses to a program prompt. Other times, only one response will be correct. If you make an incorrect entry, an error message will appear on the screen. To clear the error message press the Spacebar. You can then reenter the data. A table at the end of this project contains the error messages, the cause of the errors, and the corrective action to be taken. Review the table now before beginning this project. Anytime an error message is displayed you can exit the software project by typing the letter Q (for quit).

ASSIGNMENT 2: CHECK AVAILABLE FLIGHTS

Mrs. Beverly Johnson calls and wants to know what flights are available on October 6 to New York that depart from Los Angeles International airport. She mentions that she would like to leave between 9:00 A.M. and 12:00 noon and would like to travel first class if it doesn't cost too much.

Step 1: To display as much information as possible, airline reservation systems use many abbreviations, some of which we will use in this project. These abbreviations include:

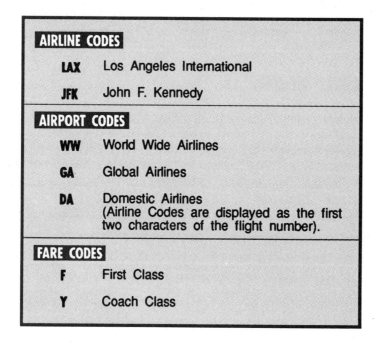

AIRLINE CODES

| LAX | Los Angeles International |
| JFK | John F. Kennedy |

AIRPORT CODES

WW	World Wide Airlines
GA	Global Airlines
DA	Domestic Airlines (Airline Codes are displayed as the first two characters of the flight number).

FARE CODES

| F | First Class |
| Y | Coach Class |

Step 2: From the Main Menu, type the number 1 after the prompt "ENTER SELECTION:" and press the Enter key.

Step 3: Enter the necessary information at the top of the Available Flights screen. For the From: code, enter LAX, the airport code for Los Angeles International airport. For the To: code, enter JFK, the airport code for John F. Kennedy airport. For the Date:, enter 10/6/92.

Question 1: What is the flight number of the earliest flight listed? _____

Question 2: Which flight numbers satisfy Mrs. Johnson's request for a flight between 9:00 A.M. and 12:00 noon? Record the flight number and departure times. _____

Step 4: Return to the Main Menu by pressing Enter.

Airline Reservations (continued)

ASSIGNMENT 3: CHECKING AIR FARES

Mrs. Johnson is happy to know that more than one flight satisfies her request. She now wants to know which of the flights offers the least expensive first class air fare.

Step 1: From the Main Menu, type the number 2 after the prompt "ENTER SELECTION:" and press the Enter key.

Step 2: Enter the necessary information at the top of the Fare Information screen. For the From: code, enter LAX. For the To: code, enter JFK. For the Date:, enter 10/6/92.

Question 1: Which airline has the lowest first class fare? Does this airline have a flight leaving

between 9:00 A.M. and 12:00 noon? _____

Question 2: What is the first class fare for this flight?

_____

Step 3: Return to the Main Menu by pressing Enter.

ASSIGNMENT 4: FLIGHT RESERVATIONS

Mrs. Johnson says that the first class air fare is acceptable and she is ready to make a flight reservation.

Step 1: From the Main Menu, type the number 3 after the prompt "ENTER SELECTION:" and press the Enter key.

Step 2: Enter Mrs. Johnson's name at the top of the Flight Reservation screen. Enter the last name first, followed by a comma, followed by the first letter of Mrs. Johnson's first name and a period. Enter the name as: Johnson, B.. At the prompt for Title, enter Mrs..

Step 3: Enter the Departure Date as 10/6/92.

Step 4: At the prompt for Flight #, enter the number of the flight chosen by Mrs. Johnson.

Step 5: At the prompt for Fare Code, type F to indicate that Mrs. Johnson wants a first class ticket. The first class fare will then display on the screen.

Step 6: Type C to confirm the reservation. Use the information on the screen to answer the following questions.

Question 1: On which flight is Mrs. Johnson booked? _____

Question 2: What time is the flight scheduled to arrive in New York? _____

Question 3: What is Mrs. Johnson's reservation number? _____

Step 7: Return to the Main Menu by pressing Enter.

ASSIGNMENT 5: SEAT ASSIGNMENTS

Mrs. Johnson wants you to assign her seat now to save her time when she checks in at the airport. She says that she would prefer an aisle seat anywhere in first class except the first row. Aisle seats are B or C in first class and C or D in coach class.

Step 1: From the Main Menu, type the number 4 after the words "ENTER SELECTION:" and press the Enter key.

Step 2: Enter Mrs. Johnson's reservation number.

Question 1: Based on Mrs. Johnson's seat preference, what seats are available? _____

Step 3: Choose a seat for Mrs. Johnson. Available seats are shown as a number and letter combination that indicates the row and seat within the row. Seats that are already selected or are not available are shown as a double asterisk (**).

Airline Reservations (continued)

ASSIGNMENT 6: OPEN RESERVATIONS INQUIRY

Mr. Fred Peterson calls and says that he needs to know the arrival time of his business flight scheduled for the middle of October. He asks if you can provide the information.

Step 1: From the Main Menu, type the number 5 after the prompt "ENTER SELECTION:" and press the Enter key.

Step 2: Enter Mr. Peterson's name at the top of the Open Reservations Inquiry screen. Enter his last name, followed by a comma, followed by the first letter of his first name and a period. Enter the name as: `Peterson, F..`

Question 1: What is the reservation number of Mr. Peterson's flight? _____

Question 2: What is the date and flight number of Mr. Peterson's flight?

_____

Step 3: Return to the Main Menu by pressing Enter.

ASSIGNMENT 7: ENTERING RESERVATIONS

During the day, the following passengers call to make flight reservations and seat assignments for flights from Los Angeles (LAX) to New York (JFK) on October 6. Use the following information to make the necessary entries. Record the reservation number.

NAME	FLIGHT	CLASS	SEAT PREFERENCE	RES #
Ms. B. Chang	GA182	Y	None	?
Dr. S. Heintz	GA182	F	Next to wife in 2B	?
Mr. T. Walker	DA356	F	Front row, window	?
Ms. G. Peacock	GA120	F	None	?
Mrs. F. Ruiz	?	?	Next to J. Ruiz*	?

* During the reservation entry for Mrs. F. Ruiz, you will be instructed to make an Open Reservations Inquiry for J. Ruiz. Copy the flight, fare code, and seat assignment information for J. Ruiz and use this information to complete the reservation for F. Ruiz.

ASSIGNMENT 8: END THE PROJECT

When you are finished with all the assignments, exit the program.

Step 1: From the Main Menu, type the number 6 after the prompt "ENTER SELECTION:" and press the Enter key.

Airline Reservations (continued)

ERROR MESSAGES

◆   The following table contains the error messages that you might encounter when you make incorrect entries. The cause and the corrective action is given for each error.

ERROR MESSAGE	CAUSE	CORRECTIVE ACTION
INVALID MENU SELECTION. ENTER 1 TO 6.	A menu selection other than a number from 1 to 6 was entered.	Enter a selection from 1 to 6.
INVALID AIRPORT CODE. PLEASE REENTER.	An incorrect airport code was entered. For this project, only two airport codes are valid: LAX for the From airport code and JFK for the To airport code.	Enter LAX for a From airport code prompt or JFK for a To airport code prompt.
INVALID DATE. PLEASE REENTER.	An invalid date was entered. For this project, the only valid date is October 6, 1992. This date should be entered as 10/6/92.	Enter 10/6/92 at the date prompt.
INVALID NAME. PLEASE REENTER.	An invalid name was entered. For this project step, the only valid name is (passenger name).	Enter (passenger name).
INVALID TITLE. PLEASE REENTER.	An invalid title was entered. For this project step, the only valid title is (title).	Enter (title).
INVALID FLIGHT NUMBER. PLEASE REENTER.	The flight number entered does not exist or no flight number was entered.	Enter one of the valid flight numbers shown on the Available Flights screen.
FARE CODE MUST BE F. PLEASE REENTER.	A fare code other than F was entered. For this project step, F (for first class) is the only valid fare code.	Enter the fare code as F.
FARE CODE MUST BE Y. PLEASE REENTER.	A fare code other than Y was entered. For this project step, Y (for coach class) is the only valid fare code.	Enter the fare code as Y.
RESERVATION NUMBER NOT ON FILE. PLEASE REENTER.	The reservation number entered is not on file. Reservation numbers are created during the Flight Reservation step.	Check the reservation number and reenter. To obtain the reservation number for a specific passenger, return to the Main Menu and run the Open Reservations Inquiry.
INVALID SEAT SELECTION. PLEASE REENTER.	The seat does not exist, is already assigned, or does not match the fare code.	Check the seating chart for available seats and reenter a seat number.
NO RESERVATION ON FILE. PLEASE REENTER.	The passenger name entered does not match any existing flight reservation records.	Reenter the passenger name.
INVALID RESPONSE. PLEASE REENTER.	The valid responses are R, C, and Q.	Type R, C, or Q.

COMPUTER LAB SOFTWARE PROJECTS
Electronic Mail

PROJECT OBJECTIVES

◆ Review electronic mail (email) messages
◆ Create and send email messages
◆ Perform administrative functions associated with an email user account

PROJECT DESCRIPTION

◆ This project consists of nine assignments requiring the use of a computer and associated software. The user enters an account name and password to gain access to an electronic mail (email) system. The student assignments allow the user to review email messages that have been sent to him or her by others, send email messages, and perform administrative tasks associated with an email account, such as adding user names and maintaining mail distribution lists. The screen below illustrates the email login screen.

```
            E L E C T R O N I C   M A I L
                      LOGIN
--------------------------------------------------
ENTER USER ACCOUNT NAME:




     Enter the name Chris at the prompt that says ENTER USER ACCOUNT NAME.
```

Electronic Mail (continued)

ASSIGNMENT 1: PROGRAM EXECUTION

Load the program for this project into main memory and execute the program.

Step 1: The method for loading and executing the program for this project will vary between different computers. Obtain the necessary instructions from your instructor or the computer center.

Step 2: Load and execute the program for this project.

Step 3: A message about the use of this computer lab software project will appear on the screen. Read the message and press the Spacebar.

Step 4: Sometimes you will be able to enter any one of several responses to a program prompt. Other times, only one response will be correct. If you make an incorrect entry, an error message will appear on the screen. To clear the error message press the Spacebar. You can then reenter the data. A table at the end of this project contains the error messages, the cause of the errors, and the corrective action to be taken. Review the table now before beginning this project. Anytime an error message is displayed, you can exit the software project by typing the letter Q (for quit).

ASSIGNMENT 2: LOGIN

Use an account name and password to log on to an electronic mail account.

Step 1: At the prompt "ENTER USER ACCOUNT NAME", enter the name Chris.

Step 2: When the prompt "ENTER PASSWORD:" appears on the screen, enter the password MYCODE and press the Enter key. (Enter the password using only capital letters. For security reasons, most passwords do not appear on the screen as they are entered.) If the password is correctly entered, the system will display the Main Menu.

ASSIGNMENT 3: VIEW MAIL

Review the mail messages on your account.

Step 1: From the Main Menu, type the number 1 after the prompt "ENTER SELECTION:" and press the Enter key.

Step 2: Review the Mail List screen. It is similar to screens found in many electronic mail packages available today. The screen shows # (message number), Type, From (who sent the message), Subject, and the Date and Time the message was sent. In this project, Type indicates if the message is new, meaning that it has not yet been read. A blank in the Type column indicates that you have previously read the message but have not yet deleted the message. Some electronic mail packages have several other type codes such as priority (1,2,3, and so on.), carbon copy, blind copy, and encrypted. For this project the Type code will either be new or blank.

Question 1: How many messages have previously been read but not yet deleted?

_____

Question 2: What is the subject of the message from Michael? _____

Question 3: What was the date and time of the last message received? _____

Step 3: Review the new mail message from Michael. To view this message, type the number 4 and press Enter.

Question 4: How much higher were this year's first quarter sales compared to last year? _____

Electronic Mail (Assignment 3 – continued)

Step 4: Review the other mail messages and answer the following questions.

Question 5: Regarding the message from Carmen; how much was the 9–15 car rental? _____

Question 6: Regarding the message from Dieter; how many copies of the marketing brochure are needed for the convention? _____

Question 7: Regarding the message from Harriette; how much is Whiz Bang Products going to be lowering their prices? _____

Question 8: Regarding the message from Frank; where is the convention next month?

_____

Step 5: After answering the last question, return to the Mail List screen by pressing the Enter key.

ASSIGNMENT 4: REPLY TO A MESSAGE

Most electronic mail systems allow you to add comments to a message you have received and return the message with your comments to the original sender.

Step 1: From the Mail List screen, choose the message from Dieter by typing the number 2 and pressing the Enter key.

Step 2: Indicate that you want to reply by typing the letter R after the prompt "ENTER SELECTION:" and press Enter.

Step 3: Enter the following reply to the original mail message. Enter the reply exactly as it is shown below:

```
I think we should order 4,000 brochures.
This quantity should be enough for the
convention and the direct mail program
that we will start in two months.
```

Step 4: To send your reply to the original sender of the message, type the letter S after the prompt "ENTER SELECTION:" and press Enter. To reenter your reply, type the letter R.

Step 5: Return to the Mail List screen by pressing Enter.

ASSIGNMENT 5: FORWARD A MESSAGE

Most electronic mail systems allow you to pass on a message you have received to one or more other system users.

Step 1: From the Mail List screen, choose the message from Michael by typing the number 4 and pressing the Enter key.

Step 2: Indicate that you want to Forward the message by typing the letter F after the prompt "ENTER SELECTION:" and pressing Enter. (The *Sales entry on the User Names list is a mail distribution list that will be explained in Assignment 8 of this project.)

Question 1: How many users are listed under USER NAMES on the Deliver Mail screen? _____

Step 3: Forward the message to the following users: Doug and José. For each of these users, enter his user number and press Enter. After you select each user, his name is added to the Deliver To list.

Step 4: After you have selected the users to receive the message, send the message by typing the letter S.

Step 5: Return to the Main Menu by pressing Enter.

Electronic Mail (continued)

ASSIGNMENT 6: CREATE A MAIL MESSAGE

Enter a message and send it to two users.

Step 1: From the Main Menu, type the number 2 after the prompt "ENTER SELECTION:" and press Enter.

Step 2: At the "Subject" prompt, enter Monthly sales projections.

Step 3: At the "From" prompt, enter Chris.

Step 4: At the "Message" prompt, enter the following exactly as shown:

```
For planning purposes it is very impor-
tant to turn in your sales projections
no later than the 5th of the month. If
you can't transmit your report, please
call Harriette.
```

Step 5: To send your message, type the letter S after the prompt "ENTER SELECTION:" and press Enter. To reenter your message, type the letter R.

Step 6: Send the message to the following users: Carmen and Doug. For each of these users, enter his or her user number and press Enter. After you select each user, his or her name is added to the Deliver To list.

Step 7: After you have selected the users to receive the message, send the message by typing the letter S.

Step 8: Return to the Main Menu by pressing Enter.

ASSIGNMENT 7: ADD A NAME TO THE MAIL ADDRESS LIST

All electronic mail systems provide for the creation and maintenance of a list of users to whom mail can be sent. This list can be called the Address List, Address Book, or Receiver List. The maintenance of this list is often under the control of the system administrator. In this project, the user can only add names to the address list.

Step 1: From the Main Menu, type the number 3 and press Enter.

Step 2: At the "USER NAME" prompt, enter Jeff and press Enter.

Step 3: To add the user, type the letter A after the prompt "ENTER SELECTION:" and press Enter. To reenter the user name, type the letter R.

Step 4: After the user is added, return to the Main Menu by pressing Enter.

ASSIGNMENT 8: MAINTAIN A MAIL DISTRIBUTION LIST

A mail distribution list is a group of user names that can be conveniently referred to by a single name. For example, distribution lists are often used to send mail to all the members of one department or members of a committee.

Step 1: From the Main Menu, type the number 4 after the prompt "ENTER SELECTION:" and press Enter.

Step 2: At the "DISTRIBUTION LIST NAME" prompt, enter *Sales.

Question 1: Who are the current members of the *Sales distribution list?

_____

Step 3: At the "NEW MEMBERS" prompt, enter the name Dieter and press Enter.

Step 4: Return to the Main Menu by pressing Enter.

ASSIGNMENT 9: END THE PROJECT

When you are finished with all the assignments, exit the program.

Step 1: From the Main Menu, type the number 5 after the prompt "ENTER SELECTION:" and press the Enter key.

Electronic Mail (continued)

ERROR MESSAGES

◆   The following table contains the error messages that you might encounter when you make incorrect entries. The cause and the corrective action is given for each error.

ERROR MESSAGE	CAUSE	CORRECTIVE ACTION
AN INCORRECT ACCOUNT NAME WAS ENTERED. PLEASE REENTER.	An account name other than Chris was entered.	Enter the account name as `Chris`.
INVALID PASSWORD. PLEASE REENTER.	An incorrect password was entered. For this project, the only valid password is MYCODE.	Enter the password as `MYCODE`. Enter only capital letters.
INVALID MENU SELECTION.	An entry other the numbers listed on the menu was entered.	Enter a selection from the numbers listed on the menu.
An incorrect message was entered. Enter the following line.	An incorrect entry was made while entering the reply during assignment 4, REPLY TO MESSAGE.	Enter each of the reply message lines exactly as shown below: `I think we should order 4,000 brochures. This quantity should be enough for the convention and the direct mail program that we will start in two months.`
An incorrect message was entered. Enter the following line.	An incorrect entry was made while entering the message during assignment 6, CREATE A MAIL MESSAGE.	Enter each of the message lines exactly as shown below: `For planning purposes it is very impor- tant to turn in your sales projections no later than the 5th of the month. If you can't transmit your report, please call Harriette.`

COMPUTER LAB SOFTWARE PROJECTS

Desktop Publishing

PROJECT OBJECTIVES

◆ Define newsletter layout
◆ Change text style
◆ Import a graphic
◆ Import a table
◆ Import text

PROJECT DESCRIPTION

◆ This project consists of seven assignments requiring the use of a computer and associated software that simulate a desktop publishing system. You can use desktop publishing software to design and produce professional looking documents that combine text and graphics. In this project, you will develop a customer newsletter for a computer store. The newsletter has already been started. You will use the Import command to merge previously created text, a graphic, and a table into the newsletter. You make changes to the newsletter using a command menu that appears on the screen. To make the menu appear, press the Slash key (/). You can then make menu selections by typing the letter that is highlighted in the menu choices. Because the use of a complete desktop publishing system was not feasible, the commands listed on the menu work only with the situation that is discussed in the student assignment. For example, the Text Style command used in student assignment 3 works only with the first line of the newsletter headline. The initial layout of the newsletter is shown in the figure to the right.

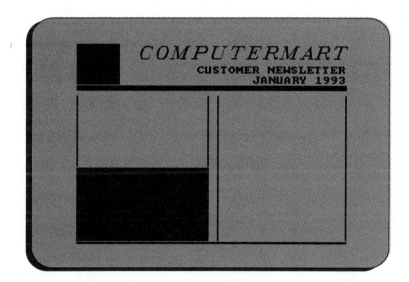

Desktop Publishing (continued)

ASSIGNMENT 1: PROGRAM EXECUTION

Load the program for this project into main memory and execute the program.

Step 1: The method for loading and executing the program for this project will vary between different computers. Obtain the necessary instructions from your instructor or the computer center.

Step 2: Load and execute the program for this project.

Step 3: A message about the use of this computer lab software project will appear on the screen. Read the message and press the Spacebar.

Step 4: Sometimes you will be able to enter any one of several responses to a program prompt. Other times, only one response will be correct. If you make an incorrect entry, an error message will appear on the screen or the system will beep. To clear the error message, press the Spacebar. Check the workbook instructions and reenter the data or menu choice. A table at the end of this project contains the error message, the cause of the error, and the corrective action to be taken. Review the table now before beginning this project.

ASSIGNMENT 2: DEFINE NEWSLETTER LAYOUT

After reviewing the existing newsletter layout, you decide to make some changes. The first change you make is to increase the number of columns from two to three.

Step 1: Display the menu by pressing the Slash key.

Step 2: Choose Layout by typing the letter L.

Step 3: Use the information displayed to answer the following questions.

Question 1: What is the Orientation? _____

Question 2: What spacing is specified for the Bottom margin? _____

Question 3: What spacing is specified for the Right margin? _____

Step 4: Choose # of Columns by typing 4.

Step 5: Type 3 and press Enter to specify three columns. The screen will redisplay with a three-column layout.

ASSIGNMENT 3: CHANGE TEXT STYLE

The next layout change you want to make is to change the style of the company name in the heading from italics to normal.

Step 1: Use the arrow keys to place the cursor at the beginning of the word COMPUTERMART in the heading. Press the Left Arrow key twice and the Up Arrow key twice.

Step 2: Press the Right Arrow key 12 times to highlight the word COMPUTERMART.

Step 3: Display the menu by pressing the Slash key.

Step 4: Choose Text by typing the letter T.

Step 5: Choose Style by typing the letter T.

Step 6: Choose Normal by typing the letter N. The screen will redisplay and the word COMPUTERMART will have changed from italics to normal-style text.

ASSIGNMENT 4: IMPORT GRAPHIC

Merge a graphic image of a personal computer into the heading of the newsletter.

Step 1: Use the arrow keys to place the cursor in the box in the upper left corner of the newsletter. Press the Left Arrow key three times and the Up Arrow key once.

Step 2: Display the menu by pressing the Slash key.

Step 3: Choose Import by typing the letter I.

Step 4: Choose Graphic and the pcimage file by typing the letter G. A graphic image of a personal computer will be placed in the upper left hand corner of the newsletter.

Desktop Publishing (continued)

ASSIGNMENT 5: IMPORT TABLE

Each month's newsletter is designed to contain a table showing selected products on sale. This month, printers will be on sale. The table with the printer sale information has already been created. Use the Import command to merge the table into the newsletter.

Step 1: Use the arrow keys to place the cursor in the box in the lower left corner of the newsletter. Press the Down Arrow key twice and the Left Arrow key twice.

Step 2: Display the menu by pressing the Slash key.

Step 3: Choose Import by typing the letter I.

Step 4: Choose Table and the prntrbl file by typing the letter A. The screen will redisplay with the printer sale information.

Step 5: Use the information in the table to answer the following questions.

Question 1: What is the speed of the LZR 2000 printer? _____

Question 2: What is the list price of the LZR 1000 printer? _____

Question 3: What is the sale price of the DM 500 printer? _____

Question 4: What type of printer is the DM 400? _____

Question 5: What is the speed of the DM 400 printer? _____

Question 6: What is the list price of the DM 300 printer? _____

ASSIGNMENT 6: IMPORT TEXT

Although most desktop publishing systems have some form of word processing capability, many users create longer text items with a separate word processor and then merge the text into their desktop publishing document. In this project, the text has been created separately and will be merged, or imported, into the newsletter.

Step 1: Use the arrow keys to place the cursor at the top of the leftmost newsletter column. The cursor should be below the heavy black line that runs across all three columns. Press the Left Arrow key twice and the Up Arrow key once.

Step 2: Display the menu by pressing the Slash key.

Step 3: Choose Import by typing the letter I.

Step 4: Choose Text and the jannews file by typing the letter T. The screen will redisplay and columns will be filled with text.

Step 5: Use the information in the text to answer the following questions.

Question 1: On what date will training classes begin? _____

Question 2: How long will each training class last? _____

Question 3: How much does each training class cost? _____

Question 4: What is the maximum number of students that can attend each training class? _____

Question 5: What is the size range of disk drives currently sold by Computermart?

_____

ASSIGNMENT 7: END THE PROJECT

When you are finished with all the assignments, exit the program.

Step 1: Display the menu by pressing the Slash key.

Step 2: Choose exit by typing the letter E.

Desktop Publishing (continued)

ERROR MESSAGE

◆ The following table contains the error message that you might encounter when you make incorrect entries. The cause and the corrective action is given for the error.

ERROR MESSAGE	CAUSE	CORRECTIVE ACTION
INVALID SELECTION.	The menu selection chosen is not applicable to this student assignment. For this project, menu selections are limited to specific student assignments and specific areas of the newsletter.	Check your workbook instructions for the correct menu selection for this student assignment.

Presentation Graphics

PROJECT OBJECTIVES

◆ Modify text
◆ Change the style used for text
◆ Rearrange the order in which slides are presented

◆ This project consists of seven assignments requiring the use of a computer and associated software that simulate a presentation graphics system. Presentation graphics software creates and organizes documents that can be used in presentations as slides, overhead transparencies, and handouts. In this project, an eight-slide presentation already exists. In the student assignments you will make changes to several slides and rearrange the order of the slides. You make the changes to the slides using a menu that appears on the screen with the slide. To make the menu appear, press the Slash key (/). You can then make menu selections by typing the letter that is highlighted in the menu choices. Because the use of a complete presentation graphics system was not feasible, the commands listed on the menu only work with the slide or portion of the slide that is discussed in the student assignment. For example, the Change Text command used in student assignment 2 works only on a specific line of slide 2. Slide 1 of the existing presentation is shown in the figure to the right.

LAB29

Presentation Graphics (continued)

ASSIGNMENT 1: PROGRAM EXECUTION

Load the program for this project into main memory and execute the program.

Step 1: The method for loading and executing the program for this project will vary between different computers. Obtain the necessary instructions from your instructor or the computer center.

Step 2: Load and execute the program for this project.

Step 3: A message about the use of this computer lab software project will appear on the screen. Read the message and press the Spacebar.

Step 4: Sometimes you will be able to enter any one of several responses to a program prompt. Other times, only one response will be correct. In most cases if you make an incorrect entry, you will hear a beep and the system will not accept the incorrect entry. In some cases an INVALID ENTRY error message will appear. You can clear this message by pressing the Spacebar. Check the workbook instructions and reenter the data or menu choice.

ASSIGNMENT 2: CHANGE TEXT

Change a portion of the text on one of the existing slides.

Step 1: Display the menu by pressing the Slash key.

Step 2: Choose View Slides. Type the letter V for View Slides. View Slides options are N for the next slide, E to exit the software project, or a specific number to go directly to a slide.

Step 3: Type either N for next or 2 for slide 2 and press Enter.

Step 4: Use the cursor control keys to place the cursor on the word at in the first line of major reasons. Press the Right Arrow key twice and then the Up Arrow key twice.

Step 5: Display the menu by pressing the Slash key.

Step 6: Choose Change Text by typing the letter T.

Step 7: Delete the word at by pressing Delete twice.

Step 8: Enter the word nearing.

Question 1: What are the three major reasons for building a new factory?

1. _____

2. _____

3. _____

ASSIGNMENT 3: CHANGE STYLE

Change the style of a portion of slide text.

Step 1: While still on slide 2, move the cursor to the letter m in the word major. Press the Left Arrow key five times and the Up Arrow key once.

Step 2: Press the Right Arrow key 13 times until the words major reasons are highlighted.

Step 3: Display the menu by pressing the Slash key.

Step 4: Choose Change Style by typing the letter S.

Step 5: Choose Italics on the Change Style submenu by typing the letter I.

ASSIGNMENT 4: CHANGE GRAPH TYPE

Change a bar graph to a line graph.

Step 1: Display the menu by pressing the Slash key.

Step 2: Choose the View Slide command by typing the letter V.

Step 3: Advance to the next slide by typing the letter N and pressing the Enter key.

Step 4: Display the menu by pressing the Slash key.

Step 5: Choose the Change Graph Type command by typing the letter G.

Presentation Graphics (Assignment 4 – continued)

Step 6: On the Change Graph Type submenu, select Line by typing the letter L. The bar chart should change to a line graph.

Step 7: Based on the information displayed on the line graph, answer the following questions.

Question 1: What are the projected unit sales for Widgets in 1994? _____

Question 2: What are the projected unit sales for DoDads in 1995? _____

Question 3: What are the projected unit sales for Gizmos in 1996? _____

ASSIGNMENT 5: CHANGE SLIDE ORDER

Change the order in which the slides will be presented.

Step 1: Display the menu by pressing the Slash key.

Step 2: Choose the View Slides command by typing the letter V.

Step 3: At the View Slides prompt, type 6 and press Enter to advance to slide 6.

Step 4: Display the menu by pressing the Slash key.

Step 5: Choose Change Slide Order by typing the letter O.

Step 6: At the prompt for new slide position, type 7 and press Enter. Slides will be switched and the old slide 7 will now be displayed as slide 6.

Step 7: Based on the information displayed on slide 6, answer the following questions.

Question 1: What is the estimated budget for Land? _____

Question 2: What is the estimated budget for Materials? _____

Question 3: What is the total estimated budget? _____

ASSIGNMENT 6: VIEW SLIDES

Use the View Slides command to answer questions about information on specific slides.

Question 1: On slide 4, Production Capacity, what is the actual production of Gizmos? _____

Question 2: On slide 4, Production Capacity, what is the percent capacity for Widgets? _____

Question 3: On slide 5, Available Capacity, what is the available capacity percentage? _____

Question 4: On slide 7, Recommended Action Plan, what are the first two recommendations?

1. _____

2. _____

Question 5: On slide 8, what is the estimate of how long it will take to build a new factory?

_____

ASSIGNMENT 7: END THE PROJECT

When you are finished with all the assignments, exit the program.

Step 1: Display the menu by pressing the Slash key.

Step 2: From the menu, choose Exit by typing the letter E.

PART III

Answers to Selected Projects

Answers to Selected Projects

CHAPTER 1: An Overview of Computer Concepts

ANSWERS TO CLASSNOTES (1.9)

What Is a Computer? (1.9)

1. data

What Does a Computer Do? (1.9)

1. input, process, output, storage
2. information processing cycle
3. words, numbers, pictures
4. letters, forecasts, presentations
5. Information processing, electronic data processing
6. storage
7. end user
8. storage
9. output
10. processor
11. input

Why Is a Computer So Powerful? (1.10)

1. input, process, output, storage
2. quickly, accurately, reliably

How Does a Computer Know What to Do? (1.10)

1. instructions
2. a computer program, program instructions software

The Information Processing Cycle (1.10)

1. Input
2. Process
3. Output
4. Storage

What Are the Components of a Computer? (1.10)

1. input devices, processor unit, output devices, auxiliary storage units
2. keyboard
3. addition, subtraction, multiplication, division
4. $<$ (less than), $>$ (greater than), $=$ (equals)
5. data, program instructions
6. printer, computer screen
7. instructions, data
8. peripheral devices

Categories of Computers (1.11)

1. microcomputer, minicomputer, mainframe computer, supercomputer
2. speed, size, price, processing capabilities
3. • $<$ $10,000
   • $15,000 to hundreds of thousands of dollars
   • hundreds of thousands to several million dollars
   • millions of dollars

Computer Software (1.12)

1. input, arithmetic, logical, output
2. system application
3. word processing, electronic spreadsheet, graphics, database

A Typical Business Application (1.12)

1. Load
2. data
3. process
4. Output
5. Save

What Are the Elements of an Information System? (1.12)

1. equipment, software, data, personnel, users, procedures

A Tour of an Information Systems Department (1.12)

1. multiuser computer
2. information systems, data processing, computer
3. terminal, keyboard, mouse
4. processor, CPU
5. printer, monitor
6. magnetic disk, magnetic tape
7. fixed, removable
8. Computer operators
9. data library
10. data librarian
11. data entry, systems analyst, computer programmer, database administrator, systems manager, programming manager, operations manager
12. Information Systems Department Manager
13. Systems Manager
14. Programming Manager
15. Operations Manager

The Evolution of the Computer Industry (1.14)

1. UNIVAC I
2. IBM
3. Dr. Hopper
4. FORTRAN
5. Transistors
6. IBM 360
7. Dr. Kemeny: BASIC
8. DEC Minicomputer
9. IBM: Software unbundled
10. Dr. Hoff: Microprocessor
11. Jobs and Wozniak: Apple
12. VisiCalc
13. Microsoft: MS-DOS

14. IBM PC
15. Kapor: Lotus 1-2-3
16. Intel 80386
17. Intel 80486
18. Microsoft Windows 3.0

ANSWERS TO SELF-TEST (1.15)

Matching

1. 6   5. 5
2. 3   6. 9
3. 1   7. 4
4. 7   8. 2

Additional Answers

1. data
2. storage
3. Information
4. T
5. T
6. F
7. computer programs
8. information
9. T
10. input device
11. processor
12. main memory
13. output device
14. T
15. supercomputers
16. T
17. microcomputers
18. T
19. applications software
20. six
21. Users
22. systems analyst
23. database administrator
24. F

CHAPTER 2: Microcomputer Applications: User Tools

ANSWERS TO CLASSNOTES (2.6)

An Introduction to General Microcomputer Applications (2.6)

1. broad
2. user friendly
3. commands
4. function keys, menus, screen prompts, icons
5. icons
6. function keys
7. screen prompts

Word Processing Software: A Document Productivity Tool (2.7)

1. spell checking, thesaurus, basic editing, faster, more accurate, grammar checkers
2. spell checking, thesaurus, basic editing
3. Spelling checkers
4. Thesaurus software
5. Grammar checkers
6. delete, insert, replace

7. copy
8. move
9. boldfacing, underlining, changing fonts
10. formatting
11. insert/move
12. delete
13. screen control
14. printing

Desktop Publishing Software: A Document Presentation Tool (2.8)

1. graphics, text
2. Clip art
3. WYSIWYG

Electronic Spreadsheet Software: A Number Productivity Tool (2.8)

1. faster, more accurate, easier to use, more efficient
2. Rows, columns, cells
3. row
4. column
5. cell
6. labels, values, formulas
7. recalculation
8. What-if
9. worksheet
10. range
11. copy
12. move
13. file
14. print

Database Software: A Data Management Tool (2.9)

1. retrieve data, manipulate data, update data
2. file
3. record
4. field
5. database
6. operations
7. output
8. editing
9. arithmetic

Graphics Software: A Data Presentation Tool (2.10)

1. pie chart
2. bar chart
3. line graph
4. Analytical
5. Presentation graphics

Data Communications Software: A Connectivity Tool (2.10)

1. data
2. data communications, equipment, telephone line

Integrated Software: A Combination Productivity Tool (2.10)

1. combine, easy-to-use
2. windows

Other Popular Microcomputer Applications (2.11)

1. personal information
2. phone dialers, electronic mail
3. analyze, project
4. data
5. analyzes, reorganizes

Guidelines for Purchasing Microcomputer Applications Software (2.11)

1. Read software product reviews.
2. Verify that the software performs the task you desire.
3. Verify that the software will run on your computer.
4. Make sure that the software is adequately documented.
5. Purchase software from a reputable software developer or software publisher.
6. Obtain the best value, but keep in mind that value might not mean the lowest price.

Learning Aids and Support Tools for Application Users (2.11)

1. tutorial
2. Online help
3. Trade books
4. Keyboard templates

ANSWERS TO SELF-TEST (2.12)

Matching

1. 5	5. 2
2. 6	6. 4
3. 8	7. 1
4. 7	8. 3

Additional Answers

1. User interfaces
2. F
3. T
4. graphics
5. document preparation
6. T
7. grammar checker
8. F
9. manage numeric data
10. formulas
11. what-if
12. multiple
13. record
14. Analytical
15. Data communications
16. windows
17. all of the above
18. documentation
19. Online help
20. document template

CHAPTER 3: Input to the Computer

ANSWERS TO CLASSNOTES (3.8)

Overview of the Information Processing Cycle (3.8)

1. input
2. process
3. output
4. storage
5. keyboard
6. printer, computer screen
7. fixed disk, diskette

What Is Input? (3.8)

1. programs, commands, user responses, data
2. main memory
3. keyboard, auxiliary storage
4. command
5. keyboard
6. user response
7. main memory

How Is Data Organized? (3.9)

1. alphabetic, numeric, special
2. alphabetic, numeric, alphanumeric
3. field, record, file
4. any single data item could be circled
5. any row could be checked

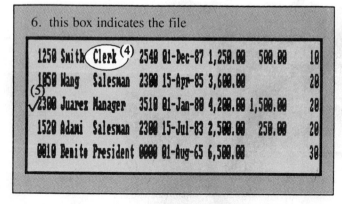

6. this box indicates the file

7. key field
8. database

The Keyboard (3.9)

1. terminal, personal computer
2. Numeric keys
3. Special characters
4. numeric keypad
5. Cursor control keys, arrow keys
6. Insert key, Delete key
7. function keys

Terminals (3.10)

1. dumb, intelligent, special-purpose
2. independent
3. processing, programmable, smart
4. uploading
5. point-of-scale

Other Input Devices (3.11)

1. mouse
2. ease of use
3. space, speed
4. rotate
5. desk space
6. touch screens
7. natural, speed
8. resolution arm fatigue
9. light pen
10. digitizer
11. graphics tablet
12. hand-printed, information
13. Voice
14. no keying

Input Devices Designed for Specific Purposes (3.12)

1. Optical character readers
2. Optical mark readers
3. laser scanner

4. page scanner
5. Image processing
6. MICR readers
7. Data collection devices

User Interfaces (3.12)

1. hardware, software, communicate
2. respond to
3. control
4. information
5. message, information, instructions
6. Data editing
7. menu title
8. menu selection
9. menu prompt
10. sequential number
11. alphabetic
12. cursor positioning
13. reverse video
14. options
15. special commands
16. training
17. guided
18. slow, restrictive

Graphic User Interface (3.13)

1. icons
2. mouse

Features of a User Interface (3.14)

1. e, b, c, d, a

Data Entry (3.14)

1. data

Data Entry for Interactive and Batch Processing (3.14)

1. output
2. online data entry
3. production data entry
4. offline
5. prompt
6. input field
7. protected fields

Data Entry Procedures (3.15)

1. Who originates the date?
2. Where will the data be entered?
3. How soon will the data be entered?
4. How will the data be entered?
5. How much data will be entered?
6. How will data errors be identified and corrected?
7. How will data be controlled?
8. How many people are needed?

Ergonomics (3.15)

1. d, c, e, b, a

ANSWERS TO SELF-TEST (3.16)

Matching

1. 6	3. 2	5. 1	7. 4
2. 7	4. 8	6. 9	8. 3

Additional Answers

1. input
2. storage
3. software
4. main memory
5. user
6. computer program
7. alphanumeric
8. record
9. file
10. key
11. random
12. database
13. cursor
14. arrow keys
15. Function keys
16. T
17. programmable
18. point-of-sale
19. F
20. resolution
21. graphic
22. digital
23. banking
24. printed
25. optical character reader
26. test scoring
27. grocery stores
28. page scanners
29. image processing systems
30. Data collection
31. user interface
32. software
33. prompts
34. Menus
35. menu selection alternatives
36. graphic image
37. System responses
38. Response time
39. password
40. data
41. T
42. reverse video
43. distributed data entry
44. screen height
45. Transaction volume
46. transcription

CHAPTER 4: The Processor Unit

ANSWERS TO CLASSNOTES (4.7)

What Is the Processor Unit? (4.7)

1. central processing unit
2. main memory
3. central processing unit
4. control unit, arithmetic/logic unit
5. fetch instruction
6. decode instruction
7. execute instruction
8. store result
9. add/subtract
10. multiply/divide
11. logical operators
12. code
13. working
14. I/O
15. address
16. byte
17. 1024
18. megabyte, gigabyte

How Programs and Data Are Represented in Memory (4.8)

1. numeric, special
2. byte
3. | J | O | H | N | | D | O | E | |
4. | $ | 1 | 2 | 3 | . | 6 | 9 | | |
5. 8
6. bits
7. on, off
8. binary
9. ASCII
10. characters
11. 2

Parity (4.9)

1. right
2. Odd
3. Even
4. error
5. even
6. transmission

Number Systems (4.10)

1. 10
2. 2
3. 16

4.

NUMBER SYSTEM	BASE	SYMBOLS USED
DECIMAL	10	0, 1, 2, 3, 4, 5, 6, 7, 8, 9
BINARY	2	0, 1
HEXADECIMAL	16	0, 1, 2, 3, 4, 5, 6, 7, 8, 9 A, B, C, D, E, F

5. zero
6. third
7. symbols
8. base
9. positional
10. zero
11. 2^2, or 4
12. 22
13. first
14. 76395
15. 4
16. 0101, 1010, C, B
17. AC

How the Processor Unit Executes Programs and Manipulates Data (4.11)

1. Machine language
2. operation code
3. value length
4. value 2 address
5. fetch instruction, decode instruction, execute instruction, store result
6. instruction
7. execution

Processor Speeds (4.11)

1. system clock
2. megahertz
3. MIPS
4. bus
5. width
6.

Buses:			
	TRANSFER SIZE (IN BITS)		
BUS WIDTH	**8**	**16**	**32**
8	BO_1	2	4
16	1	1	2
32	1	1	1
	NUMBER OF TRANSFERS		

7. one
8. two
9. four
10. 640
11. one
12. sixteen
13. word size

Architecture of Processor Units (4.12)

1. integrated circuit
2. motherboard
3. multiple
4. numeric, graphics, or special function
5. parallel
6. RISC

Types of Memory (4.12)

1. Vacuum tubes
2. core, semiconductor
3. RAM
4. ROM
5. PROM
6. EPROM
7. EEPROM

ANSWERS TO SELF-TEST (4.13)

Matching

1. 5	5. 7
2. 1	6. 4
3. 9	7. 2
4. 3	8. 6

Additional Answers

1. control
2. main memory
3. 16,000
4. ten
5. 01011001
6. ASCII
7. F
8. 1
9. T
10. base
11. 4
12. 4
13. operation code
14. machine cycle
15. MIPS
16. 4
17. word size
18. T
19. coprocessor
20. semiconductor
21. F
22. volatile

CHAPTER 5: Output from the Computer

ANSWERS TO CLASSNOTES (5.7)

What Is Output? (5.7)

1. information

Types of Output (5.7)

1. hard copy
2. soft copy
3. Reports
4. Internal reports
5. External reports
6. detail
7. summary
8. exception
9. Computer graphics
10. pie charts
11. bar charts
12. line charts
13. Multimedia
14. Video compression
15. digital video interactive

Printers (5.8)

1. low speed
2. medium speed
3. high speed
4. very high speed
5. tractor, friction
6. continuous-form paper
7. letter quality
8. typeface
9. front, hammer
10. Nonimpact

Impact Printers (5.9)

1. dot matrix
2. paper
3. ribbon
4. printing head
5. 9
6. standard
7. bold
8. bidirectional
9. 80
10. 132
11. graphics
12. daisy wheel
13. chain
14. drive gear
15. ribbon
16. hammers
17. paper
18. ribbon
19. scalloped steel print band
20. hammer
21. magnet
22. paper

Nonimpact Printers (5.11)

1. ink jet
2. thermal
3. page

Considerations in Choosing a Printer (5.11)

1. How much
2. Who
3. Where

Screens (5.11)

1. monitor, CRT–Cathode Ray Tube, VDT–Video Display Terminal
2. 80
3. pixels
4. Higher resolution
5. dot-addressable displays, bit-mapped displays
6. CGA
7. VGA
8. cursor
9. rectangular, underline, arrow
10. scroll

11. blinking
12. color
13. LCD
14. Color

Other Output Devices (5.12)

1. projection panels
2. plotter
3. pen plotters, flatbed plotters, drum plotters, or electrostatic plotters
4. Computer Output Microfilm
5. Voice output
6. voice synthesizer

ANSWERS TO SELF-TEST (5.13)

Matching

1. 2   5. 8
2. 9   6. 3
3. 7   7. 6
4. 1   8. 4

Additional Answers

1. Output
2. reports and graphics
3. external
4. detail
5. graphics
6. pie chart
7. bar chart
8. impact or nonimpact
9. lines
10. all of the above
11. 8 1/2
12. tractor feed and friction feed
13. Dot matrix
14. daisy wheel
15. heat
16. laser
17. Band
18. page
19. F
20. scrolling
21. LCD—liquid crystal display
22. plotter
23. T

CHAPTER 6: Auxiliary Storage

ANSWERS TO CLASSNOTES (6.6)

What Is Auxiliary Storage? (6.6)

1. nonvolatile
2. tape drive, disk drive
3. input/output
4. kilobytes, megabytes, gigabytes

Magnetic Disk Storage (6.6)

1. convenient, reliable, low cost
2. 3 1/2, 5 1/4
3. mylar, plastic
4. metal oxide coating
5. disk jacket
6. hub, liner, or recording window
7. plastic
8. tracks, sectors
9. track
10. sector
11.

DISKETTE TYPE	TRACKS PER DISK	SECTORS PER TRACK	TRACK NUMBERING
5 1/4"	40	9	0-39
3 1/2"	80	9	0-39

12. recording density, number of tracks, number of sides
13. 2
14. bits
15. 360K, 540K
16. seek time, latency, settling time, transfer rate
17. Don't touch the disk surface.
    Don't bend the disk.
    Don't expose the disk to excessive sunlight.
    Don't expose the disk to magnetic fields.
    Don't use an eraser on the disk label.
    Don't place a heavy object on the disk.
18. Use felt-tip marker on labels.
    Store disks in their dust jackets.
19. platters
20. larger, faster
21. mounted, sealed
22. DASD
23. 25, 80
24. online storage, large capacity, faster access
25. hard card
26. spindle
27. platters
28. access arms (actuators)
29. read/write heads
30. millionth
31. head crash
32. 10, 100
33. fast access, high capacity, portable, easily secured

34.

35. uncovered, covered
36. backup

Magnetic Tape (6.10)

1. backup, transfer
2. 300; 3,600
3. 100
4. supply reel
5. take-up reel
6. read/write head
7. vacuum columns
8. EBCDIC, 9
9. 800; 6,250
10. 38,000
11. interblock
12. logical
13. physical
14. helical scan

Other Forms of Auxiliary Storage (6.10)

1. billion
2. CDROM, WORM
3. solid-state, mass

ANSWERS TO SELF TEST (6.11)

Matching

1. 4   5. 2
2. 6   6. 1
3. 8   7. 9
4. 7   8. 5

Additional Answers

1. secondary storage
2. F
3. megabytes
4. 3 1/2, 5 1/4
5. defining the tracks and sectors on the diskette surface
6. T
7. the number of sectors on the disk

8. bits recorded per inch
9. latency
10. to position the read/write head over the proper track
11. F
12. F
13. storage features of a hard disk
14. backing up data onto a cartridge tape
15. hard card

16. cylinder
17. T
18. cartridge tape
19. logical records, physical record
20. grouping of logical records
21. inability to be reused
22. T
23. F
24. T

CHAPTER 7: File and Database Management

ANSWERS TO CLASSNOTES (7.6)

Database Management (7.6)

1. procedures, accurate, timely
2. security, maintenance
3. form, time

What Is a File? (7.6)

1. file
2. fields
3. field

Types of File Organization (7.6)

1. sequential, indexed, direct or relative
2. printing, backup
3. 55
4. key field, disk address
5. random
6. relative
7. hashing
8.

FILE TYPE	TYPE OF STORAGE	ACCESS METHOD
SEQUENTIAL	Tape or Disk	Sequential
INDEXED	Disk	Sequential * or Random
DIRECT (RELATIVE)	Disk	Sequential * or Random

How Is Data in Files Maintained? (7.7)

1. adding, changing, deleting

Databases: A Better Way to Manage and Organize Data (7.8)

1. multiple separate files
2. database
3. answer in your own words

What Is a Database? (7.8)

1.

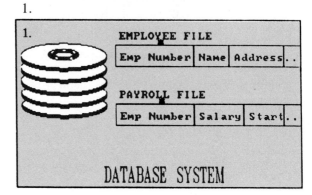

DATABASE SYSTEM

1. continued

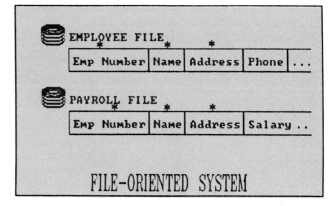

FILE-ORIENTED SYSTEM

2. database management system (DBMS)
3. file management system

Why Use a Database? (7.9)

1. reduced data redundancy, improved data integrity, integrated files, improved data security

Types of Database Organization (7.9)

1. hierarchical, network, relational
2. parent
3. parent-child
4. parent

5. child
6. child
7. parent
8. Records are in separate branches and are not easily addressed at the same time. Adding new fields means total redefinition of the database.
9. member
10. owner
11. create
12. Adding new fields means total redefinition of the database.
13. file
14. record
15. field
16. domain
17. link
18. Data relationship doesn't have to be predefined. Adding new fields only requires defining the fields in the appropriate table.

Database Management Systems (7.10)

1. Data dictionary
2. Utility
3. Security
4. Query language

Query Languages:
Access to the Database (7.10)

1. select, project, join
2. Structured Query Language (SQL)

Database Administration (7.10)

1. database administrator

Personal Computer
Database Systems (7.10)

1. mainframe

ANSWERS TO SELF-TEST (7.11)

Matching

1. 8   3. 5   5. 1   7. 9
2. 4   4. 7   6. 3   8. 2

Additional Answers

1. F
2. all of the above
3. records
4. T
5. record
6. auxiliary storage
7. sequential
8. access speed is slow
9. sequence
10. disk
11. T
12. position
13. hashing
14. collision
15. updating
16. T
17. multiple
18. Database management
19. File management
20. reduced data integrity
21. relational
22. link
23. flexibility
24. hierarchical
25. root
26. fast
27. multiple
28. T
29. English-like
30. rows
31. fields
32. relational
33. database administrator
34. F
35. dBASE
36. multiple

CHAPTER 8: Communications

ANSWERS TO CLASSNOTES (8.8)

What Is Communications? (8.8)

1. transmission
2. Telecommunications
3. telephone lines

A Communications System Model (8.8)

1. communications channel
2. communications equipment
3. computer or terminal

Communications Channels (8.8)

1. twisted pair wire
2. coaxial cable
3. fiber optics
4. microwave
5. uplink
6. downlink
7. earth stations

Line Configurations (8.9)

1. point-to-point
2. multidrop

Characteristics of Communications Channels (8.9)

1. digital, analog
2. synchronous
3. asynchronous
4. simplex
5. half-duplex
6. full-duplex
7. bits per second

Communications Equipment (8.10)

1. modem
2. internal
3. acoustic coupler
4. multiplexor
5. Polling

Communications Software (8.11)

1. dialing, file transfer, terminal emulation, data encryption

Communications Protocols (8.11)

1. information

Communications Networks (8.11)

1. information resource sharing, network control unit or hardware resource sharing
2. client
3. wide area network

Network Configurations (8.12)

1. star network
2. bus network
3. ring network

Connecting Networks (8.12)

1. gateway

An Example of a Communications Network (8.12)

1. LAN bridge
2. gateway
3. front end processor

ANSWERS TO SELF-TEST (8.13)

Matching

1. 6
2. 1
3. 7
4. 2
5. 5
6. 4
7. 8
8. 3

Additional Answers

1. F
2. Teleprocessing
3. data communications
4. all of the above
5. communications channel
6. communications equipment
7. personal computer or terminal
8. T
9. one signal at a time
10. multiple signals
11. satellite
12. Line configurations
13. T
14. a host computer
15. Digital
16. Analog
17. synchronous
18. asynchronous
19. T
20. modem
21. circuit board inside the computer
22. an acoustic coupler
23. multiplexing
24. File transfer software
25. Dialing software
26. T
27. both a and b
28. file-server method
29. all of the above
30. topology
31. network
32. star
33. all of the above
34. F
35. bus, 4
36. both a and b
37. front end processor

CHAPTER 9: Operating Systems and Systems Software

ANSWERS TO CLASSNOTES (9.6)

What Is Systems Software? (9.6)

1. system, application
2. System
3. starting up the computer, loading, executing, and storing application programs, storing and retrieving files, utility functions
4. Application
5. spreadsheet, word processing, database, graphics

What Is an Operating System? (9.6)

1. equipment
2. monitor, executive, master program, control program, kernel
3. nonresident

Loading an Operating System (9.7)

1. OS
2. computer
3. OS
4. application
5. execution
6. commands

Types of Operating Systems (9.7)

1. simultaneous
2. programs
3. single program
4. multiprogramming/multitasking
5. multiprocessing
6. virtual machine
7. more than one
8. one or more than one (multiuser)
9. more than one on each CPU
10. more than one on each CPU
11. more than one on each operating system
12. more than one on each operating system

Functions of Operating Systems (9.8)

1. allocating system resources
2. monitoring activities
3. utilities
4. time slicing
5. time slicing without priority
6. time slicing with priority
7. partitioning
8. active
9. segmentation
10. paging
11. swapping
12. multiple

13. spooling
14. response time, CPU utilization
15. security
16. utilities

Popular Operating Systems (9.10)

1. proprietary operating systems
2. UNIX
3. OS/2
4. portable operating systems
5. MS-DOS

Operating Environments (9.10)

1. graphic interface

Utilities (9.10)

1. Utilities
2. editor

Language Translators (9.10)

1. machine instructions

ANSWERS TO SELF-TEST (9.11)

Matching

1. 4   5. 8
2. 9   6. 7
3. 6   7. 5
4. 2   8. 1

Additional Answers

1. F
2. systems
3. T
4. T
5. ROM
6. T
7. multiple, multiple
8. multiprocessing
9. T
10. F
11. Time
12. Paging
13. F
14. T
15. F
16. F
17. utilities
18. instructions

CHAPTER 10: Management Information Systems

ANSWERS TO CLASSNOTES (10.5)

Why Is Information Important to an Organization? (10.5)

1. expanded markets, increased competition, shorter product life cycle, government regulation
2. Expanded markets
3. Increased competition
4. Shorter product life cycles
5. Government regulation

How Do Managers Use Information? (10.5)

1. Managers
2. planning, organizing, directing, controlling
3. goals, objectives
4. resources
5. instructing, authorizing
6. performance, corrective action

Management Levels in an Organization (10.6)

1. Senior management, middle management, operational management, functional level
2. strategic decisions, current operations
3. tactical decisions, performance variances
4. operational decisions, production, support

Qualities of Information (10.6)

1. Meaningful
2. organized
3. cost-effective
4. accurate

What Is an Information System? (10.7)

1. information system
2. equipment, software, accurate data, trained information systems personnel, knowledgeable users, documented procedures

3. Operational systems
4. Management information systems
5. EIS
6. decision support system
7. Expert systems

Integrated Information Systems (10.7)

1. integrated information

The Role of Personal Computers in Management Information Systems (10.7)

1. cost-effective, flexible

ANSWERS TO SELF-TEST (10.8)

Matching

1. 4   5. 3
2. 8   6. 5
3. 1   7. 2
4. 7   8. 6

Additional Answers

1. T
2. expanded markets
3. F
4. Organizing
5. Controlling
6. Middle
7. strategic
8. F
9. accurate
10. meaningful
11. MIS
12. DSS
13. Expert system
14. T
15. F

CHAPTER 11: The Information System Life Cycle

ANSWERS TO CLASSNOTES (11.8)

What Is the Information System Life Cycle? (11.8)

1. information system
2. analysis, acquisition/design, customizing/development, implementation, maintenance
3. planning, scheduling, reporting, controlling
4. Documentation

Analysis Phase (11.8)

1. the separation of a system into its parts to determine how the system works
2. problem definition
3. system analysis
4. interviews, questionnaires, reviewing current system documentation, observing current procedures
5. the output of the current system, the procedures used to produce the output, the input to the current system
6. design tools
7. feasibility study
8. cost/benefit analysis

Acquisition Phase (11.9)

1. evaluating, identifying, making
2. Commercial application
3. horizontal, vertical
4. request for proposal
5. Software houses
6. System houses
7. benchmark test
8. Software license

Commercial Applications versus Custom Software (11.9)

1. application package, custom software

Customizing Phase (11.9)

1. identifying
2. custom software

Design Phase (11.9)

1. logical
2. physical
3. Top-down design
4. Bottom-up design
5. output design
6. input design
7. database design

8. input, output
9. flowchart
10. controls
11. source document, input, processing, accounting
12. F
13. design review
14. prototyping
15. computer-based

Development Phase (11.11)

1. program development, equipment acquisition

Implementation Phase (11.11)

1. training and education, conversion, post-implementation evaluation

Maintenance Phase (11.11)

1. the process of supporting the system after it is implemented
2. performance monitoring, change management, error correction

ANSWERS TO SELF-TEST (11.12)

Matching

1. 3   5. 6
2. 7   6. 4
3. 2   7. 1
4. 5   8. 9

Additional Answers

1. T
2. Project management
3. Documentation
4. analysis
5. Detailed system analysis
6. F
7. commercial application
8. horizontal
9. Vertical
10. T
11. performance
12. software license
13. custom software
14. vertical application
15. both a and c
16. T
17. design
18. all of the above

19. T
20. system flowchart
21. prototype
22. development
23. F

24. implementation
25. training and education
26. T
27. maintenance
28. T

CHAPTER 12: Program Development

ANSWERS TO CLASSNOTES (12.8)

What Is a Computer Program? (12.8)

1. instructions, data, process, information

What Is Program Development? (12.8)

Step 1: review specs
Step 2: design
Step 3: code
Step 4: test
Step 5: finalize documentation

Step 1—Reviewing the Program Specifications (12.8)

1. data flow diagrams, system flowcharts, process specifications, data dictionary, screen formats, report layouts, actual documents
2. analyst, users
3. programmer

Step 2—Designing the Program (12.9)

1. logical solution
2. Structured program design
3. modules, single entry/single exit, control structures
4. subroutines
5. Structure or hierarchy charts
6. hierarchy charts, modules
7. sequence, selection, iteration
8. sequence
9. Selection structure
10. Iteration structure
11. do-while
12. do-until
13. Single entry/single exit
14. flowcharts, pseudocode, Warnier-Orr
15. decision
16. terminal
17. input/output
18. predefined process
19. processing
20. offpage
21. connector
22. preparation
23. Pseudocode, eliminates drawing symbols
24. output

25. structured walk-through
26. Systems analysts
27. review the logic, improve program design

Step 3—Coding the Program (12.10)

1. Coding

Step 4—Testing the Program (12.10)

1. desk checking, syntax error checking, logic testing, debugging
2. similar to proofreading a letter
3. identifying violations of the program language's grammar rules
4. using test data (expected and unexpected data) to test the program
5. locating and correcting program errors during testing

Step 5—Finalizing Program Documentation (12.11)

1. narrative description, program flowcharts, pseudocode, program listings, test results, comments within program

Program Maintenance (12.11)

1. errors

What Is a Programming Language? (12.11)

1. communicate

Categories of Programming Languages (12.11)

1. machine language, assembly language, high-level languages, fourth-generation languages
2. Machine language
3. converted
4. mnemonics
5. symbolic addressing
6. Macroinstructions
7. contain program statements, are usually machine independent, are converted to machine language by a compiler or an interpreter

8. source program
9. error listing
10. source program statement
11. interpreter
12. machine language instructions
13. very high-level languages, nonprocedural
14. what, how
15. database query language
16. natural

Programming Languages Used Today (12.13)

1. Beginner's All-purpose Symbolic Instruction Code
2. microcomputers, minicomputers
3. COmmon Business Oriented Language
4. business
5. systems
6. FORmula TRANslator
7. mathematical equations
8. Blaise Pascal
9. structured
10. Augusta Ada Byron
11. programs
12. Report Program Generator
13. reports
14. It uses special forms filled out describing the report.
15. ALGOL
16. APL
17. FORTH
18. LISP, PROLOG
19. LOGO
20. MODULA-2
21. PILOT
22. PL/1

Application Generators (12.13)

1. program generators
2. source programs
3. menu generator
4. screen generator

Object-Oriented Programming (12.14)

1. objects
2. methods
3. inheritance
4. instance

How to Choose a Programming Language (12.14)

1. programming standards, portability, language suitability, maintenance requirements, programmer expertise, language availability, interfacing needs

ANSWERS TO SELF-TEST (12.15)

Matching

1. 8   3. 2   5. 7   7. 3
2. 4   4. 1   6. 6   8. 5

Additional Answers

1. all of the above
2. review of program specifications
3. program design
4. modules
5. iteration
6. UNTIL
7. pseudocode
8. a single entry/exit
9. testing the program
10. all of the above
11. an ongoing process
12. F
13. T
14. programmer
15. T
16. F
17. translate
18. what verses how
19. Pascal
20. COBOL and RPG
21. generators
22. T
23. T

CHAPTER 13: Career Opportunities in Information Processing

ANSWERS TO CLASSNOTES (13.5)

The Information Processing Industry (13.5)

1. the computer equipment industry, the computer software industry, information processing professionals

What Are the Career Opportunities in Information Processing? (13.5)

1. operations, data administration, system analysis and design, programming, information center

2. Operations
3. database administration, quality assurance
4. systems analysis, forms design and control
5. system
6. consulting, training
7. Sales
8. consultant
9. T

Compensation and Growth Trends for Information Processing Careers (13.6)

1. communications
2. $27,000 $27,000
   $31,000 $30,000
   $27,000. $32,000

Preparing for a Career in Information Processing (13.6)

1. computer engineering, computer information systems, computer science
2. computer design engineer, service and repair technician
3. information processing manager, database administrator, systems analyst, business applications programmer, computer operator, data entry operator
4. computer scientist, language design specialist, systems software specialist
5. user groups

Career Development in the Information Processing Industry (13.6)

1. professional
2. Certification

ANSWERS TO SELF-TEST (13.7)

Matching

1. 1   3. 7   5. 9   7. 4
2. 5   4. 6   6. 3   8. 2

Additional Answers

1. computers
2. computer equipment
3. IBM
4. all of the above
5. programmer
6. T
7. teaching and consulting
8. Sales representatives
9. T
10. Consultants
11. demand
12. all of the above
13. business
14. Computer science
15. Computer engineering
16. T
17. Professional organizations
18. T
19. T

CHAPTER 14: Trends and Issues in the Information Age

ANSWERS TO CLASSNOTES (14.6)

Information Systems in Business (14.6)

1. batch processing
2. word processing
3. electronic mail
4. voice mail
5. desktop publishing
6. facsimile
7. image processing
8. teleconferencing or video conferencing
9. computer-aided design
10. Computer-aided engineering (CAE)
11. factory
12. product design
13. production planning
14. manufacturing
15. product distribution

Bringing the Information Age Home (14.8)

1. personal
2. personal services, control of home systems, telecommuting, education, entertainment
3. Computer-aided instruction (CAI)
4. Step 1: Become computer literate.
   Step 2: Define and prioritize the tasks you want to perform on your computer.
   Step 3: Select software packages that best meet your needs.
   Step 4: Select equipment that will run software you have selected.
   Step 5: Select the suppliers for software and equipment.
   Step 6: Purchase software and equipment.

Social Issues (14.8)

1. software theft/piracy, unauthorized access and use, malicious damage, viruses

ANSWERS TO SELF-TEST (14.9)

Matching

1. 9   3. 1   5. 3   7. 4
2. 6   4. 7   6. 2   8. 5

Additional Answers

1. productivity   10. T
2. word processing   11. telecommuting
3. Electronic mail   12. education
4. T   13. F
5. CAD   14. T
6. CAM   15. security
7. CAE   16. T
8. T
9. T